DATE DUE

DE 8 '95		
MY 4 '98		

DEMCO 38-296

MANAGING WITH DUAL STRATEGIES

MASTERING THE PRESENT
PREEMPTING THE FUTURE

Derek F. Abell

THE FREE PRESS
A Division of Macmillan, Inc.
NEW YORK
Maxwell Macmillan Canada
TORONTO
Maxwell Macmillan International
NEW YORK OXFORD SINGAPORE SYDNEY

The Free Press
A Division of Macmillan, Inc.
866 Third Avenue, New York, N. Y. 10022

Maxwell Macmillan Canada, Inc.
1200 Eglinton Avenue East
Suite 200
Don Mills, Ontario M3C 3N1

Macmillan, Inc. is part of the Maxwell Communication Group of Companies.

Printed in the United States of America

printing number

1 2 3 4 5 6 7 8 9 10

Library of Congress Cataloging-in-Publication Data

Abell, Derek F.
    Managing with dual strategies: mastering the present, preempting the future / Derek F. Abell.
        p.   cm.
    Includes bibliographical references and index.
    ISBN 0-02-900145-5
    1. Strategic planning. 2. Management. 3. Marketing.
4. Organizational effectiveness.   I. Title.
HD30.28.A243   1993
658.4'012—dc20   93-8016
                                                                CIP

To my wife Rose Marie, and three grown daughters Susanne, Julia, and Thérèse, who unstintingly supported me all the way through the struggle to define and write this book.

To my Mother and Father, both now 84, who tightened already tight belts, to put education ahead of their own personal needs.

And to my friends in Central and Eastern Europe whose deep instincts for excellence and capacity for change provided constant inspiration.

CONTENTS

PREFACE

The concepts and ideas in this book, like so many others in the field of management, emerged from working alongside senior managers who were struggling to conceive and implement strategies for their businesses. I had been struck, for some time, by the paradox that many companies who wanted help with their "strategic plans" really needed help to put straight what they were trying to do today—as a quite separate task from anticipating and planning for the future. "Putting straight" what they were already doing usually meant first clarifying and sharpening up the *current* definition of the business and its target segments, and second making sure that given this sharpened definition, those factors critical to success were attended to with painstaking dedication.

I also could not help being struck by the fact that changing the business as opposed to just running it had increasingly become a major management preoccupation. After the relatively steady growth and continuity of the three decades that followed the Second World War, the world's business environment, from the early 1970s onwards, became increasingly turbulent and competitive. Only those managements that made change a focus of their attention seemed capable of survival. Paradoxically again, change was often driven by the need to catch up with the present as well as to anticipate the future.

I began to ask myself therefore whether the conventional concept of business strategy was really the right way to look at it. Wasn't there some danger that a company that tried to conceive *a* single strategy for its business would fall between two stools—neither fully capitalizing on its current opportunities, nor getting itself properly positioned for the next phase of its development.

This book attempts to shed some light on this complex subject. It is based on a wide set of personal experiences spanning more than a decade, as well as in-depth observation of some ten leading multinationals in 1990 and 1991. The conclusions suggest that these companies are indeed feeling the dual pressures of superior present performance on the one hand, and improved change management on the other. Few, however, have yet fully redefined their management processes to deal with this duality.

This work may therefore be likened to trying to piece together a jigsaw puzzle, using pieces from several different pictures. While no company alone exhibited a complete picture, taken as a group, a picture does begin to emerge—and that is what is reported here. I have tried to find a sensible balance between scientific rigor and speculative insight.

Part I serves as an introduction. Chapter 1 distinguishes *running* a business from *changing* a business, and thereby introduces the concept of dual strategies. Chapter 2 draws on the experience of four leading multinationals to show how duality is handled in practice.

Part II addresses the issue of developing dual strategies from three different analytical perspectives: that of the customer; that of the company vis-à-vis its competitors; and that of costs. For each we must ask "How do things look today?" and "How will they look tomorrow?"

Section A of Part II, "The Customer Perspective," discusses what we mean by "customer analysis" in both its present and future dimensions. Chapter 3 broadens the meaning of customer analysis to include nonproduct as well as product needs, the time dimension of customer satisfaction, and multiparty influences in the buying process. Chapter 4 goes into depth on market segmentation and its use as a strategic weapon, not just as a research tool. Chapter 5 focuses explicitly on the dynamic nature of markets and changes in customer needs and behavior over time.

Section B of Part II, "The Company Perspective," aims to provide a sound understanding of both the demand side and the supply side of the market. This means, above all, recognizing current and potential future possibilities for differentiation between our own company and our competitors. Chapter 6 introduces this subject by examining what we mean by the word "industry," and reminding us that even within a so-called industry, different competitors may define businesses quite differently. Chapter 7 then examines the points of more obvious differentiation between a company and its competitors; while Chapter 8 examines sources of differentiation which often lie hidden from direct view.

Section C of Part II, "The Cost Perspective," presents the concept of cost analysis as a fundamental ingredient to both strategies for the present and change strategies aimed at preempting the future. Chapter 9 takes up in detail the analysis of present and future costs; Chapter 10 shows how good cost management can become an effective strategic weapon.

In Part III, the orientation shifts from the more analytical orientation of Part II to a more decision-making orientation. Analytical perspectives gained in Part II are now put to work to develop dual strategies—a strategy for the present on the one hand, and a parallel strategy for transforming the company and preempting the future on the other. Chapter 11 focuses exclusively on present strategy—how to use existing competences and resources to their best advantage in the *current* marketplace. Chapters 12 and 13 deal with strategies for transforming the company to equip it for the future. Chapter 12 draws on the practical experiences of five major multinationals who are deeply engaged in the management of change. Chapter 13 provides a more generalized and prescriptive view of how transformation and change management can be conceived and implemented.

The book concludes with some implications. Certainly, shifting from a single-minded approach to strategy and its implementation, to the recognition that there is a need to operate with dual strategies is easier said than done. In most organizations it does in fact require a major upheaval in virtually all aspects of organizational structure, processes, and operations, as well as in managerial thinking and behavior. Part IV highlights just three of these: Chapter 14 examines the need for new organizational structures and processes; Chapter 15 deals with the need for new approaches to planning; Chapter 16 suggests the implications for the age-old problem of managerial control. In fact control itself takes on a dual meaning. Current strategies must be controlled against performance benchmarks; change strategies must be monitored against agreed upon milestones.

Who is this book for? It would be too simplistic to say "all managers," but something close to this is not far from the truth. The issues raised certainly *concern* all managers. Certainly all those with general management responsibilities or those senior functional managers who make up the general management team responsible for a business unit will find it relevant. It is written for practicing managers. Having said this, I imagine that some teachers running executive programs or MBA programs may also find it grist for the mill. It provides another view of topics that normally get taught in marketing courses, strategic management courses, planning courses, and general management or "business policy" courses.

Many organizations and individuals have contributed directly or indirectly to this book. The generous support of Nestlé S.A. and the Harvard Business School provided the means to make it possible to explore these ideas and bring them into written form. IMD (The International Institute for Management Development) provided the time, and the intellectual framework, and the collegial environment with which practice and theory could be joined. The ten companies who opened their doors at the most senior level, namely Aegon, Bertelsmann, Caterpillar, Ericsson, Heineken, Imperial Chemicals Industries, Nestlé S.A., Procordia, Schering AG, and Sulzer Brothers provided me with critical insights. Throughout, many individuals gave me the encouragement to continue when the way ahead looked bleak or ambiguous.

Although the book strikes new ground, I am deeply indebted to my co-author in a previous book, John Hammond, for allowing me to quote extensively from his insights—all of which have stood the test of time.[1] I am also grateful to the publisher of that book and another book which I authored a decade ago, for allowing the inclusion of several key pieces of text in this new book.[2]

During the gestation period of this book, I was working actively not only in the United States and Western Europe, but also extensively in Central and Eastern Europe. My gratitude to those friends and colleagues there whom I was fortunate enough to work with cannot be fully expressed in just a few words. It was in this "New Europe" that I discovered that the instinct for excellence and capacity for change are things that we have no monopoly on, and where I saw in stark relief how the two have to be managed side by side.

Lastly, I would like to express my great appreciation to Anne Bellmann for her many contributions in turning this book into reality. Without her help, it would not have been possible, and without the tireless, speedy, and accurate stenography of Anne and of Debbie Brunettin, there would be nothing legible to read.

Derek F. Abell
IMD
Lausanne, Switzerland

PART I

INTRODUCTION

CHAPTER 1

THE DUAL NATURE
OF MANAGEMENT

U sing present capacities to their fullest advantage and developing new ones in anticipation of the future characterizes the high performer in all fields of human endeavor. Athletes train and compete, and train further to enhance capacities for future events. Armies fight battles deploying whatever materiel and personnel they have at their disposal, and in more peaceful times develop new military capabilities in anticipation of battles still unfought. More generally speaking, we "consume" and "invest"; and as the old proverb warns (to remind us that there is a downside also): "We make our bed and lie in it."

Management as a human endeavor differs from the above examples in one important respect: Running the business and changing it are not sequential but parallel pursuits. Even armies are seldom on full alert all the time, at least not for limitless periods. War and peace are punctuated—providing the breathing space to build and regroup. Managers enjoy no such luxury, competing today and preparing for tomorrow with no letup on either front.

Because the two activities go on continuously and in parallel, we tend to forget that they are in fact very different in character. *Running* a successful business requires a clear strategy in terms of defining target markets and lavishing attention on those factors which are critical to success; *changing* a business in anticipation of the future requires a vision of how the future will look and a strategy for how the organization will have to adapt to meet future challenges.

Until recently, most organizations have successfully managed to run and change their businesses under the umbrella of a single strategy. As long as neither present competition was too demanding, nor change too severe, this approach proved to be quite adequate. This did, in fact, characterize most business activity in the long period of expansion following the Second World War and lasting until the early 1970s. In spite of a few nasty jolts in which management was rudely reminded of the necessity for change, and in spite of a few outbursts of intense competitive activity when supply and demand were temporarily out of balance, or a competitor made a radical breakthrough, a "business as usual" philosophy prevailed. Singular strategies encompassing present and future did the job. Not so today. As competition for current markets has heated up and as change has become increasingly pervasive, a single strategy encompassing the near to medium term runs the risk of providing neither the basis for effectively running the existing business, nor the basis for managing change.

The idea of duality is not entirely new. In 1968, a far-sighted publication of the Boston Consulting Group revealed that the planning practices of a sample of their large client companies were of two distinct types: "Action planning" was used to plan the necessary present and future actions to ensure "operational" success; while "planning for strategic change" was used to improve the organization's capability to have current major decisions "properly weighted by in-depth study of long-term environmental change."[1] In many cases, this was found to mean changing traditional assumptions and policies in order to facilitate the organizations' adaptation to future conditions.

Curiously, this distinction, articulated nearly twenty-five years ago, has not been given a great deal of further attention. One reason may indeed be that times were less demanding and the need to distinguish between present and future strategies was less evident; another may be that it was an insight ahead of its time; strategic planning was then in a very experimental stage and innovative approaches and insights—good and bad—were used and discarded with some rapidity.

Whatever the reasons, most companies have continued to develop strategic planning practices without discriminating clearly between the two modes—often in fact, adopting systems and approaches which are a "halfway house" between the two, and which meet neither today's short-term needs for excellence nor the long-term needs for change as well as they should. Critics of current planning approaches which are built primarily on "fitting" existing distinctive competences to market opportunities have, in fact, argued that articulating such strategies and making them explicit can actually limit flexibility, and "block out peripheral vision!"[2] It is certainly true that an undue focus on the present at the expense of the future can have this very undesirable result. But there is nothing wrong at all with making present strategy explicit *if* this is combined with a parallel undertaking to determine the direction of future change.

The fact is that companies' options to perform with excellence today are highly dependent on decisions made in the past; and decisions to pursue this or that future direction today inevitably shape future options. As the old proverb has it: "In the present lies the past, and in what is now is hidden what will be."[3] One executive, articulating the same idea in managerial terms, put it as follows: "Short-term success is mainly a feature of long-term moves made earlier."[4]

The distinction between a present and future orientation is *not* the usual short-term, long-term distinction—in which the short-term plan is simply a detailed budgeting exercise made in the context of a hoped-for long-term market position. Present planning also requires vision—a vision of how the firm has to operate now given its unique competences and choice of target markets. The long-term plan, by contrast, is built on a vision of the future—and even more importantly on how to get there.

Planning for today requires a clear *definition* of the business—a precise delineation of target customer segments, customer functions, and the business approach to be used; planning for tomorrow is much more concerned with how the business should be *redefined* for the future.

Planning for today is focused on *shaping up* the business to meet the needs of customers today with excellence. This means identifying those factors that are critical to success and smothering them with attention; planning for tomorrow is often focused on *reshaping* the business to compete more effectively in the future.

Planning for today is focused on achieving *compliance* in the various functional activities of the firm with whatever definition of the business has been chosen; planning for tomorrow is much more likely to involve *bold moves* away from existing ways of conducting the business.

And, while planning for today requires *organization*, planning for tomorrow quite often requires *reorganization*.

In a nutshell, planning for today is about *managing for results;* planning for tomorrow is about *managing change.*

I have deliberately used the word *managing* here together with the words *strategy and planning* because the present/future dichotomy goes into all aspects of managerial work. What we are in fact talking about in this and ensuing chapters are two parallel *managerial* agendas—one aimed at managing today's activities with excellence, the other aimed at preparing for the future.

Few firms have clear "20/20" vision when it comes to discriminating adequately between these two types of plan. All of the usual human ailments with respect to vision are reproduced in companies. Myopia can extend well beyond the "marketing myopia," that Theodore Levitt identified three decades ago.[5] Companies can, in fact, be so consumed with the present that they fail completely to prepare themselves for the future. When change comes, it is unexpected and unprepared for—and these companies are left high and dry, the victims of their short-term focus. But just as dangerous is to focus most of the attention on the future, overlooking the needs for excellent performance today. Change should be a management preoccupation, but in addition to, not instead of, present performance.

As we shall see subsequently, the appropriate *balance* between a present and future orientation is related to the situation at hand. In some circumstances, particularly those characterized by rapid or extreme change, the future component must be given the lion's share of attention; in more stable circumstances, the present component is predominant. But whatever the situation, both components must always be attended to in parallel.

Underlying the failure of companies to achieve the proper balance between present and future is usually the inability of individual managers to wear these two hats simultaneously. Some managers, especially at lower levels, do of course spend most of their time on current operations as opposed to the requirements for future change. And the reverse is true at the top of the corporate hierarchy. But the more organizations flatten and responsibilities are pushed down, the more *every* manager has to have a sharp eye on both horizons. In fact, it is a critical requirement to develop 20/20 vision up or down the whole organization if the present and future are to be well managed.

Different companies are adjusting their practices in different ways in recognition of the dual nature of managerial work. While some continue with a "catchall" process which lumps together present and future into a two-, three-, or five-year business plan, others are making a clearer distinction between the long-term framework and shorter-term plans, reserving the former more for corporate headquarters while delegating the latter more to business unit management. Only a few are making a more fundamental distinction between present and future, and between the roles of corporate and business unit management in attending to each. It is to current managerial practice that we now turn to see how some leading companies are responding to the dual challenge of present and future in increasingly competitive and changing markets.

CHAPTER 2

DUALITY IN PRACTICE

F our of the leading multinationals that were studied in depth are described in some detail in this chapter. Between them, Swiss-based Nestlé, U.S.-based Caterpillar, German-based Schering, and Dutch-based Heineken provide important contrasts and comparisons with respect to how dual strategies are conceived and implemented in practice.

NESTLÉ S.A.

The world's largest food company provides us with a good starting point and a "benchmark" to understand current practices. Nestlé has traditionally operated with a highly decentralized country-by-country structure, with some sixty country markets grouped into four main geographic "zones." Headquarters has played largely a coordinating role in two specific ways: first by providing functional expertise and coordination in the fields of marketing, the "technical" areas of manufacturing, R&D, and facilities management, and finance and control; and second by providing some degree of product management at the center. In the overall balance of power, there was little question that final decision-making responsibility—and indeed profit responsibility in a formal sense—lay with individual market and zone management. Not surprisingly, markets carried the major planning responsibility, and the so-called "long-term plan" drawn up market-by-market provided the strategic framework within which each market managed its current business.

The comments of several members of Nestlé's senior management revealed, however, that by the early 1990s, this approach to planning and managing Nestlé's worldwide business was running into trouble. According to Ramon Masip, general manager for Eu-

8

rope: "These long-term plans are in reality three-year budgets—bottom-up in origin, with some inputs from the top. Their focus is on investments and sales/cost figures. I am personally not so interested in these projections—which are increasingly uncertain as one looks forward; but I am interested in the key issues that have to be tackled in each market—such as digesting and consolidating the production system following a recent major acquisition, or figuring out ways to compete effectively in the absence of having our own distribution."

Statements such as this suggest that there are, in fact, two facets to be dealt with: one side focused on current business, the other side characterized by the need for change in certain areas of the company's operations.

Nestlé's corporate finance director, R. F. Domeniconi, observed that the mechanics of Nestlé's planning approach worked well, but pointed to several shortcomings: the plans were often characterized by "high hopes"; planning was not a constant state of mind—but an event taking place for one or two months each year; planning was too often an extrapolation of current trends; and there was often too much financial data around a single option, instead of real strategic alternatives. He lamented: "We do not have a long-term plan—we do a three-year budget. There are few alternatives—and too much figure crunching. People are overworked and do not think much about the future. In our industry, there are few with real vision."

A senior product division manager at Nestlé, Peter Brabeck, explained other dimensions of the current planning process. A "top-down" process, driven by product management, provides the framework for running each business. He described this as "a continuous circular, pragmatic process—starting with a vision of the marketplace today, and our vision of the marketplace tomorrow—up to ten years ahead."

According to Mr. Brabeck: "This framework is first discussed with zone management, with central technical and R&D functions, and ultimately with senior corporate general management. When approved, it is adapted to the different zones and becomes an input to the "bottom-up" planning process. This takes place in May, June, and July of each year, and the questions are then asked: Does the plan fit the overall frame? Does it suggest any revisions to the frame? Is it a good basis for the one-year plan?"

We see clearly in this description the attempt not only to deal with current realities, but to think ahead to what could be done differently in the future. This future orientation originates however with corporate product management, not in the markets themselves, and as pointed out by Messrs. Masip and Domeniconi, with the balance of power weighted in favor of decentralized markets as opposed to centralized product management, short-term consideration apparently often prevailed.

In 1990, Nestlé embarked on a fundamental reevaluation of its organizational structure and processes. According to Helmut Maucher, Nestlé's chief executive: "We wanted to find a way to strengthen product management, while retaining strong market and zone management—and to make product management more responsible for the whole range of business issues confronting a product, not just marketing."

This reassignment of roles has its origins in deep-seated changes in Nestlé's markets—restructuring for region-wide and increasingly global competition in some lines, and internal changes in Nestlé itself—new more diversified product lines, a substantial overall size increase resulting from acquisitions, as well as organic growth, changing "values" concerning the need for team work, and a general need to speed up on all fronts.

Previously the focus of product management had been on medium- and long-term thinking, and marketing in particular, with zone management having a more short-term profit orientation. Increasingly, product managers found themselves under two conflicting pressures: On the one hand, there was an increased need for *short-term* coordination as new competition put pressure on speed, the coordination of new product launches, and day-to-day management issues arising from these; on the other hand, there was a *longer-term* need to coordinate, across countries, plant rationalization, distribution restructuring, cost reduction projects, and marketing activities. According to Peter Brabeck:

> This marketplace is moving so fast, we cannot continue to separate the long-term and the short-term as we now do. Even before the reorganization which is now underway, the organization was finding interim, "informal" ways to adjust to the need for greater integration,

greater speed, and a closer relationship between strategies and implementation. Short-term moves must be guided by some long-term vision—some sense of overall direction—but "plans," in the conventional sense of the work, may not provide this.

The repeated reference to the need for long-term vision and strategic considerations in the current three-year business planning process is, however, a clear sign that the future, change-oriented component of planning is likely to be more important in the new structure than it was in the old. Left previously mainly in the hands of product management, it apparently failed to get sufficient attention. The product manager's role, in the old system, was clearly subordinate to that of zone and market management; product management was largely restricted to marketing issues; day-to-day management increasingly encroached on product managers' time. According to Brabeck, some product managers were spending up to 80 percent of their time on operations and project coordination before the organizational change.

Change of a more fundamental nature *was* being managed at Nestlé, but in an organizationally separate process. One of its most important aspects was an acquisition activity which added such well-known names as Carnation, Rowntree, and Perrier to the Nestlé stable in the late 1980s and early 1990s. Nestlé was also continuously engaged in "project" oriented change at a variety of levels, and in a variety of organizational locations. These included *corporate* organizational changes (the main one described above being under the label of "Nestlé 2000"), changes going on at the *zone* level, *country* level, in *functional* departments and in individual *business* areas. Among them were projects to improve information flows between units, improved logistics systems, cost reduction projects, and projects aimed at rationalizing manufacturing.

In summary, we see that Nestlé is evolving steadily towards a more comprehensive system of planning and management, more attuned to current market realities and to its own internal development. It combines a focus on current operations with attention to future change in a number of key ways: through the current planning process itself, and particularly now by strengthening the role of product management—traditionally the custodian of the longer-term vision of a business or major segment of activity; but also through project based activities where the main focus is on change as opposed to operating strategies.

CATERPILLAR

This company provides an interesting contrast to Nestlé in the sense that, while Nestlé was increasingly *integrating* decision making region-wide, and even worldwide, at least for some product lines, Caterpillar was in the midst of a process of greater *decentralization* to individual businesses and markets. Caterpillar's attention was also significantly directed to the question of how to manage the substantial *changes* needed to compete effectively against its Japanese rival Komatsu in the growing smaller machine side of its business.

Bob Petterson, manager of the International Region for Caterpillar Overseas S.A. (COSA), described the situation in the early 1990s as follows:

> In the early years, it was clear what the company was trying to do. We controlled the parts business, so that CAT would benefit and nobody else. We had 60,000 people all going in the same direction. Today's vision is less cohesive—and not everyone is going in the same direction. The current problem is costs—CAT is traditionally driven by engineering with a tendency to build in high cost features. This was OK when people bought CAT equipment for the most rugged uses—but it is not OK for small backhoe loaders!
>
> Part of our long-term strategy therefore is to sort out whether and which CAT brands are right for a particular low-cost segment. It is almost heresy to talk about subcontracted brands. And we also have to sort out whether each step in our distribution/marketing chain adds real value for the customer. We have at all costs to protect our traditional dealer system *and* at the same time try to shift to new segments and serve them in new ways. On the other side, dealers must trust CAT to stay with them, and yet change.

The implication of this statement is quite clear. Caterpillar has two quite different agendas to manage in parallel. On the one side it has to continue to manage its existing highly successful large machinery business, using the tremendous strength of its engineering traditions, and indisputable leadership in distribution; on the other side it has to manage a process of substantial change to allow it to compete successfully in newer segments such as the smaller machinery business.

According to Sig Ramseyer, managing director, "there has been an implicit rejection of the more focused strategy of sticking to the large machine and traditional user markets, where Caterpillar has unquestioned superiority. This would have implied shrinking the company to around $5 billion from the current $11 billion! On the other hand, Caterpillar has a famous name and an unparalleled distribution system. If ways can be found to exploit these in new markets, as the new vision envisages, it would be an unbeatable company."

In 1990, Caterpillar was reorganizing to support this new strategic vision and direction. U.S. headquarters in Peoria had reorganized into thirteen profit centers, some related to geographic markets, and others related to product or user segments. The European-based COSA, one of the major geographic profit centers, underwent its own internal reorganization, recognizing a number of key product/market segments as a basis for organization, and the appointment of "product" management.

While these changes were being worked through, there was also at Caterpillar a clear understanding that the current business had to be managed in the meantime. Among the main aspects of this "current strategy," Sig Ramseyer reported the following:

–fine tuning of plans by segment—especially getting dealers to develop strategies for segments and subsegments

–consolidating CAT/dealer inventories in selected field locations, as part of an overall review of costs and effectiveness in the distribution chain

–improved asset management via information management systems

–boosting the current Caterpillar image

At COSA, the division between planning for the current business and planning for future change was made explicit in 1990. The company thus had a "short-term" planning process, which included the annual budget, and a separate "long-term" planning process. The

first long-term plan—going beyond the conventional five year projection of sales and costs, and dealing with the real agenda for
change—was presented to Caterpillar's executive committee in
March of 1991—three months after presentation of the 1991 short-
term plan. Although this process will certainly be refined as time
passes, Caterpillar stands out as a prime example of what this book
is all about. This must certainly be attributed in large part to the
very substantial pressures for change that Caterpillar faced in the
late 1980s and early 1990s, and the consequent need to devise managerial processes to run the current business successfully while
managing massive change in parallel.

SCHERING A.G.

Schering provides us with yet another perspective on how companies are facing the parallel problems of managing change while running their existing business, and what roles headquarters and business-level management play in this process. Prof. Dr. Klaus Pohle,
Schering's vice chairman of the board and chief financial officer, described the company as follows:

> Schering is a research-driven company. Long-term thinking is bril-
> liant. But on basic operational matters like inventory control, Scher-
> ing continues to be weak. We have brilliant vision, but sometimes
> so-so execution. On the other hand, with our leading edge products
> commanding high margins, is this really a critical success factor?

These somewhat harsh self-judgments on Schering's operating capabilities were tempered by two important compensating factors.
First, 82 percent of Schering's business is done outside of Germany.
The subsidiaries were described as being "extremely well run"—
largely by country general managers who have been "apprenticed"
in tough operating jobs before taking over. Second, Schering
charges a shadow interest rate on capital employed as an expense
when assessing operating performance—thus assuring a certain
discipline in the use of working capital.

Nevertheless, the main point remains: Schering is a company that
is highly R&D driven and future oriented. It concentrates on small
markets with specialized pharmaceutical needs, and on relatively

price insensitive segments, mainly in the most developed economies such as the United States, Germany, Japan, and Switzerland. It
studiously avoids the more "mainstream" segments of the pharmaceutical market—such as antibiotics, cough and cold remedies, and
analgesics, where day-to-day operating discipline and tight controls over performance would be critical.

In practice, planning at Schering takes place between division
and corporate controllers as well as between division general management and corporate board members. The corporate board in this
way develops a broad overview of corporate strategies and priorities, and can "feed in" the tradeoff between short-term performance
and longer-term investments in key areas of opportunity. Once the
overall strategic framework is set, "the divisions parcel out the business requirements country-by-country."

Pohle described Schering as an "unorthodox consensus-driven
company." He noted: "We do exceptionally well in development—
especially when this is close to our 'core competence.' An example
would be tumor therapy which the company knows from its hor-
mone technology associated with birth control. But we made errors
in central nervous system applications—where we had to go beyond our competence. We just didn't appreciate all the abilities that
are needed to succeed there. In fact, the question was raised: Do we
really understand our core competence?"

Schering's future-oriented, "high-end" approach was compared
by Pohle to that of BASF and Merck—two other large German-
based participants in the world chemicals and pharmaceuticals industry. He described BASF by contrast as a "more commodity-
oriented, lower-margin, operations-driven company," while Merck
was classified as having a "chemicals' versus pharmaceuticals culture—with less research vision, but more tightly controlled rollouts
of products into 'big' markets."

In spite of the obvious orientation to the future, and to R&D,
Schering announced in late 1990 that as of January 1, 1991, it would
move to a "segment management system." According to Pohle, this
change was necessary.

> to redress the previous underestimation of the importance of seg-
> ments. We previously did not realize how diversified we were by
> segment. Our division structure was simply not fine enough. Our

> hope is to create a new "tension" between division/corporate man-
> agement and segment management. We might say, "If you can get
> inventories down by X, we can find some (extra) funds for develop-
> ment."

Interestingly, Pohle's point of comparison for this exercise was not
other pharmaceutical or even chemical giants. It was instead a company named Herlitz, a small German manufacturer and distributor
of paper pads. Herlitz was well known in Germany for creating an
automatic inventory and logistics systems to supply and resupply
stationary outlets with extremely short delivery times. Herlitz was
noted for its excellence in operations and for its ability to run its
current business with consummate skill. Apparently, Schering, like
Nestlé and Caterpillar, was finding in the early 1990s that it could
not content itself with only a forward-looking management system;
operations also had to be managed with excellence—and in doing
so funds might even be boosted to reinforce long-term positions.

HEINEKEN

To complete this picture, we turn to Dutch-based Heineken—a
company also in the midst of far-reaching change—in this case in-
spired by fundamental shifts in consumer tastes and values, and by
a quest for global leadership.

The "old" Heineken was a family-owned and family-managed
company made up of a group of local operating companies (Holland being the largest and strongest), each with five-year plans,
each with an assortment of products, and each with different product positioning, widely varying market share goals, and considerable freedom to make decisions. The "new" Heineken is envisioned
as a professionally managed company with a focus on premium
specialty beers, strong international brands, and an integrated (but
not necessarily standardized) approach to its different markets
worldwide. Change has been initiated from the top with a major
reshuffle of executive board tasks—away from regional responsibilities to functional responsibilities on a worldwide basis. This would
all add up to more central policy control and less autonomy market-
by-market.

The change process at Heineken was encapsulated in eighteen separate "projects"—all starting in early 1991, and all slated to finish within three years or less. Heineken's chief executive, "Ray" van Schaik, commented:

> Not everything can be changed simultaneously, especially against a background of possible worldwide recession. Pushing for change is the concern that performance over the last five years has not been as high as the company's potential would indicate. Performance must be higher to support the kinds of investment that will be needed by the future "global brand" strategy—especially with some environmental costs now making themselves felt. . . . So a critical point is finding ways to keep the company running smoothly and profitably, while making the necessary changes.

The difficulty of simultaneously managing change while managing for current results was highlighted by B. Sarpriati, corporate director of human resources:

> If everything works, we will have shifted from strong family management to "management for the 90s" without a real crisis. Perhaps it would be easier if there were a crisis! It is much more difficult to stay on the track and avert a crisis while we are changing. The danger will be if the market softens and people attribute bad results to the changes and not to the recession.

Heineken's approach to managing the change process and the existing business in parallel was to keep the two apart—at least initially. Sarpriati commented:

> The current planning system drives today's business. It starts in February/March of each year with a discussion of mission and scope for each operating unit, continues in May/June with the development of policies and plans for the next five years (but with a concentration on the next three), and finishes in November with an operational plan and budget.

The changes coming out of the eighteen project teams, each comprised of corporate staff and country management, were expected to gradually impact the existing planning process via new guidelines. Under the old system, regional and country market managers were profit responsible; under the new system, they were expected to retain profit responsibility but work more within frameworks determined by the Corporate Centre. In this respect, changes at Heineken closely resemble changes at Nestlé.

J. B. H. M. Beks, Heineken's Finance Director at the time of the study, described the changes as follows: "In the past, the head office focused on the future; operating companies largely focused on the present. In the new company, the future and present must be better integrated."

But he also recognized the difficulty of actually accomplishing this: " 'Duality' does not really go much down the line—nor should it. Don't give *too* (author's emphasis) much chance for people down the line to think about the future—they should concentrate on running successful operations." He added, "Our current five-year plans are really 'present plans for the future,' mostly focused on the operating company level."

Describing the company's current planning system, Beks commented:

> Today, the company simply "adds up" the operating company plans. At the moment, local operating companies are intent on building local business; we at the Centre are intent on building the Heineken brand. But we also look primarily at return on assets compared to budget—and not enough at the key success factors *behind* (author's emphasis) the numbers.

Our picture of Heineken, and indeed of the problem of attending simultaneously to today and tomorrow, would be incomplete without the perspective of an operating unit general manager. R. V. Strobos, general manager of Heineken Holland, made it clear that the problems of managing change in parallel when managing operations are not limited to the top:

> Heineken Holland was always very profitable, and therefore a bit "fat and happy." Now competition is tougher and our financial position is under more pressure. We therefore have to reduce costs, change our organizational mentality, increase production flexibility, add new low-alcohol products, bring "services" closer to the market, and start subcontracting some of our internal requirements for transport, warehousing, and facilities management.

These changes, *at the operating level,* were expected to extend over a three-year horizon, and had started by 1989. They involved cost reduction plans on the one side, and new marketing approaches on the other. Strobos summarized the overall dilemma of attending simultaneously to the present and future as follows:

> I am concentrating on these longer-term improvements, but trying to avoid present problems which would endanger the long-term plans. Some of my subordinates more naturally look at short-term operations; some more at the long-term. As far as change is concerned, we have spent a lot of time preparing to change—now we have to start implementing. . . . On top, everyone knows that something important is happening at the corporate level.

Nestlé, Caterpillar, Schering, and Heineken all tell a similar story, albeit in different industries and different settings. Headquartered in four different countries, all are undisputed world leaders in their respective fields. The story they tell is of a new but persistent challenge: how to manage change while at the same time managing their existing businesses with excellence. Managing with excellence today is for each a precondition for excellence tomorrow, because future-oriented investments depend on high levels of current earnings. And managing the change process successfully is the precondition for earnings tomorrow.

All the companies are also facing the challenge of defining the respective roles of corporate, country, line of business, and functional management in planning and managing the agendas for today and tomorrow. Some, like Nestlé and Caterpillar, are edging towards a closer integration of the two; others, like Heineken and Schering, foresee a closer integration in the future. All see the shortcomings of viewing planning simply as a three-year or five-year extended sales forecasting and budgeting process.

These four companies have been picked out from the ten that were subjects of in-depth study only because they provide the most complete set of contrasts and comparisons. *All* the companies exhibited, to a greater or lesser extent, the same underlying dilemmas—and these issues are certainly not limited to these ten companies only. Managing change and managing with excellence today is becoming a pressing problem for all firms and all managers—in whatever industry and geographic setting they participate.

Before dealing with present strategy and change strategy in detail, which are the subjects of Part III, some foundations have to be laid. To understand dynamic, ever-shifting modern markets we must look at these markets from three very different perspectives. Thus Part II takes first a customer perspective, second the perspective of the company and its competitors, and third the perspective of costs. Armed with these three perspectives, we shall be in a better position to understand the real nature of dual strategies and how each should be conceived and implemented to master the present and preempt the future.

PART II

PERSPECTIVES ON TODAY AND TOMORROW

THE CUSTOMER PERSPECTIVE

CHAPTER 3

THERE'S MORE TO CUSTOMER SATISFACTION THAN MEETS THE EYE

Tom Peters, in one of his excellent video tapes on excellence, describes a "full service" gasoline station that resembles a pit stop in the world of automobile racing.[1] Four trained "attendants" descend on the car (and driver) as it pulls in, checking tires, oil, battery, windshield wipers, and a number of other safety points. They pump gasoline, clean the whole car outside, vacuum clean the inside, provide coffee and a newspaper, and have you on your way in ninety seconds! This clearly redefines current standards, not only in terms of how well the service is provided, but also in terms of the scope and variety of benefits offered.

If it can be done for gasoline service stations, why can't it be done for other products or services just as well? Is the problem a technical one? Is it a question of costs versus benefits? Or is it just mediocrity in our thinking, and too easy acceptance of existing norms of product and service quality? In fact, combing through recent experience reveals that, while such "mutations" are the exception rather than the rule, they do nevertheless occur with some regularity. Benetton made a similar breakthrough in the clothing market; IKEA in the furniture market; Apple in personal computers; Sony in consumer electronics; and Canon in home copiers. Earlier examples are also evident: Polaroid did it in the photography market, while Club Med did it in the vacation/leisure market. Each of these companies *redefined* existing notions and standards of customer satisfaction, rather than just aiming for incremental improvements. They each laid a new challenge at their competitors' doors, not because they were intent on "gaining a competitive edge," but because they were intent on providing a new and better way of doing things. In searching for an explanation, it is tempting to ascribe the underlying driving force for change to either "entrepreneurship" or "creativity," or "technology." It is in fact all of these things and more—the ability to see the world in a new way.

The question before us, as managers, is whether we can do anything to improve the likelihood of redefining standards in our *own* sector of activity. Is the process random or can it be managed? In fact, there seems to be surprisingly little recognition among managers that breakthroughs of the type made by Polaroid, Club Med, Benetton, IKEA, Canon, and others may be fundamentally different than incremental "product development." Nor is there any widespread questioning about whether these types of breakthroughs can become more the rule than the exception. Even where there is a steady drive for quality improvement, it is more often than not manifested in terms such as becoming more "differentiated," or "gaining competitive advantage" than in radically improving customer satisfaction. Is the purpose just to stay ahead of competitors, or is it to do an exceptional job of meeting customers' needs? Just "beating the next guy" may turn out to be a limiting rather than mind-expanding philosophy.

Some would, of course, correctly argue that competition is the underlying mechanism by which the customers' lot can be continually improved. But to put the quest for competitive advantage ahead of the quest for customer satisfaction in our *thinking* is to put the cart before the horse. Competition and competitive advantage are, in fact, only part of the story. If firms compete without the imagination and passion to provide better offerings for their own sake, even competition cannot be relied on to do the job. The "differentiation" sought by many managers turns out to be a rather modest objective; even "long-term sustainable competitive advantage" pales before the idea of dramatically serving customers better as an objective in and of itself. If customers are served with excellence, long-term sustainable competitive advantage will result of its own accord.

The picture is further clouded by the fact that quality and customer satisfaction are themselves terms that are ambiguous and difficult to define. Do we mean by quality something absolute, in the sense that product A may be considered superior to product B in every circumstance by all customers? Almost certainly not. Beauty, they say, lies in the eyes of the beholder—and so it is with quality. Features of the product itself, or features of service that may be provided along with its purchase or use, may have a very different appeal to different groups of customers. Part of this may hinge on customers' own shopping habits or uses to which they put the product; part of it may hinge on their own level of experience with such products and their power of discrimination between one product and another. Each segment is defined by its own configuration of needs. We risk comparing apples with oranges, therefore, if we judge quality differences across substantially different segments. In a nutshell, quality and customer satisfaction are theoretically, as well as practically, elusive.

As we look to the future, a reasonable prediction is that as the competitive race continues to heat up, only those companies that can emulate the real breakthroughs of the past will survive. This is a frightening prospect for many, if not most, organizations. Most have barely scrambled to keep up with new standards, let alone taken the lead in redefining the very basis of customer satisfaction.

But the signals that the exception may become the rule seem persuasive. Global competition is drawing new, previously unheard of competitors who intrude into each local marketplace, and "our" standards, whatever they are, are often found to be wanting by our customers. New competitors often deliver not only higher levels of customer satisfaction than we do, but they provide new *dimensions* of satisfaction. U.S. consumer electronics producers were forced to abandon their markets to Japanese producers, not because of incremental product differences, but because the Japanese redefined the very nature of customer satisfaction in this industry in the

1970s and 80s. And it seems safe to assume that radical improvements in customer satisfaction may not be the sole preserve of large multinationals with their origins in the so-called "triad" of affluent Western Europe, Japan, or the United States. New customer-satisfying possibilities may emerge from human experience and imagination as well as from technology and financial investment. The so-called "developed" world has no particular monopoly in these respects.

On the demand side, there are also strong signals of impending change in required standards. Customers are ever hungrier for real improvements, sensing that in spite of burgeoning new technology, there is still a big gap between what they really want and what they get. In fact, if we look across a wide array of industry and service sectors over the past several decades, we see that while there are many cases of successful redefinition, there are far more cases of continuing "me-too" approaches. It is of course not easy to gauge to what degree standards are improving overall, since there are few absolute yardsticks. Expectations also change with time and may affect judgments. But even the casual observer could be forgiven for questioning whether customers are really making enough gains. It might even be argued that in some sectors, regress rather than progress more aptly describes the evolution of customer satisfaction. Such appears to be the case where the "secondary" effects of the product on the environment are not properly factored into product development, where side effects produce more harm than good (as in the case of cigarettes or some pharmaceuticals), and where the opening up of mass markets for products or services is accompanied by a degradation of quality. And we can all think of examples in individual companies, or even whole sectors, where quality "slippage" has occurred. This is not just limited to our favorite hotel, restaurant, or corner store which, falling into new hands, fails to live up to our old expectations. It has occurred in sectors as large and important as airline travel, which with overcrowding, inadequate infrastructure, and poor profitability, showed declining levels of punctuality, service, and convenience in the late 1980s. Against this mixed picture, the only certainty seems to be that as life-styles are rapidly changing, customer demands are rapidly changing in response. No industry and no company can remain immune from such powerful forces. Each must find new ways to not only meet, but *exceed,* customer expectations.

Improving customer satisfaction via product innovation (or service innovation in the case of service industries) often takes precedence in managements' eyes over improving distribution, communications, services, and "softer" attributes such as perceived image, the nature of the buyer/seller relationship, and a host of others. A product focus on innovation is especially prevalent in technology-oriented companies, where an "engineering mentality" may predominate. Too little attention is also usually paid to opportunities for satisfying customer needs at stages of the purchase and use cycle beyond the purchase itself. And seldom is enough consideration given to the need of individuals other than the direct purchaser.

The remainder of this chapter puts product innovation into a broader perspective—as one way, but by no means the only way, to devise true "breakthroughs" in customer satisfaction. In fact, the closer the product or service is to the commodity end of the spectrum, the more we have to look beyond the physical product itself as a basis for excellence. We start therefore with possibilities for improving the physical product, but we shall by no means end there. It's just the top of the iceberg, as illustrated in Figure 3–1. Each of these successive levels can provide the basis for breakthroughs in customer satisfaction.

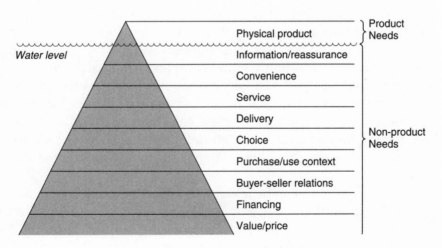

Figure 3–1. The Customer Satisfaction Iceberg

IMPROVING THE PHYSICAL PRODUCT

In some industries, the opportunities for improvement in the product itself seem to abound, while in other, more "commodity-like" areas, opportunities seem relatively few and far between. And even if ways are found to improve the product, these are relatively easily copied by competitors so that product differentiation is short-lived. Product improvements seem particularly hard to come by in the more mature stages of the life cycle for virtually all products, whatever their inherent characteristics, as technological innovation slows and products become more standardized. It is small wonder therefore that managers usually carry a mental image of their products as situated towards the commodity end of the spectrum.

In fact, opportunities for increasing customer satisfaction via product improvement are never exhausted—even for so-called commodities. Much depends on the perspective which management takes. And while in most such cases nonproduct dimensions of customer satisfaction carry substantial weight, product innovation possibilities should never be ignored. U.S. consumer electronics producers were convinced, for example, that they were operating in a mature, commodity-like industry in the early 1970s. Cathode-ray tube technology had apparently plateaued, consumer demand for television was thought to be saturated, and picture quality, color, and definition appeared to be more than acceptable by local U.S. standards. It took Japanese insight into customer-satisfying possibilities, and the application of new electronic technology, to prove how wrong U.S. producers were. In the intervening years, a whole new industry with a complex variety of products and services has developed, virtually monopolized by Japanese producers. And the story is still far from over as new syntheses between computers, communications, home entertainment, and education are coming into view, and as high-definition television, prodigious memory capacities, and other digital technologies become commonplace.

Two perspectives can be taken with respect to product development. The first, that apparently taken by U.S. TV producers, is to start with the existing product and look for ways to improve its qualities. This can often take us so far and no further. We can easily become the captives of existing solutions and overlook other, often better, solutions that lie outside the concept of the current product offering. Technological innovation is then often constrained to the improvement of existing technological solutions rather than to the development of totally new approaches.

A more fruitful perspective, that apparently taken by Japanese consumer electronics producers, is to take as a starting point the *function(s)* that the product is performing for the customer, and the particular *benefits* that are, or might be, sought. This puts the existing product offering in another light, as one, but only one possible solution to the customer's problems. This customer-oriented approach to product development is aptly captured in the old adage that a customer doesn't really want a quarter-inch drill, he wants a quarter-inch hole. Instead of thinking about how to improve our drill, it gets us thinking about how to make better holes. We may go even further and ask why the customer needs the quarter-inch hole. Is it to bolt two pieces of metal together? If so, can we find an alternative solution to this broader problem? Soon we find ourselves thinking about improved ways to join metals rather than about improving quarter-inch drill bits or even making quarter-inch holes. Following this approach, General Electric Medical Systems Division, a leader in X-ray technology, diversified early into CAT scanning devices, and into imaging diagnostic devices based on ultrasound technology. They conceived new product development in terms of providing customers with an improved imaging diagnostic function as opposed to incrementally improving conventional X-ray devices.

It may be fairly argued that taking a customer perspective can lead companies into fields that lie beyond their particular areas of technological competence. The counterargument is that such competences must be built internally or acquired if customer satisfaction is the ultimate goal. In reality, as we shall see later, every successful company has to synchronize the development of underlying competences with its business definition to assure that it operates from strength and not from weakness.

Taking the function/benefit approach, the various possibilities for increasing customer satisfaction via product improvement may be conceptualized along two distinct lines. First, better ways may be found to perform existing functions. Second, the functions performed by the product may be redefined.

Better Ways to Perform Existing Functions

One or more existing aspects of the product can be singled out for special attention with the objective of redefining the current standards of quality. The gas station example quoted at the beginning of this chapter provided a graphic example. High-definition television is another. In every product or service category there are new untapped potentials to redefine standards. Conceptual imagination rather than technological innovation is often the limiting ingredient.

Another alternative is to develop entirely *new* dimensions of customer satisfaction. Polaroid built its reputation by pioneering the "instant development" attribute of photography. Prior to this breakthrough, development times were as long as it took the photo shop to do the job—always a few hours and usually a few days. While its main competitor, Kodak, was focusing on new technical characteristics of the camera and film, Polaroid took another track completely. New, hidden, or partly hidden dimensions of customer satisfaction are waiting to be uncovered in virtually all industries. But a customer perspective is needed to uncover them, and technological know-how may be needed to take advantage of them.

In practice, many improvements in customer satisfaction result from product developments that fall somewhere between these two extremes. One existing aspect or another of the product may be highlighted that had not previously been considered to be that important—or perhaps in reality was actually not that important. Manufacturers of bathroom and kitchen faucets and shower fittings, for example, have seen a progressive shift over the past two decades from the "engineering" qualities of the fittings, such as brass content, hand polished finishes, and ease of installation, to design, ease of use, and brand image. Design is in fact of increasing importance in a wide range of consumer and industrial goods as basic functionality is assured. Manufacturers who have paid attention to these emerging needs in their product development activities have outstripped their rivals who have ignored them.

Redefining Functions Performed by the Product

Two or more functions, previously met with separate products, may be combined into a single product offering. Computer terminals offering on-line fax capabilities are an example, as are the growing number of food products offering health-related properties.

Conversely, several functions that were previously combined in a single product may be "unbundled" and provided separately. Such is the case today with a great deal of computer hardware and software purchases—providing far more options for the customer to select specialized software appropriate for his needs rather than standard packages.

Or, alternatively, opportunities may even exist for increasing customer satisfaction by developing products that perform entirely *new functions*. Such products as telefax, windsurfers, snowboards, voice mail, video cameras/recorders, and garbage compactors are not just extensions or improvements of existing products. They are entirely new additions in their respective categories, offering not only new benefits but performing previously unperformed functions.

I have deliberately limited this discussion of ways to improve customer satisfaction to improvements aimed at *existing* groups of customers. Product development may also be required as a company extends its activities to new customer groups or diversifies into entirely new markets. This, however, is the subject of later chapters. As a first step, we need to understand the myriad ways in which, for any one customer segment, satisfaction can be radically enhanced.

While not exhaustive, these examples give some flavor for the almost unlimited possibilities for improving customer satisfaction through the product itself. Even for so-called commodities, raising standards in certain selected benefit areas, pioneering new dimensions of customer satisfaction, bundling or unbundling functions, and developing entirely new functionalities can help to create competitive advantage. For inherently more differentiated products, or products at earlier stages of their life cycle, these approaches can provide even more powerful differentiating possibilities.

While technology is often a key ingredient in improving customer satisfaction, there is almost always a strong element of *conceptual* innovation involved also. By conceptual innovation, I mean *mental* conception of a new way to satisfy the customer. In fact, technological innovation is often most effective when it is used to *support* conceptual innovation, rather than when it is itself directly the origin of the innovation. Too often, product creation processes are technically driven by R&D or engineering staff, rather than taking their cue from the market and from the conceptual innovation which a market-oriented company may come up with.

All that has been said here about the physical product as a center-piece of providing customer satisfaction can also be said of services. Exactly the same logic applies. We have to think of functions being performed and specific benefits sought as the starting point for improving services—not the particularities of the service currently being provided—by whatever means. And the same four areas provide options for new innovation—upgrading of existing standards, pioneering of new dimensions of customer satisfaction, bundling and unbundling of functions, and the addition of entirely new functionalities. But whether we are talking about products or services, the improvement of the product or service itself is only part of the story. It is to the nonproduct dimensions of customer satisfaction that we now turn.

NONPRODUCT DIMENSIONS OF CUSTOMER SATISFACTION

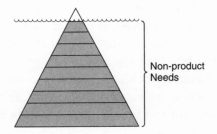

Non-product Needs

Helping the customer through the purchase process, getting the product to the customer at the right time, in the right place, with the proper assurance that he has bought what he needs, with guarantees that it will do what it is supposed to do, providing needed services before, during, and after the sale, arranging financing, and providing an attractive context within which the product is purchased and used, all at an attractive price—all these factors vye in most situations with the product (or service) itself in providing customer satisfaction. Managing these processes, with the right priorities for a chosen customer segment, therefore is of major importance. When these dimensions of customer satisfaction are addressed with excellence, the company may be well on the way to making the kind of breakthrough that was described earlier in this chapter.

It is difficult, if not impossible, to construct a complete list of mutually exclusive nonproduct customer needs. And in each particular situation, some may take on considerably more significance than others. The main need areas in which new degrees and levels of customer satisfaction are being added by innovative companies will be taken up in turn.

Needs for Information and Reassurance

Customers are particularly susceptible to information and reassurance concerning a product or service when it is of high value, complex, has "hidden qualities" (a mattress is a favorite example of mine—you don't know whether it is good or not until you have slept on it for twenty years!), and when they lack experience in purchase or use. Information and reassurance can range from purchasing advice and instructions on how to use the product, to extensive problem solving and consulting support required in the purchase of high-value investment goods or large-ticket consumer durables. It may be directed at "real" product attributes or at creating a perceived image of the product, or both.

New breakthroughs are being made in recognizing the importance of these needs for particular customer segments at particular times for particular purchases—and investing with much higher selectivity to meet these needs. Bland advertising, uninformative packaging, and listless, uninformed point-of-sales sales personnel are being replaced by customer-satisfying communications, carefully conceived and professionally delivered. The wholly owned and managed cosmetics stores of Shu Uemura break totally new ground in providing levels of information and reassurance to cosmetics purchasers—as well as providing brilliantly conceived displays, product variety and choice, point-of-sale consulting, and the highest quality products.

New ways are also being pioneered to *convey* information and reassurance—via video, fax, at-home marketing devices, and a host of other means. New communication technologies are opening the door to communication innovations—but it takes a managerial imagination and a customer perspective to put these wonderful technologies to work.

Convenience Needs

Convenience means getting the product into the right place at the right time. It means literally "to make things easy" for the customer. Customers are particularly susceptible to convenience for frequently purchased so-called "impulse" items—like newspapers, toiletries, and foodstuff. If these are not conveniently distributed, they will not be sold.

What is new is the recognition that convenience is a hot issue for many other items too. The provision of several in-flight telephones on long distance transcontinental flights was a major breakthrough in convenience in the 1980s. In the 1990s, new standards of convenience have been set by providing a telephone on the back of *every* seat on many short distance flights as well. Computer hookups in all major hotels, showers for the weary traveler, and just-in-time delivery of components to industrial manufacturers are all examples of managerial imagination applied to improving the convenience of the product as opposed to product improvement itself. Even for high-ticket items, where traditionally the needs for information and reassurance have outweighed the needs for convenience, new ground is being broken. Rental and car leasing companies, for example, are challenging car dealers by making it more convenient to lease than to buy—even if there is a substantive price difference.

Service Needs

Service has a wide range of connotations. It ranges from personal contact between buyer and seller (or seller's agent) at the point of purchase or use, to various kinds of logistical backup or repair, to services that may be required by the customer before, during, or after purchase. There are elements of service provision associated with practically every physical product transaction. And in so-called service industries, service *is* the product.

Customers are susceptible to service at the point of sale or use when the transaction is complex and otherwise time consuming. They are susceptible to logistical, backup, or repair services when the absence of these would cost substantial amounts of money or time. Purchasers of office equipment such as copying machines are, for example, highly sensitive to prompt service (or its product counterpart, reliability) because the cost and inconvenience of downtime is high. The risk and cost of downtime for a process control computer controlling a multimillion dollar chemical production process is even higher—and customers are willing to pay hefty price premiums to guarantee reliability. For a nuclear plant, the risk is even higher, and the "price" of service guaranties even heftier.

Service needs, like information and reassurance needs, are being reassessed by virtually all leading, innovative firms. Service quality in most industries leaves much to be desired and there is very substantial room for radical improvement and innovation. Examples now abound of new concepts and standards of service to fill the gap. The gas station example again helps us to envision the potential that exists in most industries for a redefinition of standards.

The steady spread of "self-service" across a whole range of retail products—from supermarket items to soft goods, to semidurables, gasoline, banking, and now large-ticket items such as furniture—testifies to the changing tradeoffs that customers are making between the cost and benefit of information and personal service at the point of sale. But self-service is itself a new service concept that extends beyond retailing. IKEA is able to provide low-cost, value-oriented furniture with immediate delivery because part of the manufacturing task has been transferred to the customer. All DIY (do-it-yourself) products have self-service elements inherent in them.

Delivery Needs

Delivery is always important, and it can almost always be improved. Both the period between order and delivery and punctuality are important dimensions of customer satisfaction. Conventional standards are rapidly becoming obsolete as manufacturers and service providers increasingly address the underlying reasons for poor delivery. East German customers for the now famous Trabant car had to wait up to fourteen years for delivery! Mercedes operated regularly with waiting lists of one year and more until the 1980s. Today, some Japanese car producers are reputed to be able to deliver a *customized* vehicle seven days after the order is placed! Records are being slashed daily for industrial deliveries. "Just-in-time" delivery means getting the product to the customer not one hour earlier and not one our later than it is needed in the subsequent production process—and failure to meet such standards automatically disqualifies suppliers from the marketplace.

The Need for Choice

Customers do not always know exactly what they want or need, and if they think they do, the "shopping" experience may change their minds or allow them to more precisely define their requirements. Industrial goods purchasers are also susceptible to this phenomenon—the process of exploring "what's out there on the market" helps to define the eventual purchase. Providing a choice of products or services may therefore be indicated—if only to satisfy this "shopping" requirement. But choice is valuable in and of itself because it allows an even finer segmentation than we can provide with a single offering. Shades of difference in customer needs can be satisfied by the process of self-selection that customers go through as they sift through choices to see what is exactly right for them.

Choice is important when there are a large number of product or nonproduct attributes, and/or when the possible variations of any of these attributes are many. Clothing is traditionally in item where the element of choice is high—mainly because of the almost infinite variations possible in design, style, color, and size. But for other more prosaic products such as bottled water, choice has become an important criterion as customers increasingly distinguish between bottle design, carbonation, mineral content, bottle size, multiple-pack alternatives, and the like. Failure to provide choices may limit the potential market.

Innovative companies are providing choices—often where none was provided before—as an important dimension of their overall offering. Information technology is providing a new means to provide rapid feedback between the point of purchase and manufacturing and logistic systems, so that favored choices can be given priority. Benetton's system of dying textiles only weeks before purchase in the store is feasible only because of such a computerized information feedback system. But, more importantly, choice is now being provided in product areas where it was previously considered impractical or only of marginal value. The newspaper industry is a case in point. Until recently, readers all received the same newspaper, perhaps with minor variations by geographic region. Today, teletext and data text systems (such as France's Minitel) are enabling the user to pick out that information which he or she specifically wants, from a vast array of information possibilities. And what is happening in newspapers is happening in television programming (via cable as well as video recording), in computer software, and even in durable goods such as automobiles. BMW claims to offer more than one million variants of a single basic car!

Contextual Needs

Few products or services are purchased or consumed in a vacuum—although failure to realize this may be one of the many reasons for failure to deliver real customer satisfaction. Coffee comes in a cup, and the cup may be plastic, ordinary ceramic, or fine porcelain. The cup may be gripped in the hand, for want of an alternative, or it may be placed on a silver tray, accompanied by a small silver cream jug and a bowl of sugar. The tray may be set on a pink linen tablecloth on the sunny terrace of a Swiss mountain restaurant by a beautiful waitress (or handsome waiter) who takes the time and has the willingness to exchange some interesting words with you—all against a backdrop of snow-capped peaks, in resplendent sunshine. If she or he takes the time to introduce you to the people at the next table, or to find you your favorite newspaper, your coffee may be a substantially different product than that obtained at a machine dispenser in a basement a few feet away from the company restrooms!

Worrying about context may be as or more important than worrying about the product quality itself. And even when the user context cannot be completely controlled, as in the case of many consumer or industrial goods purchased for off-premise use, the *purchase* context usually can. Control or influence over the retail distribution environment is one such way—which explains why so many high-quality product manufacturers are integrating forward to own and control their own retail outlets.

In many cases even the user context, while ostensibly in the hands of the customer, can be substantially improved if thought is given to improving it. Easy to open, attractive, and easy to dispose of packaging is one example; the provision of interior design support to buyers of home furnishings is another.

Creative marketers are coming up with all kinds of ways to meet the needs of customers for a radically improved purchase or use context. The first step in the process is simply to start thinking about it!

The Need for a Sound Buyer-Seller Relationship

The buyer-seller relationship is likely to be particularly important when a *series* of repeat purchases are made from a single supplier, when the product life is long and interim service arrangements are required, or when there is a need for assurance as to *future* competencies—such as technical know-how needed to develop a stream of compatible follow-on or replacement products. The relationship may be directly between buyer and seller or between the buyer and supplier channels of distribution. It can take the form of interpersonal relationships, contractual relationships, or simply perceptions.

IBM recognized the importance of such relationships early in the history of the computer industry. Manufacturing and selling excellent products was not enough—and the strong relationships that it built with its customers played an important role in protecting IBM from competitors as long as product/price divergences were not too great. But the need for managing sound relationships is not limited to IBM and the computer industry. Firms everywhere are discovering that being customer oriented has a long-term effect. It has been likened to a marriage. The relationship has to be nurtured continually so that individual transactions between the partners take place against a backdrop of security and trust. Nordstrom, the leading San Francisco-based retail department store, exemplifies concern for the buyer-seller relationship. *All* merchandise is returnable at no charge, if the customer is not satisfied—whatever the reason!

The Need for Financing

Customers are likely to be susceptible to credit or other forms of financial support when there is a discrepancy, for whatever reason, between cash available and cash needed for purchase, or when the cost of credit from other sources is prohibitive. Sometimes the discrepancy is simply a matter of timing—as in the traditional problem of providing farm credits during the crop cycle; in other cases credit is an integral part of the customer's satisfaction, as in the case of a house mortgage. Credit needs have increased dramatically over the last two decades, as consumption aspirations have expanded against a backdrop of level or even shrinking disposable resources. Many firms have unwisely provided credit to noncreditworthy customers and now find themselves with uncollectible receivables or bad debts on their hands. Nevertheless, the selective use of credit and other financing instruments remains an important aspect of customer satisfaction. Financing distributors' inventories or financing field stocks to drastically improve customer service deserves just as much attention from marketers as it does from corporate financial staff—who often view it as a cost rather than a customer benefit.

Budgetary and Value Needs

Last but not least, the customer has to be satisfied in terms of the price paid and his perception of the total value achieved. Prices may or may not reflect costs but they must reflect perceived value. Pricing at "what the market will bear" may be a good way to maximize *short-term* profitability, but in the long term it may backfire if there is not a basic *long-term* concept of a "fair price," that is, a price at which both buyer and seller feel that they are in a "win-win" situation.

Meeting Needs

The section of this book entitled "The Company Perspective" goes into depth concerning the ways in which firms meet needs for information and reassurance, convenience, services, delivery, choice, context, relationships, financing, and value. Here, I shall simply point out that technical and product know-how is only the tip of that iceberg. Below the surface is a dazzling array of hidden marketing tools ranging from branding, packaging, advertising, promotion, and other marketing communication, as well as retail and wholesale distribution; further below the surface are other elements of the firms' own business activities, including manufacturing and logistics systems, engineering and development, information technology, finances, and management systems; even further below the visible surface are corporate-wide resources and competences which may be brought to bear, directly or via alliances; and at the base of the iceberg the customer-satisfying possibilities of the whole vertical "business system," from raw material supply at one end to customer distribution at the other.

A BROADER CONCEPT OF "CUSTOMER"

So far we have concentrated on broadening the concept of customer satisfaction beyond the purely technical aspects of a product or service. Another way in which companies achieve innovative breakthroughs is to take a broader perspective with respect to who their "customers" really are. It is too easy to assume that either the purchaser or the user is the *only* customer whose needs have to be satisfied. This flies in the face of common sense when we pause for a moment to consider the often substantial number of individuals who play some role in influencing the purchase, or who subsequently are involved in the use, service, or even disposal of the product, as shown in Figure 3–2.

Consider for a moment the purchase and use of an automobile. While one particular family member may be the "purchasing agent" in the sense of taking charge of the overall purchase process, several if not all immediate family members may participate and express their own needs and preferences; so may friends, solicited or unsolicited for their opinion, as well as acquaintances or even complete strangers who offer a chance remark or comment. Further, the automobile may have, once it is purchased, multiple drivers, each with different needs; parked in the driveway or on the neighborhood street, it may be an eyesore or a source of pride not only to

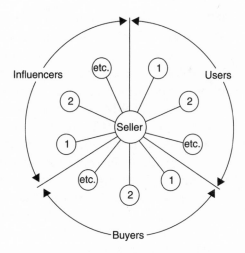

Figure 3–2. Multiple Buying Influences

its owners but also their neighbors. Even more important perhaps, it may bring reputation and profit for the local franchised dealer or service station if it functions well, or disrepute and wrath on their heads if it functions badly. Who is the customer to be satisfied in these circumstances? The answer is *all* of the above! All needs have to be carefully considered and where there appears to be an important point of leverage, these needs have to be met with excellence.

Industrial goods marketers often seem to be more aware of the multiplicity of buying influences than their consumer goods counterparts. But even then this may not go far enough, and important influences and influencers are overlooked. Too often, the purchasing agent, as the main point of contact for the industrial marketer, is regarded as the customer, and buying needs are taken as they are manifested and expressed by this person alone. For all but the most routine purchase nothing could be further from the reality, and it is necessary to go behind purchasing to understand by whom the product will be used, for what purposes, and what benefits are sought by the different parties involved.

A second important perspective to take, after that of the immediate customer, is of the customer's customers or customers at subsequent stages in the vertical business chain. This is particularly true of industrial goods customers, but is also true of consumer goods purchasers who may eventually contemplate reselling their products to the secondhand market. It is obviously also true of purchases by wholesalers or retailers who will eventually sell to customers. For industrial goods, the satisfaction of customers lower in the chain may be critical to selling successfully to immediate customers. Automobile components manufacturers, for example, have a much higher likelihood of winning OEM contracts, if they can develop products that provide clear benefits to the end customer. Tire suppliers thus develop their products as much with the eventual customer in mind as with the automobile manufacturer in mind.

Developing the habit to "look downstream" and to understand customer needs at each successive stage of the vertical business chain can often be a source of a breakthrough in providing new important product or service possibilities and standards. Providing customer-satisfying benefits at downstream stages is a powerful way to create "pull" for the product at the next immediate customer level. It provides your immediate customer with a way to differentiate his own offering. One result of this increasing adoption of the "downstream" perspective by suppliers is increased competition between one whole vertical business system and another for the end customer's dollar. Benetton competes for the end-customer purchase by controlling the whole vertical chain from manufacturing through distribution to retailing—making sure that "customers" are satisfied at each stage along the way.

THE TIME DIMENSION
OF CUSTOMER SATISFACTION

The possibility for providing customer satisfaction begins at the moment the customer first considers, in any way at all, the product purchase, and ends only when the product is disposed of. The many, many steps along the way can each be considered as separate opportunities for meeting, exceeding, or *failing* to meet customer needs (see Figure 3–3).

At the front end of the process we are often talking about the acquisition of information which stimulates the customer's interest in the product category and particularly in our product, and helps him to define his needs and match them with the available offerings; at the back end of the process we are increasingly talking of product disposal, recycling, and even "demanufacturing" possibilities. We

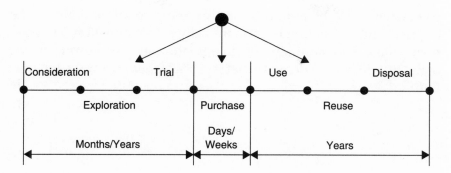

Figure 3–3. Purchase and Use Chronology

may also be talking, as in the computer industry, about providing for compatibility between old and new systems, trade-ups, trade-ins and overall long-term system planning.

It is necessary to think through this chronology carefully and look for specific opportunities at *any* stage to do a superior job of meeting customer needs. Too often management takes a too restrictive view of this time dimension, concentrating on the immediate purchase and postpurchase period. This is a producer perspective, not a customer perspective. "From womb to tomb" is a good motto for marketers as well as health care specialists. BMW and Volkswagen have both now embarked on extensive investments to ensure "demanufacturing" of used cars, recycling of key automotive components, and the limitation of negative environmental and energy effects increasingly considered important by their customers as well as the general public.

CUSTOMER SATISFACTION— A MANAGERIAL APPROACH

We have seen in this chapter that there is almost an infinite number of ways to satisfy customers' needs, and to develop new standards of quality. They range from improvements to the product or service itself, to nonproduct need satisfaction, to taking a broader perspective on who is actually to be satisfied, to thinking of possible improvements over the whole chronology of purchase and use. If this is done rigorously and creatively, it should be apparent that there is no such thing as a commodity. Standards can always be raised somewhere and the opportunities for doing so are unlimited. The biggest single limitation is normally only the imagination. Management's task is to stimulate this imagination in every corner of the organization, and to demand that it starts from a customer perspective.

CHAPTER 4

MARKET SEGMENTATION

Most companies pay lip service to the definition of markets and market segments; few practice it with the care it deserves. When well done, it provides a key input to the definition of a company's business, which in turn can be one of the most powerful factors behind growth and profitability. It often requires as much creativity as it does science. Effective definition of markets and market segments circumscribes each market, and divides these markets into pieces that are identifiable, accessible to specialized business approaches, substantial enough to be profitable, and above all defensible against competition.

Few subjects can have produced as much confusion for managers. Many regard segmentation as a research tool, and believe that it is primarily the responsibility of market research staff. In fact, it should be one of the major preoccupations of the chief executive and his top management team. The importance of market definition and market segmentation goes far beyond marketing—affecting literally every aspect of the firm's activity.

Management usually experiences difficulty with market definition and segmentation because they lack any kind of overall road map to guide their thinking. In the absence of such a map, it is not surprising that definitions often tend to be naive, indiscriminate with respect to sharply focused strategies and activities, and hardly different from those used by their main competitors. It is also not surprising therefore that sharp differentiation in the marketplace is so difficult to achieve.

A typical shortcoming is to rely too heavily on the *physical* properties of the product and on the sociodemographic characteristics of customers in defining "product markets." Further precision, if provided at all, often includes the somewhat pious ambition to be at the "quality" or "specialty" end of the market (reflecting of course management's hopes—but not necessarily concrete plans—to achieve higher margins). Other dimensions, which might provide considerably more strategic insight, like the products' inherent characteristics, or patterns of purchase and use, often receive less attention.

Focusing on differences is important for *all* competitors—whether they are in growth markets or mature markets, in high-value products or in low-value products, and whether they are market leaders or market followers. Bringing these differences into focus, so that we may deliver exactly what is needed, where it is needed, when it is needed, in the way that is needed, is what this chapter is all about.

DEFINING MARKETS AND MARKET SEGMENTS

Customers have, as we have seen in Chapter 3, a wide variety of needs to satisfy. Needs for sophisticated industrial products and services costing millions are usually more complex than needs for simple consumer items costing cents. The "market" for any one of these items may range from a single buyer to hundreds of millions of buyers, concentrated geographically or spread worldwide.

Any time there is more than one buyer, it is rare that they will have exactly the same needs. One buyer of engineered plastics, lacking his own development capability, may be more interested in getting technical support from the seller than another who has competent technical support in-house. A third may be more interested in lower-grade plastics because of different price/quality constraints in his own chosen customer market—and so on. Or, to take an example from consumer markets, one customer may buy a Swatch and another (or even the same customer for a different occasion), a Rolex.

There is of course an extensive literature dealing with market definition and segmentation—part of it originating with the economists and lawyers who need to understand and define the basis for antitrust violations. There is also an extensive marketing literature, much of which regrettably goes unread by those who most need it—senior general management.

At different times over the last two or three decades, one or another dimension of segmentation has been claimed as *the* way to define and divide markets. These have included so called "benefits" segmentation, psychographics and "life style" segmentation,[1] and other schemes related to various aspects of customer buying behavior or customer use of the product, such as heavy versus light users. But none of these has proved to be the panacea that its authors promoted it to be—and practitioners continue to grapple with the complexity of definition and segmentation as best they can. This does not mean that companies and their leaders do not sometimes come up with brilliant and creative ways to define markets, segments, and their own businesses—they do. But it happens more rarely than it should or could. And when they do, it is often more the result of serendipity, intuition, and good old trial and error than an organized strategic thought process.

Care is needed! Before we set out on the difficult task of attempting to bring some conceptual order to a subject full of ambiguity, we must recognize that the words "market" and "market segment" may be used at a variety of levels of aggregation and in a variety of ways. If, for example, we talk of *international* air travel as a market, then *transatlantic* air travel might be defined as a market segment; if instead we define *transatlantic* air travel as a market, then *business class* travel might be defined as a segment. Whatever level of aggregation and whichever way is chosen, however, a market segment can be regarded as *part* of a larger market, different from other segments in that market in some definable way.

A useful way to approach the question of aggregation is to distinguish "coarse segmentation" from "fine segmentation"—just as we do in tuning a radio. Coarse segmentation, like coarse tuning, is needed to define the overall area in which we have an interest; fine segmentation, like fine tuning, is used to pinpoint our choice exactly.

COARSE SEGMENTATION
Defining Markets in Terms of Products

At the highest level of aggregation, it is quite common to hear markets described simply in terms of the product involved. We speak therefore of the "textile market" or the "cereals market" or the "automobile market." The implication, in the absence of any statement to the contrary, is that we are talking about worldwide markets for these products, although in fact one or another geographic region of the market may really be implied, such as the *U.S.* automobile market. Still, such unidimensional descriptions of markets at such high levels of aggregation provide us with little insight as to the nature of the market, or how companies may compete for parts of it.

We may obtain more precision and still stay with a unidimensional product definition by subdividing product-defined markets. Thus textile markets may be subdivided into apparel markets and nonapparel markets; and apparel markets, in turn, into suits and shirt markets. Many further subdivisions are evidently possible along these same lines.

Defining Markets in Terms of "Product Markets"

An additional way to add further precision to the coarse definition of a market is to add another descriptor—most often the definition of the customer for whom the product is intended. Thus we may speak of the *pet* food market, or the *women's* apparel market, or the *business* travel market. Either of the two dimensions may then be further subdivided to provide further precision. Taking pet food as an example, this may be further subdivided into *dog* food (subdividing the customer dimension) or *dog biscuits* (subdividing customer and product dimensions).

Sometimes the second dimension used for defining a market is not the customer but the type of use to which the product is put, or the need which it fulfills. Thus we may speak of the *breakfast* cereals market, or the *sports* car market or the *outerwear* apparel market. Such definitions may also of course be further subdivided, such as *nutritional* cereals, *convertible* cars, or *rainwear* apparel.

FINE SEGMENTATION

Instead of further subdividing one- or two-dimensional descriptions of a product market, fine segmentation requires a different approach. On the one hand we must *precisely* identify the segment; on the other hand we must identify the specific needs or benefits that are sought by that segment.

Segment Definition

A complete description of a segment requires three dimensions to be specified: (a) the customer group(s) who buy(s) the product, (b) the functions that the product performs for those customers, and (c) the form that the product takes.[2] When these three dimensions are used, the product itself is not explicitly defined, but is implied by the other three descriptors.

It is sometimes helpful to display such segment definitions on a three-dimensional chart of the type shown in Figure 4–1. Thus we may refer to *business* (the customer) *transatlantic* (the function) *air travel* (the form). Equally, *men's cotton rainwear* defines a submarket within the larger men's rainwear market. As before, any one or more of the three dimensions can itself be subdivided to provide more precision to the market definition. We might, for example, define *large corporate* users of transatlantic air travel as a specific segment of the business transatlantic air travel market—because of their special characteristics and needs.

Sometimes specification of the use or purchase *situation* provides additional precision to the definition of a market segment—precision which cannot be obtained by descriptions of customers, functions, or form. As an example, we may describe a segment of the watch market by young upper-income customers (the customer group), needing timekeeping but not calendar (functions), using battery-operated electronics (the form). But if we add that these

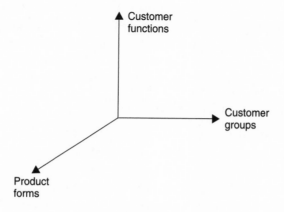

Figure 4–1.

watches are particularly to be used for scuba diving (the use situation), it helps us considerably to define the segment and how its needs might be met.

Customer Needs and Benefits

Further, and often highly useful, precision can be added to the definition of a market by specifying not only customer, function, and product (or service) forms, but by adding a description of the *specific benefits* sought by the occupants of a particular segment. We may, for example, distinguish between the *high-value, fashion-oriented, relatively price insensitive* segment of the men's cotton rainwear market, and contrast it with that segment which is interested more in a *low-price* garment.

We could of course consider this fourth dimension as really only an extension of the product form dimension—arguing that product form is really also a "sought benefit." Many times, however, it is useful to make this additional distinction—especially when discriminating between segments in the same broad market.

It is important to realize that under the heading "benefits sought," we do not limit ourselves to benefits derived from the product itself. We must also include nonproduct needs as described at length in Chapter 3, the needs of those other than the direct purchaser or user, and needs over the whole purchase/user cycle.

Any of these dimensions, customer groups, customer functions, product forms, or needs/benefits can be subdivided to increase the precision of the segment definition. This subdivision is often a matter of *both* creativity and science. Let us look further, therefore, at what creativity and science mean in practice.

CREATIVE SEGMENTATION AND MARKET DEFINITION

From a competitive viewpoint, it is important to find ways to "cut" the market into segments and/or subsegments that lead to ways of defining your own business uniquely. It is usually far more difficult for a competitor to imitate a creative definition of the business than it is to imitate a particular new product, a new channel, a new promotion or advertising campaign, or certainly a simple price cut.

This is usually true because a creative definition of the business leads to a series of coordinated changes in *all* aspects of the business, not just in one individual activity or another.

I like to think of creative segmentation as a way of cutting the cake another way. Imagine a nice fruit cake which has been cut into segments—with each "competitor" at the dining table greedily eyeing one or more pieces of it. (The largest pieces usually attract the most attention!)

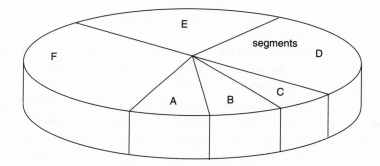

Imagine everybody's surprise when you reach down and neatly slice away the whole top layer—segment H!

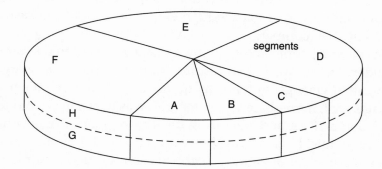

A creative definition of a market is like cutting a cake creatively; it subdivides any one or more of the dimensions used to describe the market in a new and unusual way. The following examples illustrate how the managements of two large companies actually did this.

When working some years ago on a strategic study for a major telecommunications equipment supplier, management suggested to us that they begin to segment their market by customers, and not only by product lines as had previously been the case. In addition to the basic division between standard home and office telephone equipment, PBX exchanges, and the newly emerging office terminal network equipment, they wanted to deal differently with different classes of users. They were therefore considering specialized marketing approaches, and even special organizational arrangements, to customize their efforts to banks, local government, educational institutions, large and small manufacturing firms, travel providers, and professional organizations such as consultants, accountants, and lawyers—to name but a few.

But after analyzing this proposal more carefully, they began to realize that a bank in the early stages of acquiring telecommunications equipment is not much different than a professional organization, a manufacturing company, an educational institution, or in fact any other type of customer in its early stages of acquisition. The key is not the *type* of customer, but the *amount of experience and the scale of the installation* that the customer already has in place. With this new insight, they were able to make drastic modifications in their whole marketing approach to different customer segments—not only in terms of products offered, but in terms of sales activities, sales support, customer education, and the like. Further, their customized approach to each market segment could not easily be copied by their competitors.

A second example is offered by a major international insurance provider. The company had resulted from a merger of two organizations that were geographically quite distinct. The first instinct of management, immediately post merger, was to retain the old territorial distinctions and operate with two regional organizations. This quite quickly gave way, however, to consolidation of the two regional organizations and "resegmentation" around major lines of insurance, including life, home, casualty, automobile, health, and industrial risks. With this move they nicely paralleled their competitors' approach to the same market, but did little to beat them!

The breakthrough came when the company recognized that insurance needs are closely related to the individual and family situation. Young, single individuals who have recently left home have unique insurance needs that are quite different than those they had when they lived with their parents; and young married couples differ again from the young singles. All aspects of insurance and financial planning—life, home, casualty, automobile, health, and personal investment requirements—are affected. As the family cycle progresses and young children appear, insurance needs evolve again, and continue to change as children grow and in their turn leave home for further education or jobs. Retirement and eventually widowhood bring yet other needs. Segmenting the market in this new creative way allowed the company to take a big step ahead of its competitors and to maintain a long-term competitive advantage.

In both of the foregoing examples, the company cut up the customer side of the market in a new and creative way—using previously unused attributes of the customers to define important market segments.

To complete our understanding of the conceptual underpinnings of market and market segment definition, we must now enquire what "science" is available to explain how markets may be divided and possibly subdivided—conventionally, or better, creatively. Are there any typologies or classifications of customer groups, customer functions, product/service forms, use situations, or benefits that the manager can usefully turn to?[4] It is important to keep in mind that the purpose of such an exercise is to provide a basis for dividing the market into segments that are *different* from one another in terms of their eventual requirements.

SUBDIVIDING CUSTOMERS INTO GROUPS

There are seemingly endless ways to describe customers which would provide a basis for dividing them into groups, but few of these ways provide the basis for *discriminating* between one group of customers and another. We may, for example, divide the market for a particular product into male and female users—and several decades ago this might have provided important information about their needs. Today for many "unisex" products, gender does little to discriminate. We may generalize this proposition and argue that sociodemograhic data in general provides relatively low discriminating power.

Another example of a customer characteristic that is apparently losing some of its discriminating power is geographical location.

The advent of large regional or global markets, for some products at least, suggests that differences among customer needs country-by-country are narrowing. So far we have been talking of consumer markets but similar issues arise in industrial and services markets. We must choose attributes for dividing industrial or service customers that provide maximum discriminating power. Statistical data like company size, industry type or location may offer less discriminatory power than other less obvious descriptions.

So far we have talked about descriptions of customers that do *not* provide substantial discriminating power; so which *do?* The answer is that any descriptor that has a substantial influence on purchasing behavior, use behavior, or the needs and benefits sought from the product or service can be important. "Experience" in purchase or use of the product is one such variable; so is "salience" of that product for that particular customer. With respect to sports equipment, for example, we would expect those who play sports regularly to have different requirements than those who lead more sedentary lives. This might well translate into the use of age and life-style measures to define particular customer groups. Many other fruitful ways exist to "cut the cake," and only the particularities of each individual situation can really suggest which is more or less useful. Depending on the circumstances, age, income, socioeconomic class, sex, education, location, family status, profession, health status, recreation habits, and general life-style characteristics may all be useful discriminators in consumer markets. In industrial markets, size, growth rate, market share, industry sector, financial health, innovative character, or relative importance as a potential "key account" may provide a basis for division into customer groups.

SUBDIVIDING THE MARKET IN TERMS OF CUSTOMER FUNCTIONS

Products or services perform certain functions for the customer. Functions have to be separated conceptually from the *way* the function is performed ("technology") and the attributes or *benefits* that a customer may perceive as important criteria for choice. Thus, transportation is a function; taxi transportation is a way of performing the function; price, comfort, speed, and safety are attributes or benefits associated with the choices. Likewise, teeth cleaning is a function; fluoride toothpaste and regular toothpaste are ways of performing the function; flavor, brightness, decay prevention, and price are attributes or benefits associated with a particular purchase.

The dividing line between "functions" and "benefits" is not always as clear as is indicated above. Sometimes, as functions are subdivided, the subdivisions approximate benefits. Take, for example, the function of providing a power source (say, by AC electric motors). This "function" may be subdivided into the provision of low-horsepower sources and high-horsepower sources. Are these properly categorized as "functions" or as customer benefits? Further subdivision may result in a description such as "operating low-horsepower, high-torque drilling equipment under arctic conditions." Such a narrowly defined function already implies some of the specific benefits which a specially designed motor could provide.

Further semantic difficulty is introduced by the word "needs." Indeed, at lower levels of aggregation, the words "function," "benefit," "attributes," and "needs" all appear as close relatives.

Assuming for a moment that most analysis takes place at a sufficiently high level of aggregation to allow unambiguous identification of functions, how are functions related to each other? There are three broad possibilities:

First, functions may be *complementary* in the sense that performance of one entails performance of another. Loading implies unloading; data analysis implies some sort of display; writing implies something to write on. In such cases different but complementary functions may be performed by a single multifunctional product or product system.

Often there are several different ways in which functions can complement one another. In the bank teller business, for example, customer functions may be viewed as teller functions, such as cash dispensing, depositing, and transfer from one account to another, or as bank information systems functions, such as recording, account updating, check clearing, and account analysis. Alternatively, teller functions may be associated with security functions, such as security deposit, cash protection, and burglary prevention. These alternative ways to consider the set of functions being performed for the customer have resulted in companies as diverse as computer manufacturers and security firms both manufacturing automatic teller machines.

Likewise, in the forestry equipment business, functions might be listed as logging functions, such as cutting, delimbing, loading, skidding, transporting, and shipping trees; yard functions, such as storage and drying; and mill functions, such as the production of pulp and paper. Alternatively, forestry functions associated with tree cutting and removal might be associated with other forestry management functions, such as replanting, controlled growth, thinning, and soil care. These are different ways to think about customer function segmentation and to divide up the customer function "pie." Functions can often be combined in new and creative ways by an imaginative management.

Second, functions may be *similar* in the sense that performance of one function is very similar to performance of another. Hauling a tree from stump to roadside may be almost identical with hauling it from roadside to a central dispatch point in some environments. In such cases, a single product may suffice for the performance of two essentially separate but similar functions.

Third, functions may be *unrelated* to each other. Such is the case when a customer has a range of needs to satisfy, each of which is quite separate and different. An example would be the purchase of a broad line of unrelated industrial supply items, such as fittings, parts, and small machines, for a wide range of different unrelated tasks.

Not only can functions be combined in different ways (i.e., logging and mill yard functions versus logging and forest management functions), they can also be segmented in creative ways. Sometimes segmentation along the customer function dimension can lead to a more precise satisfaction of customer needs. For example, the first hand-held calculators were intended to be multipurpose. But by the late 1970s it was possible to purchase calculators specifically designed to perform such diverse functions as checkbook balancing, interest-rate and mortgage-rate calculations, and engineering design calculations. And whereas one rubber-wheeled tractor with a variety of attachments initially performed many different forestry functions, by the early 1980s customer-function segmentation had resulted in a wide variety of different equipment, each performing a specialized function.

SUBDIVIDING THE MARKET IN TERMS OF THE "FORM" OF THE PRODUCT OR SERVICE

"Form" (which I previously labeled "technology") describes the alternative ways that a particular function can be performed for a customer. In this sense it is a "form" of solution to the customer's problems. If the function were, for example, transportation, the alternative forms of solution might be regarded as road, rail, sea, or air travel. Further subdivisions into private car, rented car, bicycle, or mass transportation might be possible.

Technology is, in fact, one important ingredient of the form that a customer solution takes. We have to remember that technology is dynamic. One technology may slowly *displace* another over time. Sometimes this displacement is complete; sometimes it proceeds only to some point of equilibrium where two or more technologies coexist as alternative solutions to a customer function.

Displacement is generally slower at higher levels of aggregation. For example, imaging diagnostics may very slowly be displaced by biochemical methods as a means of diagnosing cancer; X-ray, by contrast, may be more quickly displaced by ultrasound, nuclear medicine, and CT scanning as alternative imaging diagnostic techniques; at an even lower level of aggregation, third-generation CT scanners have almost completely displaced first- and second-generation scanners, and fourth-generation scanners are rapidly displacing the third generation. The cycle time for displacement of imaging diagnostics may be measured in periods of fifty years or more; the cycle time for displacement of X-ray may be measured in a decade or so; the cycle time for replacement of a generation of scanners may be measured in one or two years.

In assessing what are indeed the alternative "technologies" or ways of fulfilling a particular customer function, a *customer* perspective is vital. Customers may perceive the different alternatives quite differently than does an engineer. As an example, tea bags might be regarded as a technological alternative to loose-leaf tea. From a customer's perspective, however, the relevant solutions might be regarded as tea and coffee.

Technology segmentation can also take place on alternative bases. We may, for example, divide teller machines depending on whether they are electronic or electromechanical, or whether they are completely automatic or operated by a human teller.

SUBDIVIDING THE MARKET IN TERMS OF CUSTOMER BENEFITS SOUGHT

The benefits that customers wish to obtain from the purchase of a product or service may extend timewise over the whole purchase, use, *and* disposal cycle, and they include benefits that may go far beyond those provided by the product itself. For example, one set of industrial product buyers may put substantial weight on the development of new applications for the product, another may value convenient distribution, and a third, some form of guaranteed resale value. In each case, the other potential benefits assume no importance at all; they are just ranked differently. We must therefore always think in terms of a "mix" of benefits—some of which are ranked higher or lower by particular customers under particular circumstances.

Subdividing the market in terms of benefits sought amounts to distinguishing one "mix" of benefits sought from another. Some "classic" typologies are suggested here without limiting in any way the almost infinite numbers of permutations and combinations that may be imagined.

"Push" Versus "Pull"

For many products and services two contrasting approaches exist which reflect a basic difference in the *amount* of service, information, and support sought by the customers, and the *channels* through which these benefits are delivered. At the two extremes, one set of customers seek substantial service, information, and support at the point of sale—often delivered personally by a salesperson; others seek less service, information, and support, and receive it primarily through mass media channels and/or impersonal displays of the product at the point of sale. We label these approaches Push and Pull respectively because in the former the manufacturer "pushes" the product or service via wholesale and retail distribution channels to the customer via substantial personal marketing efforts in the channels; in the latter, the customer "pulls"the product off the shelf and through the upstream distribution channels usually as a result of brand advertising or promotion aimed directly at the customer by the manufacturer.

High Value Versus Low Price

Another important way of subdividing the market in terms of benefits sought is to distinguish that segment seeking primarily value—of one kind or another—and who are prepared to pay for it, from that segment seeking low price. Of course, there are many combinations possible between the two extremes, and different price-value combinations can provide important ways to segment the market. If Roles Royce is at one end of the automobile spectrum and the Citroen "deux-chevaux" at the other, we can imagine Mercedes and Volkswagen being positioned for segments that lie somewhere between these two extremes.

Critical Success Factors

A third way to divide markets in terms of benefits sought is to ask which particular attributes of the product or service itself—distribution and delivery, promotion, and before- or after-sales services—are "critical" for one particular segment or another. Again, an almost infinite variety of combinations may exist, but some main groupings often stand out: for example, one segment for which convenient supply is critical; another for which the product's technical features may be critical, and a third for which after-sales service may be critical. Creative and imaginative market definition often hinges on developing a comprehensive understanding of critical success factors, segment by segment.

Redundancy

Increasing precision on one dimension may reduce the need for precision on other dimensions, but it seldom *completely* eliminates the need for the other dimensions. Examples have been given in the foregoing text of how increasing precision in terms of customer groups or product forms is increasingly suggestive of the benefits that are likely to be sought.

As a general rule, the finer we wish to segment markets, the more we are likely to use an increasing number of dimensions to describe these segments—and the more subdivision is likely to be necessary. In practice, managers tend to err in the direction of insufficient precision in their definitions of markets and segments rather than the reverse, so it is usually wise to use customer groups, functions, forms, and benefits sought (and even use occasion where appropriate) even at the risk of some redundancy, when we are seeking precise definitions of possible target markets.

MARKET CONTRASTS

Now that we have established some conceptual basis for describing and dividing markets, we may well ask whether there are any significant differences *overall* between one market and another. Using an analogy from geographic maps, every region obviously has a unique set of features. But many maps look very similar in terms of their *broad* features, while others look totally different. Some, for example, may have sharply contrasting areas of mountains and flatland, while others are much less contoured; some may feature large areas under water, while others picture only land masses; or some may combine dry hot desert with more northerly cold areas, while others show more temperate areas throughout.

Market maps are similar. Some are highly segmented, exhibiting sharp differences in any one or more dimensions; others are less contoured, and differences are smaller. The market for specialty chemicals is, for example, highly segmented in any number of different ways, while the market for crude oil—its upstream counterpart—shows much less segmentation. Only as we carefully examine customer differences and benefits sought or any other dimension under a magnifying glass, can we observe that these apparently less segmented markets in fact still exhibit quite important differences. These differences often have less to do with product features than they do with nonproduct benefits such as service or convenience. One senior executive at Nestlé, comparing the markets for two of the company's main product businesses, soluble coffee and chilled products, put the differences in the following terms:

It is not more difficult to manage instant coffee than frozen foods. It is just *different*. It is like the difference between soccer, where a normal score is 3–2, and basketball where a normal score may be 87–76.

What he was referring to was the fact that the underlying *character* of instant coffee business is quite different from that of the frozen foods business. Instant coffee, historically at least, has long product cycles, relatively stable production technology, and quite often centrally driven market strategies; frozen foods are reinvented constantly as one new product innovation follows another.

We may also see that the markets differ in terms of the relative *importance* of one dimension or another at each successive level of disaggregation. We may divide airline travel into international and domestic routes at one level; into business and pleasure travelers at the next; and into those who value add-on hotel and rental car functions versus those who do not, at even lower levels. In other words, even though we may use "several" dimensions to describe markets and market segments, some of these dimensions may be considerably more important than others in shaping our map of the market as we zoom in on the details.

PUTTING MARKET DEFINITION
AND SEGMENTATION INTO PRACTICE

Managers frequently fail to put the foregoing ideas to work because they do not clearly separate the two processes of *creating a road map* of the market and its segments, and making *choices* about which parts of the market they wish to operate in. A company may thus end up with one or other definition of its activities with *neither* a systematic scan of the full range of possible opportunities, *nor* a careful weighing of the relative merits of each. Although this shortcoming is most common in decisions to add new products or extend to new markets, the same can often be said of choices of approach to one segment or another—choices which should be preceded by an overall definition of the market and detailed definition of its various segments.

The process of defining markets in practice should start not with market research, but with *speculative discussion* about the definition of the main segments and subsegments and, as part of this, the benefits sought by each. This kind of discussion usually highlights a certain number of "facts" about which there is already substantial knowledge, a certain number of quite strongly held hypotheses, and inevitably some questions where market research data is clearly needed. This initial speculative analysis, when done well, can be a critical ingredient in the subsequent design of market research—specifically aimed at getting answers to questions where management is still guessing, and where hypotheses need to be confirmed.

A good practical way to *start* the process of speculative discussion about differences among market segments is for senior management to ask itself the following questions.[5]

What
- benefits does the customer seek?
- factors influence demand?
- are important buying criteria?
- is the basis of comparison with other products?
- risks does the customer perceive?
- services do customers expect?

How
- do customers buy?
- long does the buying process last?
- do various elements of the marketing program influence customers at each stage of the process?
- do customers use the product?
- does the product fit into their life-style or operation?
- much are they willing to spend?
- much do they buy?

Where
- is the decision made to buy?
- do customers seek information about the product?
- do customers buy the product?

When
- is the first decision to buy made?
- is the product repurchased?

Why
- do customers buy?
- do customers choose one brand as opposed to another?

Who
- are the occupants of segments identified by previous questions?
- buys our product, and why?
- buys our competitors' products, and why?

Several points should be kept firmly in mind when using questions such as these to facilitate segmentation. First, the list of questions is only *suggestive;* in any given situation some questions will be more important than others or questions not contained in this list might be profitably asked. Second, data of *some* sort is usually needed to supply the answers. Often this data is already available from sources inside or outside the company. Third, it is important, as pointed out in Chapter 3, to consider customer needs from the very beginning of the buying process to the very end of the use process. This may span a period of several years. It may begin at a time when the customer is not even yet aware of the product, and end when the customer is plagued with the problem of disposing of it at the end of its useful life—or often before the end of its useful life. In many cases, substantial opportunities may exist for satisfying needs at times between these two extremes which provide excellent ways to differentiate the offering from competitors.

Discussions about the "shape" of the market and definition of segments are above all the responsibility of top management, but this does not mean that others lower down in the organization cannot add insight and ideas. The process should be *overseen* by top management but should involve management from a variety of levels and organizational vantage points. An engineering or R&D manager might, for example, be the best placed to provide insight about current and future forms that the product or service might take; a sales manager might be in the best position to suggest areas in which customers' needs are not properly met in the purchasing process itself, while someone from the distribution side might be able to identify ways to provide new after-sales service benefits to a particular segment. Financial management should be able to add the vital perspective, often overlooked, of how customer financing needs vary from one segment to another, and how they can be met. In other words, market definition and segmentation is *everybody's* business. Top management's responsibility is to make it everybody's business and to devise processes that bring the diverse experiences of the firm's management to bear in the most creative ways possible. However good the firm's formal strategic planning processes are, they seldom deal adequately with problems of market definition and segmentation. Special processes are usually needed therefore to bring together the right people, and to develop a common understanding of the territory in which the firm operates.

Another good reason for including levels below the top in the process of defining market segments is simply that the top has inevitably a more aggregate view of the world. This was made abundantly clear in the approach of one very large machinery manufacturer. At U.S. headquarters, where worldwide design and engineering were carried out, the company defined some dozen major segments of international business activity. At European headquarters, a far finer segmentation was used involving each of the different European countries on one hand, and a breakdown into six major "product-market" businesses on the other. Even further down, the company's main distributor organizations—usually one per country each operating multiple branches—used segmentation schemes for their own purposes which offered even more precision, and focused at least as much on sales and service requirements as on the product itself. Developing a common view of the market which can be shared between U.S. headquarters, European headquarters, and European field and distributor organizations is one of this company's major challenges.

Such processes work best when individual managers, whatever their hierarchical level or functional vantage point, are continually asking themselves in the course of their work how one segment is distinguished from another, what benefits are sought or might be sought, and how they are met or might be met. This requires constant and close contact with customers, a keen eye for what competitors are offering, and a sure sense of how needs can or could be met. Management by walking around (or MWA as it is called) means walking around externally with customers (and, of course, distributors), walking around internally to see what is realistic and possible, and walking around in the competitive marketplace to see what others are doing.

While each individual firm may design its own variation of the process needed to bring its markets and market segments into better focus, a few "basics" should be observed.

First, it makes sense to keep things *simple*. Segmentation is above all an eclectic process in which we are trying to identify major (and sometimes minor) "chunks" of business opportunity worthy of attention. We are not interested in writing down an exhaustive list of every possible permutation and combination of customer groups, functions, forms, benefits, and use situations.

Secondly, it usually makes sense to look at markets at *several* different levels of aggregation, not just one, and to be as explicit as possible about each. As described earlier, the higher the level, the fewer dimensions are likely to be needed to describe the market; the more we segment and subsegment the market, the more dimensions are likely to be needed.

Thirdly, we must be aware that at each step there are two alternative ways to add further precision—either by further subdividing on an existing dimension, such as further subdivision of target customer groups, or by adding new dimensions with which to describe the segment. There are few rules to guide the beginner, but facility grows with experience of the process itself and with a deep and intimate knowledge of the business.

Fourth, as emphasized before, market definition and segmentation is in large part a creative process. That is one reason that often "many heads are better than one." We are not looking for ways to define markets and segments that are symmetric and evident, and that every competitor can imitate. We are looking for ways that are asymmetric, unusual, and will provide a basis for avoiding rather than meeting competition.

CHAPTER 5

MARKETS IN MOTION

Markets are never stationary. Customer groups rise and fall in importance. Customer functions are redefined—or recombined; new technologies usher in new product forms; benefits that are sought change in importance over time (and indeed new unthought-of benefits make their appearance as competitors innovate and provide improved products and services), and purchase and use situations multiply as human life-styles become more complex and diverse.

This motion amounts to much more than product changes and improvements—any of the elements that make up the complete package of benefits which the customer purchases and uses may change. And the relative importance of different segments may shift, or segments may be fundamentally redefined as the market evolves. Take, for example, the market for wristwatches. These were originally conceived as pieces of jewelry with many hidden value attributes. People sought out a jeweler, and the security of a jewelry store, to make a purchase. Customers were inexperienced and ill-informed with respect to judging qualities then considered important—such as timekeeping, overall reliability, fashion, and the real presence of precious stones. The wise old jeweler with an eyeglass also provided the reassurance of assiduous repair capacity—just in case!

How times have changed! Today's Swatch is a far cry from those family heirlooms of yesteryear, and the segmentation of the watch market would hardly be recognizable to those old jewelers; Swatch is sportive, fashionable, for young (and old!), almost unbreakable, waterproof, not expensive, reliable, accurate, guaranteed, and almost infinite in the variety of design, color, and motif. It was being marketed as a collectors item—even as the first ones were in the channels of distribution. You can buy one, ten, a hundred! And the channels are almost anything *but* jewelry stores—supermarkets, kiosks, airports, gasoline stations, and specialty stores. Swatch is an idea that goes beyond a wristwatch. Swatch "Eyes," a line of sunglasses with interchangeable lenses introduced in the early 1990s, is another step in the product line development which reflects a customer approach to segmentation—trendy, fashionable, youth-oriented with a collector's flair for variety—rather than a product approach, which might well have limited the company's development to watches. This orientation led naturally from watches to sunglasses and even to cars—something that most major automobile manufacturers have difficulty even contemplating.[1] Might they make the same mistake as Swiss watchmakers who, confronted with the first cheap Timex, said "it's not a threat, it's not a watch!" The "Swatchmobile" may not be a car in General Motors' or Ford's eyes, but it certainly may be in the eyes of one of Swatch's ardent followers.

It is vitally important, therefore, that as managers we never become complacent about our working definition of markets and segments—and that we constantly review and rethink the maps of the market territory in which they operate. At a minimum, we would like to understand what the market has looked like, and how it now looks; better still, we would like to look ahead and see how it is likely to unfold in the *future*. As competitors, we may then be less surprised when "out of the blue" (or so it seems) we are suddenly confronted with new major competitive threats from directions we could scarcely imagine before—the advent of low-price "fashion" watches, like Swatch, satisfying previously unmet needs for changeability, novelty, and disposability.

Where does change originate? What are the forces that set markets in motion? Swatch is an interesting example because it shows the complex interplay between forces *external* to the market, such as life-style changes of watch customers, and forces *internal* to the market, such as life cycle phenomena, technology, and specific competitive initiatives that serve to influence buying behavior. When change is most rapid, it is usually because one competitor has capitalized on an underlying phenomenon influencing the market, and thereby changed the whole nature of doing business in that area or segment. Notwithstanding this important interplay between external and internal forces, I shall nevertheless address the main forces behind change one by one—and later look at the complex overall patterns that emerge as one or another player rides these waves of change.

LIFE CYCLE PHENOMENA
Defining the Unit of Analysis

It is only possible to assess the duration of a life cycle and its individual stages if the unit of analysis is carefully defined first. When a manufacturer successfully improves a product, the life cycle of any one version is obviously shorter than the life cycle of the product class overall; and if the product class is replaced by a whole new generation of products, based for example on completely new technology, the life cycle of any one class of product will be shorter than that of the whole sequence of successive generations. Ultimately, if we think of a *function* that successive generations of products may perform, the concept of a life cycle tends to give way to a concept of continuous development. Even when the unit of analysis is described in functional terms, the function itself may follow a life cycle curve. The function that buggy whips performed simply ceased to exist with the advent of the automobile, for example. We may diagram this concept of life cycles within life cycles as shown in Figure 5–1.

It is also necessary to distinguish whether we are talking about the life cycle of our *own company's* product(s) or the life cycle of the *industry* as a whole. The life cycle of an individual company's products tends to be less predictable since it is influenced not only by trends affecting the overall product category but by competition among producers within the product category. A company's growing business may, for example, move from infancy to maturity, or even abrupt decline, almost overnight when a competitor imitates its products, or worse completely supplants its products with new, better ones. In general, it is more useful to conceive product life cycles on an industry-wide basis than on a product-specific basis.

This still leaves open the question of definition of the product category. This depends on whether we include only close substitutes

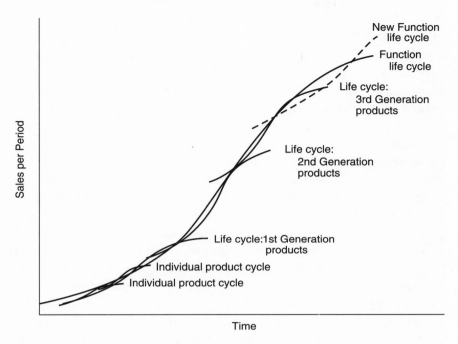

Figure 5–1. Life Cycles Within Life Cycles

in the definition, or all products that bear some competitive relationship to the product in question—albeit based perhaps on different technology, using different channels, or performing similar but not identical functions. Such would be the case, for example, if we were talking about the life cycle for watches. Should we look at all watches? Quartz watches? High-priced watches? Stopwatches as well as regular watches? Men's watches as well as women's watches? The answer is, of course, that any definition is possible, and several alternative definitions could shed light on the nature of change in the watch industry. Usually, we have to look at several alternative definitions, to be as selective as possible, and above all, in order to avoid ambiguity, to carefully define whatever unit of analysis is being used.

Patterns of Buyer Behavior

Probably the *least* interesting phenomenon related to life cycles is the shape of the *sales* pattern for an individual product or product category as the cycle progresses over time. Curiously, many managers associate life cycles first and foremost with sales patterns, and puzzle over how to apply the generalized concept of infancy, growth, approaching maturity, and maturity to their own specific forecasting needs—but sales patterns are to product life cycles as height or weight are to human life cycles. Of much more interest are the changing *characteristics* and *behavior* of individuals as they pass through their life. Analogously, the more interesting phenomena associated with product life cycles are the underlying changes in *the character* of markets and the *behavior* of customers.

In early life cycle stages, customers tend to be relatively inexperienced, unknowledgeable buyers, and as a result they are willing to pay premiums to have their information and reassurance needs satisfied. They may also be willing to sacrifice on dimensions other than price—such as convenience, delivery, and choice. Producers are also learning in early life cycles stages, so product varieties tend to multiply, and standards are not yet clearly established. As the market develops, the "early adopters," who were in the market first, accumulate important experience in purchase and use of the product, while the larger mass of latecomers to the market go through a similar learning process to their predecessors.

In later stages of the cycle, standards begin to be set, and purchasers, as a result of their enhanced experience, pay more attention to criteria other than information and reassurance. These almost always include price, but may also include convenience, delivery, choice, service, financing, and the like. This shift in the relative importance of different needs cannot easily be generalized; different product characteristics and different circumstances play an important role. Complex jet engines, for example, obviously require considerably more attention to information and reassurance needs at all life cycle stages than do relatively simpler products such as basic industrial supply items. But it is important to recognize that customer needs change over the life cycle for every product or service, and that this requires a shift in the way the business has to be managed.

It is important not only to rank the relative priority that the customer gives to each of these requirements, but also to understand the particular form the need takes in each category and how it can be satisfied. And as pointed out in Chapter 3, there is usually more than one customer, and each one goes through a long history associated with becoming aware of his or her needs, gathering information, purchasing, using, and disposing of the product.

Patterns of Seller Behavior

Sellers adjust to the changing patterns of buyer behavior described above in only partly predictable ways.[2] Some struggle to adapt *after* the event; some fail to adapt at all; and a few stay abreast of life cycle change or even occasionally anticipate it. A general pattern can nevertheless often be observed.

In the *infancy* stage, the essential questions confronting suppliers are what segments of the market to target initially, and how broad or narrow an entry should be made. Questions of "skimming" the market with a high-price approach to a narrow segment or "penetrating" the market with a lower price designed to expand volume more quickly imply related choices of channels and communication strategy. The early entrants into the market are more concerned with expanding the market as a whole ("primary demand" stimulation) than they are with fighting for market share ("selective demand" stimulation). Each early entrant is likely to have a monopoly, albeit temporary, in the segment or segments it chooses.

Strategies that initially target a large proportion of all the potential customers of the product have the advantage of preempting competition. The cost of such broad-scale marketing activities may, however, be prohibitively high, especially if the individual adoption and diffusion process is long. On the other hand, strategies that target only a selective group of potential customers, while requiring less initial investment, often invite competitive imitation before the full benefits of the innovation can be realized.

In the *growth* stage of the life cycle, companies face a new challenge. Either they may decide to spend the majority of their resources fighting to protect and fortify their existing positions in the markets they have established, or they may decide to seek new opportunities for market development where they can. They may then operate, temporarily at least, in a more monopolistic mode by virtue of being the first entrant into a new market segment. The basic choice, then, is between developing new primary demand and fighting a selective demand battle with imitative competitors who are "nipping at their heels".

If the choice is new primary demand development, this may take a variety of forms. It may, for example, mean developing *new applications* as many computer software companies do continually to expand sales; it may mean extending *geographic coverage* as multinationals usually do following limited introduction in selective areas; or it may mean *trading down* to lower-priced "mass merchandise" types of products and distribution channels in order to broaden the market. This latter process of market expansion via lower prices, more intensive distribution, and a shift in communications strategy from *push* through the channels to *pull* through mass media has typified the pattern of evolution of many consumer soft goods, semi-durables, and even durables.

These patterns of seller behavior are evident when the original market leader retains or tries to retain his leadership in the market by undertaking new primary demand development to keep his distance from competitors. In some cases, however, the original leader apparently fails to take such initiatives and wakes up (often too late) to find out that a competitor has staked out a dominant position in a new and growing market segment. The choice facing the originator is then whether to further consolidate, fortify, and defend his existing position or to react to the "leapfrogging" competitor on a me-too basis—that is, to contend for at least a share of the new market segment. In some situations, options often exist for developing still newer primary demand, by leapfrogging the leapfrogger, with the result that each competitor operates in a virtual monopoly and has to worry little about selective competition. This situation perennially confronts the established scheduled airline carriers. They have historically responded primarily to the needs of the business traveler and paid less attention to the low-price, vacation market. This creates a vacuum in the market into which new low-price competitors, offering no-frills travel, enter. These newcomers usually develop new primary demand for air travel, while the scheduled carriers continue to "slug it out" for a share of the business market.

As the life cycle *approaches maturity*, the opportunities for identifying and stimulating new primary demand begin to be exhausted, and competition increasingly revolves around selective demand stimulating activities. Competitors jostle for advantage in a variety of ways which usually include further improvements in the product or proliferation of the product line to more precisely meet the needs of subsegments of the market; sharper positioning of the product in the marketplace by careful targeting against chosen segments; and cutting out frills to lower costs. This latter approach is often called for because the pace of innovation slows and customers become more proficient at differentiating between competitive offerings. Some customers become expert enough to be unwilling to pay any longer for expensive "peripheral services," such as technical advice (or in-store services in the case of consumer goods). The dual forces of increasing competitive imitation and increasing customer skill herald the beginning of nose-to-nose competition based on dimensions other than product performance.

In the *mature,* final phase of life cycle development, the structure of the market stabilizes as no new primary demand opportunities remain to be explored, and the jostling for position which occurs during the late growth and early maturity phases is replaced by nose-to-nose competition in each market segment. Unique positions achieved during the growth stages are eroded by competition. Any selective advantage that can now be achieved is usually very temporary. Seller competition during this phase may take a variety of forms depending on which dimensions are critical to customer satisfaction. It is often price-oriented—with substantial efforts being expended on process innovations designed to reduce costs; it may revolve around minor, easily copied product feature improvements; or it may mean advertising, promotion, or merchandising activities often at a level in excess of that needed to provide adequate consumer information and reassurance (sometimes such advertising "wars" between major national brand competitors proceed to the point where a vacuum is created for the entry of a nonadvertised "private label" at a lower price). At this stage of life cycle development, "positioning" is often primarily a matter of trying to develop a differentiated *image* for the product rather than real performance differences.

Usually this evolutionary process occurs with considerable overlaps between stages. Several major segments of a business may in fact be at different stages of evolution. Some parts of a business may even be approaching maturity while others still provide opportunity for new primary demand development. Often, a product improvement breakthrough, of the type described in Chapter 3, or a new technology, or new source of economic demand in the marketplace, will restart the whole process. This provides the impetus for another cycle of innovative entry, new primary demand development, competitive jostling, and eventually nose-to-nose competition. It may even take the innovator into completely new markets which were not previously considered as being part of the relevant market. As we talk about patterns of evolution, therefore, we must be prepared to look at the ways in which competitors progressively open up nooks and crannies in, and eventually beyond, the original market definition.

Aggregate Patterns

Changing customer requirements over the life cycle combine with changing seller behavior to produce aggregate patterns which are often associated with life cycle progression. These patterns are therefore not themselves the underlying forces prompting change, although sometimes they are mistaken for such. Managers may *recognize* change by such patterns but should ask, following the lines of the previous two sections of this chapter, what is happening to buyer and seller behavior "behind the scenes" which produce these patterns. Broadly speaking we may classify these aggregate patterns in two groups: first, patterns described in terms of the *behavior* of buyers and sellers; and second, patterns described in terms of *market structures*.

Buyer-Seller Behavior

The combination of growing customer experience, product standardization, and less rapid growth as the market approaches maturity normally results in narrowing of real and perceived differences among competitive offerings and a growing emphasis on price comparison. This overall process can be termed *commoditization*. It is a pervasive force whose effects can only be reversed by the superimposition of new life cycles resulting from product improvements, the introduction of new generations of products, or entirely new functional replacements.

Commoditization of the product offering is almost always accompanied by *reductions in cost* which make some downward price movements possible. The dynamics of costs will be one of the important subjects treated in Chapter 9; here we shall simply note that experience effects associated with increased volumes, better capacity utilization, and process improvements can all contribute to cost reductions as the life cycle progresses.

Associated with commoditization and behind cost reduction is also a progressive shift from *product innovation to process innovation.* The development dollar has to be put behind those forms of innovation that have the biggest payoff in customer terms, which often means increases in efficiency to combat increased pressure on prices and margins, as opposed to further investment in the product itself.

In parallel with commoditization, cost and price reductions, and process innovation, changes are usually also taking place in the channels of distribution. The most common aggregate pattern is the progressive shift from *narrow "specialty" distribution to broader mass merchandising.* This change is associated with a decreased need for customer information and reassurance or experience with the product in general, and with the need to use broader channels to reach an ever-widening market as the life cycle progresses. It is accompanied by a shift from marketing communications reaching buyers via the channels of distribution—i.e., push—to marketing communications reaching buyers via the mass media—i.e., pull.

Structural Changes

Commoditization threatens suppliers with price-oriented competition, lower margins, and lower profits. In response to this threat, suppliers usually seek segments of the market where they can retain some degree of differentiation from competitors, and thus retain some control of prices and margins. Thus the commoditization process actually triggers *a counterprocess of segmentation and differentiation.* This is particularly apparent as the market approaches maturity and as fierce competition ensues to maintain company sales growth against a backdrop of leveling overall demand. When, for example, the overall market for regular colas began to mature, diet cola was introduced to appeal specifically to that group of customers concerned about sugar; further segmentation occurred with the introduction of sixteen-ounce, thirty-two-ounce, and then sixty-four-ounce bottles—with the net result that the overall segmentation of the cola market increased as Pepsi and Coca-Cola both tried to find new ways to achieve competitive distance from each other.

As well as more segmentation, there is also often a shift from *product segmentation to market segmentation* as the life cycle progresses. In the early stages of the life cycle, products themselves often provide the basis for segmentation, since customers are not yet well defined. Du Pont, for example, divided its synthetics fiber markets into submarkets for dacron, rayon, and acetates in the early phases of overall market development. Only later, as the submarkets for these products grew rapidly, was it useful to think about the different needs of identifiable customer groups such as men's apparel, women's apparel, and industrial markets. This allowed not only a finer segmentation but one that provided considerably more insight into differences in customer needs and buying behavior for each respective "end-user" market.

This change in emphasis from product segmentation to customer segmentation is in reality a shift from "coarse" to "fine" segmentation in the terms of the previous chapter. Coarse product segmentation is useful in early life cycle stages when customer groups, customer functions, possibilities for alternative product forms, and specific benefits sought still remain imprecise. With increased market experience and increased competition, finer and finer segmentation becomes possible, and with it a shift to definitions that are more likely to be based on customers, customer functions, and sought benefits.

The progression of the product life cycle sometimes entails not only resegmentation, but *redefinition of the market boundaries*. This can occur in three main ways: first the market may be redefined by the successive inclusion of new customer groups. Such has been the case, for example, with branded fashion goods. Once the preserve of a small group of affluent buyers, labels such as Georgio Armani, Yves St. Laurent, and Christian Dior are now marketed to a much wider customer market. Second, the market may be redefined through the addition of products or services performing new but related functions. One manufacturer of semiconductor manufacturing equipment prompted a redefinition of their market by shifting from selling related items in the manufacturing line to offering a full line of integrated equipment at a point in the market's evolution where single-item sales were faltering. Thirdly, a market may be redefined by the addition of alternative forms of the product. These new forms may result from the application of successive generations of technology, or from new materials, or from other new concepts of the product which perform the same function for the same customer in an improved fashion. The personal computer industry has, for example, seen successive generations of PCs being supplanted by machines based on new hardware and software technology. Diagrammatically, we may depict this redefinition of market boundaries along the three familiar dimensions of customer groups, customer functions, and product forms as shown in Figure 5–2.

Market boundaries may be redefined in vertical as well as horizontal dimensions. This process will be explained in greater detail in the following chapter. The process of commoditization in the latter stages of the life cycle forces companies to look for ways to differentiate their offerings and improve customer satisfaction. Often this means improving supply conditions in terms of quality, cost, or both, and on the downstream side, improving distribution. Some-

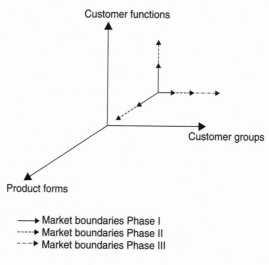

Figure 5–2. Market Redefinition

times this may go as far as achieving direct control over suppliers and/or distributors; in other cases it may mean improving systems to tie activities more tightly together. The result is increased integration along the vertical business system in the latter stages of the life cycle.

Finally, it may often be observed that life cycle progression causes temporary imbalances between supply and demand, which in turn change the structure of the industry. In the early stages of rapid growth, demand often outstrips supply, inviting capacity additions and new entrants into the market. Often this process "overshoots," there is overcapacity, and as the market approaches maturity, there has to be a correction. The result may include "shake-outs" of weaker firms, and generalized reduction in capacity for those that remain.

"EXTERNAL" FORCES FOR CHANGE

Life cycle phenomena may be regarded as "internal" forces for change. They have their origins in changes in buyer behavior as the market develops and in sellers' responses to these changes. But other forces also buffet markets continually. Some of these, such as technology, may be regarded as a mixture of internal and external forces; others such as the business cycle lie outside the domain (and control) of the firm itself and its particular markets. I shall describe six broad types of forces for change under the "external" heading: technology, internationalization/globalization, business cycles, longer-term shifts in social and demographic conditions, steadily rising aspirations, and lastly under one "catchall" heading, "discontinuities." This list is of course not exhaustive, but it gives an idea of some of the main forces at work.

It must, however, always be born in mind that change is a complex process in which many forces act together to produce the final result. Describing these forces separately runs the risk of oversimplification. When a ladder slides away from a wall leaving its occupant swinging from the gutter, it is usually a combination of a slippery floor, poor placement at too shallow an angle, and a chance movement that triggers the collapse, not any one of these things taken separately. So it is with the forces sweeping markets—which also may leave firms swinging in the air! It must also be born in mind that *each* of the five forces which are the subject of the next five short subsections deserves a much more complete coverage, and could be a book-length subject in and of itself. But the intention here is not to be exhaustive; rather it is to show in a general sense what forces are at work and how markets may be shaped by these forces—as we did with life cycle phenomena.

Technology Effects

Technology is too often only associated with product development or manufacturing process improvement. One reason perhaps is that most of the technically trained people in companies usually work either in research and development, engineering, or manufacturing or other similar "technical" departments. There is thus a cleavage between these functions and other functions. But Chapter 3 makes it clear that customer needs extend beyond product needs and that innovation can make a real difference in any organizational area that contributes to customer satisfaction. Technology can thus be a powerful influence on stimulating and realizing innovations in sales, marketing and distribution, customer communication, service, upstream and downstream coordination with suppliers and channels respectively, and in the management process itself. Sometimes a technical breakthrough in one of these areas has an impact on others. Tetrapak's new "long-life" packaging technology for dairy products has also affected their distribution, marketing, and overall supply approaches. It should be evident, then, that to comprehend the impact of technology on shaping markets, we must conceive of these impacts broadly on all aspects of the firm's operations, and indeed on any supplier or channel activities that might ultimately affect customer satisfaction.

Technology must also be conceived in terms of specific *internally* generated technologies which are peculiar to the firm's own "know-how," and activities and technologies that originate *outside* the firm or its industry, but find internal application. For most firms, technologies originating externally make up the bulk of what is used, so that assessing the effects on any of the firm's markets requires a very broad understanding of their development and potential impact. Since multiple technologies, including materials technologies, microelectronic technologies, and computer-aided design technologies, may be embedded in a single product, assessing the impact of technological change on markets can be a daunting task. It suggests, as a starting point, that good marketing executives need to be technologically literate!

Finally, technology's impact on markets has to be assessed at several levels of abstraction. At the highest level, it is apparent that there have been successive replacements, first of mechanical technology by electromechanical technology; then electromechanical technology by electronic technology; and now just beginning, of electronic technology by biotechnologies. At the moment we can only dimly perceive the vast changes that will be wrought on markets as electronics give way to biological sciences in many or most product and process technologies. At a lower level of abstraction we must assess the impact of *specific* new electronic technologies on *specific* markets, and of their eventual replacement by *specific* biotechnologies on these same markets. This is a key question confronting the computer industry right now, in terms of assessing the future performance possibilities and costs of computers even three to five years from now. And at a lower, very specific level of abstraction, we must assess the impact of one particular technological breakthrough, for example, of integrated circuits with previously unheard-of memory capacity on the market for PCs.

To summarize, technology has wide application throughout all aspects of the business; many relevant technologies are developed outside the firm and its industry, and these technologies must be considered at multiple levels of abstraction. Technology can be an enormous force for market change. It has transformed, and continues to transform, the markets for virtually every conceivable product and service. Like gas, it spreads itself into every conceivable nook and cranny in the market, and with instant global communications, technology travels worldwide with great speed. New technology lies behind a large proportion of the dazzling array of new products and services now reaching the market, and also lies behind many of the breakthroughs in services, distribution, and communication that are transforming notions of customer satisfaction. Such changes can fundamentally change the basis for market segmentation, alter the relative size and importance of different segments and upend customer requirements. The manager's job is to comprehend these changes well enough to exploit them for improved customer satisfaction and competitive advantage.

The Effect of Internationalization/Globalization

Although by no means all products are becoming "global" products, and by no means all businesses operate globally (or even regionally), there is nonetheless a clear trend towards *thinking* in terms of global opportunities. Occasionally the answer comes out in favor of a high degree of standardization worldwide and sometimes it comes out in terms of completely separate approaches to each local market; more often than not it comes out in terms of a mixture of the two approaches in which some elements of the business approach are relatively standardized (e.g., product design), whereas other elements remain tailored to each local environment (e.g., distribution strategies). Global *thinking* does not imply global *standardization* for all products in all elements of the business approach.

From the point of view of understanding the effects of globalization on markets, we are interested in *change*. Which markets considered as local markets now have to be considered globally? And for these markets, which particular elements of the approach have to be more standardized than before?

The overall effect of such changes is that many markets segmented historically by geography are becoming segmented instead along other dimensions. For example, a new global market is emerging for high-performance luxury cars—to name just one example. The segments of customers who buy these products are almost indistinguishable from one another worldwide, and buying behavior and usage patterns are nearly identical. In *each* country these segments differ substantially, however, from other car-buying segments.

The Effect of Business Cycles

Recession has very uneven effects on different sectors of the economy. It usually hits "investment goods" hardest, resulting in severe decline in "postponable" expenditures such as housing, machine tools, new plants, and advertising. For most products and services there is a negative effect as buyers have less money in the pocket and begin to husband resources more carefully. But for a few products, recession produces gains: cigarette and alcohol consumption are sometimes used as examples. But more evidently, products and services at the lower end of the market in terms of price and quality may gain ground at the expense of products and services at the upper end, as customers substitute cheaper alternatives and look for bargains. In boom times, just the reverse may be true: investment goods markets show huge upturns, and markets for lower-end products and services suffer as people trade off in expectations and spending. Apart from the expansion and contraction of various segments of demand over the business cycle, changes in buying behavior and usage patterns can also fundamentally affect customer requirements and products. They may, for example, make different tradeoffs between convenience and services provided through the distribution channel, and price. One example is the shift towards do-it-yourself home improvement items in recession periods. This occurs firstly because people have less money available to spend, but secondly because unemployment provides time that can be fruitfully employed. Another example is the increased need for credit to support the purchase of many durable tools or investment items.

There are few generalizations that we can make about the effect of the business cycle on any *particular* market or market segment; each situation has to be evaluated on its own merits. Almost always, however, the business cycle plays a powerful role in changing segmentation, changing the requirements of buyers within the segment, and changing the size and profitability of business opportunities that the segment provides.

The Effects of Social and Demographic Changes

This is again such a huge topic that we can here only illustrate the point with some typical examples. A fundamental social change is the rising concern for our ecology and the rapidly increasing interest in environmentally "safe" products, reusability, recycling, and the like. A second important social phenomenon affecting many consumer markets is the increase in one-person households, and the increase in the proportion of women in the workforce. These social forces are reshaping many markets, changing the nature of customer requirements (for example retail store opening hours), and resulting in new segmentation possibilities. And the demographic shift towards a much larger percentage of old people in the population is having, and will have, an effect on product requirements, as well as requirements for distribution, service, communication, and convenience—in fact on virtually every aspect of customer satisfaction across virtually the whole range of product and service requirements, from food to clothing, to housing, to recreation, to transportation, to health care, to leisure.

Rising Aspirations

One of the most important forces affecting today's, and certainly tomorrow's, markets is the seemingly generalized phenomenon of almost universally rising aspirations. And "universal" means here not only *geographically* universal—that is, that the populations of less developed countries aspire to the consumption possibilities of their more fortunate neighbors—but *economically* universal, in the sense that the well off as well as the less well off are raising their consumption sights.

Worldwide communication has played some role in this process; increased individual mobility and travel has also played a role. But another important reason for rising aspirations is the growing awareness and education of consumers, prompting them to evaluate more carefully their life's goals, ambitions, and personal value systems. Often the result is not "more" but "better" when it comes to consumption expenditures. The effect is a growing scorn for second-class or shoddy products, and a migration towards the upper end of the market. The biggest boom of all is likely to be at the very top end of most markets, particularly for products or services where there are only limited opportunities for increasing supplies. The rising worldwide demand for champagne, for Havana cigars, for luxury homes, and for entrance to first-class educational institutions testifies to this phenomenon. At the moment, only a fraction of the so-called consumers in the triad of Western Europe, Japan, and the United States are potential customers for these "quality" products, but if and when increasingly affluent populations in Asia and elsewhere join in, then markets will be under huge demand pressure. But the phenomenon of rising aspirations is not limited to luxury products. A manufacturer of caravans and mobile homes described the changes in that product over the last two decades as a shift from "little more than a box-on-wheels, to a real home-from-home with all possible modern conveniences." These are not so much the result of technical improvements as the result of manufacturers using their imagination to reconceive the idea of a traveling home as customer aspirations have risen.

At this time, aspirations appear to be rising faster than incomes. But this provides almost unlimited opportunities for suppliers to meet such needs—either by improving quality of so far run-of-the-mill products, or by lowering costs (and therefore prices), or both. Fashion manufacturers have taken the lead here, making high-quality "designer" clothes available to a much broader market at (nearly!) affordable prices. This has implied not only new products, but also new concepts of distribution, branding, promotion, advertising, and sales support. What clothing manufacturers have done, in terms of providing high-quality merchandise to mass markets is a trend that we can expect to see repeated in market after market—with as-yet hard to imagine consequences for the size, shape, and composition of segments within these markets.

Discontinuities

By definition, we cannot easily forecast discontinuities. But we do have numerous examples from the past. We can only assume there will be numerous other examples in the future even though we cannot yet determine their shape. The oil shocks of the late 1970s, the reforms in Eastern Europe, the Gulf War, and the demise of the Soviet Union should forewarn us that markets are not only affected by the more or less predictable forces described above.

SUPPLIER INITIATIVES

So far I have described the forces for market change as originating either "internally" with their origins in the product life cycle, or "externally" with their origins in technology change, globalization, business cycles, social change, rising aspirations, or unanticipated discontinuities. Yet markets are also changed by the initiatives undertaken by one supplier or another. To return to the Swatch example, with which this chapter started, it was the ingenuity of SMH's (Swatch's mother company) management and engineering staff that produced the Swatch idea, which redefined the very nature of the reasonably priced watch business.

In other words, underlying forces may exist to change markets, but they have to be exploited by manufacturers or service providers before the market is actually changed. Sometimes supplier initiatives are in the target area, but rarely, as I described in Chapter 3, do they result in real breakthroughs, and often they misfire. It is this trial-and-error process, often with three steps forward and two back, that results in the aggregate market motion that we can observe.

COMPANY "DIVERSIFICATION" VERSUS MARKET CHANGE

Up to now in this chapter we have talked exclusively about changes in *markets,* assuming the company as a constant throughout, and indeed companies do have to adapt constantly to these market shifts. This will be the subject of subsequent chapters in the next section.

But companies also move from one market to another as new opportunities appear and existing businesses opportunities reach saturation. Just like market change, diversification into new product or market areas implies change in operating requirements which the company has to cope with. This will also be taken up in detail in the next section. From the company view, dealing with such change can be just as taxing as dealing with major change in existing markets—and the further the diversification goes away from existing areas of competence, the more taxing the shift is likely to be.

UNDERLYING MARKET DIFFERENCES

To complete this chapter on "Markets in Motion," it is important to ask whether all markets can be looked at through the same lenses, that is, the lenses of internal and external change, and their effects. Or are there also *underlying* market characteristics to take into account that are likely to influence the way these other internal and external driving forces affect the markets in question. The answer is certainly "yes," and without going into great detail, the main underlying characteristics certainly include the following three main categories.

First, there are underlying *structural* characteristics of the market which seem to affect both life cycle and other changes. These may include such factors as (1) supply concentration, that is, is it a market with a few major competitors or one with a large number of players, (2) barriers to entry and exit, and (3) extent of product differentiation.

Second, the degree to which *technology* plays a role in gaining and maintaining competitive advantage appears to distinguish the way some markets change compared to others. Markets are likely to be more fundamentally redefined where technology is a key factor than when technology plays only a marginal role.

Thirdly, *cost structure*, in the sense of the underlying proportion of fixed and variable costs in the industry, usually plays a key role with respect to the rapidity of market change. High fixed cost industries are typically slower to change, and firms that choose strategies of owning rather than "renting" high fixed cost assets have more difficulty adapting to rapid change. This subject will be taken up in detail in Chapters 9 and 10.

We now turn from these introductory chapters on markets from a *customer perspective* to a look at industries as a whole. It is the *industry* which provides the setting within which the individual firm and its competitors seek to satisfy customers and struggle for supremacy.

THE COMPANY PERSPECTIVE

———————— ⚫ ————————

CHAPTER 6

DEFINING AN INDUSTRY

The previous section of this book took a customer perspective. It argued for not just meeting but exceeding customer expectations. It argued for doing so with the passion to constantly improve, rather than to simply meet or beat competition. And it argued for applying this passion to well-defined segments of opportunity.

But this should not lead us to ignore competition. There are not only innovators—struggling to exceed customer expectations in often new and exciting ways—there are imitators too—ever ready to plug the holes that we fail to fill as precisely as is needed.

An important question then is who are these possible competitors and what is the basis of their competitive challenge? And this question raises immediately the question that is closer to home: What is the basis of *our* competitive position, and from which vantage points can it be reinforced? To answer these questions, and the related questions of where value and costs are created, which are the subjects of succeeding chapters, we need to start with some concept of how to define the space within which competition takes place, in other words how to define a so-called "industry."

The terminology itself is not well-defined. What do we need to define to define an industry? And what do we mean by even the word "industry"? I shall use the concept here of a space within which one or more firms compete for the customer's purchase. But as we shall see, what happens *beyond* the space is usually as important as what happens within the space itself.

CONVENTIONAL DEFINITIONS

The "steel industry," the "automobile industry," or the "chemicals industry" situate us within a broad sectoral classification scheme without telling us much about the nature of competition within these broad sectors. And as shown in Chapter 3 of this book, such definitions are certainly too broad to be precise about the nature of customer needs. In fact the characteristics of demand for specialty steel products and basic commodity steel products may be more disparate than those of commodity steel and commodity chemicals.

As we saw in Chapter 4, segmentation of an industry produces more precision about customer needs. We might talk therefore of the "specialty steel industry," the "sports car industry," or the "basic chemicals industry" if the objective is to better understand the customer. And as was pointed out, we often have to define segments in ever "finer" terms than this to really isolate a group of customers having a relatively homogenous set of needs within an overall industry.

Conventionally this approach, which has as its main objective a better understanding of *customers,* has been presumed to be identical to the approach needed to understand the *supply side* of the market equation. Nothing, in fact, could be further from the truth. In fact, the progressive subdivision of an industry into segments and subsegments to understand the nature of demand usually obscures rather than illuminates the nature of competition. Paradoxically, taking a customer perspective usually argues for a relatively narrow definition, while taking a supply side perspective usually argues for a broad one.

Let us take an example from the previous chapters. To understand the requirements of *customers* in the "earth-moving machinery" industry, we certainly need to clearly segment large, heavy-duty machinery used for major road and civil engineering construction projects (traditionally dominated by Caterpillar) from the newer, lighter, smaller machines used for a large variety of smaller-scale construction and local "works" projects (in which

Komatsu has successfully challenged Caterpillar). But this is not nearly segmented enough to design and market machinery for specific applications such as "backhoe tractors" or "small excavators"—where differences among specific buyers, users, technologies, and benefits sought show considerable variation.

The problem is that when we reach a level of segmentation that enables us to understand demand, we may have narrowed the focus much too much to properly understand the basis on which competitive advantage can rest. Caterpillar's ability to compete for a particular segment of small excavators depends not only on its position in the small excavators business but also on its position in *all* excavators and possibly even on its position in all earth-moving equipment. Brand reputation, for example, is a corporate-wide phenomenon; some manufacturing and product technologies may be common to a wide range of products; and marketing advantage may have its roots in the breadth of the product offering. Similarly, cost advantages (or disadvantages) may be related to volume and/or experience generated in related product lines using common assemblies or components.

These "horizontal" relationships which have their origins in the scope and differentiation of a competitor's overall product or service offering are themselves only half of the story. "Vertical" relationships, upstream with suppliers and downstream with other intermediaries, can also have a major influence on competitiveness. Thus for Caterpillar, having access on the supply side to low-cost and high-quality power sources, and on the downstream side to a strong distribution and dealer network, is critical.

This same paradox between the narrower definition of a market needed to understand customer behavior, and the broader definition needed to understand competitive behavior exists to a greater or lesser degree in all businesses. Take, for example, the fashion industry. Moderately priced men's lightweight suits sold in department stores may be a meaningful definition from the viewpoint of defining customer requirements, but is not meaningful for understanding competition in this segment: A broader "horizontal" definition of the "industry" would be required which takes into account the synergies which competitors achieve in cost and quality by participating in a variety of related fashion segments; a broad "vertical" definition is required to understand the benefits which accrue to ventrically integrated producers who own or control various stages of the production and marketing chain, as Benetton has done.

It should be apparent from the foregoing examples that good business strategy, like good military strategy, focuses broad resources on a narrow target. It is analogous to using a magnifying glass to focus the enormous energy resources of the sun. The stronger the resources and the greater the focus, the more effective the result.

With these examples in mind, let us now examine more closely how to define an industry, if our objective is to understand competition within it. First, we shall look at "horizontal" definition; secondly at "vertical" definition. Both are important if we are to understand the basis on which we, as well as our competitors, derive competitive advantage.

DEFINING AN INDUSTRY
IN "HORIZONTAL" TERMS

Several competitors competing for the *same* customer segment rarely, if ever, have identical product or service portfolios. Differences often show up within the business itself, in terms of specific product and market choices; they are likely at the business unit or division level where different approaches to business definition may result in the inclusion of substantially different product or service lines; and they are almost always present at the corporate level where substantial divergence of activities usually results from internal development and corporate diversification and acquisition.

These differences, at the product-market level, in divisional, product, or service portfolios, and in the corporate spread of activities, play a crucial role in the way one or another competitor gains its competitive advantage. As we shall see in the chapters that follow, these definitional differences affect both qualities offered as well as costs. But these differences also affect the definition of the "industry," that is, the overall competitive space. The "industry" may be viewed as a series of overlaps of differently defined businesses, intersecting with one another but not necessarily congruent with one another.

Again, an example may be useful to illustrate the point. General Electric and Carrier compete "head on" with one another in the central air conditioning (CAC) equipment market. Carrier achieves a strong product quality and manufacturing cost position by having the largest CAC market share of any single producer. General Electric has a considerably lower share of the CAC equipment business, but a major share of *all* electrical devices, appliances, and equipment that go into the new home. Their strength, therefore, is drawn from their close relationship to new home developers, and from their ability to distribute a large variety of disparate "electrical" items to this particular market segment. Carrier's is essentially a product-specific advantage; General Electric has a market-specific advantage.

It is common in many industries to refer to companies as full-line manufacturers, part-line manufacturers, or specialty firms. Various bases for classification may be used in establishing such a trichotomy, including product features, price points, or technologies. Sometimes product breadth and market breadth are measured separately. If so, various combinations of product and market breadth can be delineated. Several authors, realizing that a typology based solely on product or market scope is inadequate, have sought to add to this concept a supplementary measure of *differentiation*. Originally proposed by Wendell Smith,[1] and elaborated by Philip Kotler[2] and later by Michael Porter,[3] this measure classifies three main approaches, as "undifferentiated" (cost leadership), "differentiated," and "concentrated" (or focused).

The problem with this classification is that it tells us about the position of a competitor in the *market* but does not tell us how the breadth or narrowness of participation relates to resource efficiency or effectiveness—especially as they may be affected by synergies between activities at the divisional or corporate levels (nor, in fact, does it tell us anything about competitive advantages resulting from *vertical* arrangements which may substantially differentiate one competitor from another, as we shall see in the next section).

A more complete conceptual scheme for understanding how the range of a company's overall activities may influence its competitive position in a particular segment was originally suggested by me in a previous book.[4] This requires a description of each competitor's activities along the now familiar three dimensions:

–customer groups served

–customer functions served

–technologies (or product forms or "approaches") used

These same three dimensions were used in Chapter 4 to help us understand market segmentation. When we *contrast* different competitors' approaches on these three dimensions, it also provides us with a basis for defining the industry space within which competition takes place.

These distinctions clarify some of the confusion that exists between "demand side" and "supply side" criteria for defining market boundaries. "Interchangeability of use" is a frequently accepted criterion for defining market boundaries from a demand side perspective. But competition between firms is influenced heavily by their "extra-market" activities. A view of the supply side along these three dimensions is therefore essential to understanding the resource efficiencies and synergies achieved by each competitor. The "overlaps" of various competitors on customer-group, customer-definition, and technology dimensions often create a competitive envelope extending far beyond any single market. From an analytical viewpoint, demand side definitions represent arenas where competitors meet; supply side definitions are necessary for explaining their actions.

Classification of "Industries"

Broadly speaking, there are two types of industry: First there are those where the major competitors are *similarly* defined in terms of the customer groups they serve; customer functions provided for; and technologies used. Second, there are those where the major competitors, like Carrier and General Electric in the earlier example, define their activities *differently*.

If activities of competitors are similarly defined, this still leaves very much open the question of *how* they are defined. In an earlier book I depicted eight variants depending on whether major competitors were narrowly or broadly defined on each of the three dimensions.[5] For example, the Big Three U.S. automobile manufacturers define their businesses very similarly, and each of them boasts a car line that appeals to diverse (but similar) segments, diverse (but similar) functional needs, using diverse (but similar) technology and marketing approaches. At the other extreme, competitors in much more segmented markets take a narrower, more focused approach on each of the three dimensions. Between these two, there is the possibility for a mixture of broad and narrow approaches on each of the three dimensions—the distinguishing features being, however, that the major competitors are *all* similarly defined.

In the second major type of industry, when competitors are *differently* defined, the possibility exists for an almost infinite number of combinations and permutations. One competitor may focus on a narrow customer segment but offer a range of products (or services) serving a range of functions, and base the product line on several different technological approaches; another competitor may focus on one main function, using one unique technology, but market products broadly to a wide variety of customer segments. Pictorially, this may be diagrammed as in Figure 6–1.

An example of contrasting approaches to the same business is demonstrated by Avon and Revlon. Both appeal to similar customer groups; both offer cosmetics that perform similar functions and satisfy similar needs; but Avon's "technology" is to demonstrate directly in the home via a huge direct sales operation; Revlon's approach is to utilize retail channels of distribution, and mass media.

Of course, industry definitions are seldom static. One or another competitor may extend or contract its activities on any of the three dimensions and in so doing alter the basic definition of the industry. Industries once identified as having similarly defined competitors may evolve into industries with differently defined competitors—and vice versa. And industries in which the similarity is based on a narrow focus in one dimension or another may change when competitors, in parallel, broaden their activities to take advantage of new market opportunities.

The Corporate Portfolio

As we shall see in the next two chapters, our understanding of value creation and costs would be incomplete if we limited ourselves to the scope of each competitor's participation in that *particular* prod-

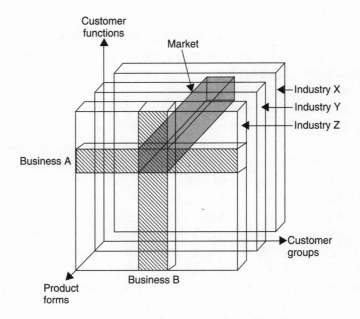

Figure 6–1. Businesses, Industries, and Markets
SOURCE: Derek F. Abell, *Defining the Business: The Strategy Point of Strategic Planning,* © 1980, p. 180. Prentice Hall, Englewood Cliffs, New Jersey.

uct-market area. Where synergies are present *among* one or more business areas in which a competitor engages, these synergies affect either customer value or costs, or both.

General Motors, for example, competes in five broadly defined price-value segments of the automobile industry, represented respectively by its Chevrolet, Oldsmobile, Buick, Pontiac, and Cadillac divisions. Clearly its position in any one of these is affected by the others because there are many shared technologies, manufacturing processes, and marketing activities. But it is not stretching the point too far to say that GM's position in the automobile business is also affected by what it does in the truck business, and vice versa. In fact, GM also operates in many other business areas including the defense industry and financial services industry. These also have some indirect—if not direct—effects on the automobile business which we cannot afford to ignore totally if we wish to understand the nature of competition in automobiles.

To summarize, supply side, "horizontal" definitions of an "industry" must take into account the *full* range of activities of each major competitor corporate-wide as well as business-wide. This is particularly the case where major synergies are present between one product-market activity and another. How these activities actually affect customer value and costs will be the subject respectively of the following four chapters.

Existing Competitors and Potential New Entrants

So far we have talked only about *existing* competitors in an industry. These competitors all compete currently for the same segment of the market as we do, albeit from substantially different as well as similar definitions of the business.

But *potential* competitors entering our business, or threatening to enter our business, also pose a threat and must be considered. Such a potential competitor seldom enters "out of the blue." He may enter from any one of several starting points, for example:

- He already sells to our customers, but expands his participation to include new customer functions which we currently satisfy.
- He already satisfies customer functions that we satisfy but expands his participation into our customer market from activities in other customer markets where we are not currently active.
- He previously operated in the same markets and functions with products based on an entirely different and so far noncompetitive technology, but moves to a technology directly competitive with ours.
- He enters from an upstream or downstream position.
- He enters as a result of an "unrelated" diversification—often bringing a new "substitute" product into the market.

Michael Porter uses a four-way schema to array these various entry alternatives as shown in Figure 6–2. Understanding the competitive arena and its possible evolution requires us to keep a sharp eye out for these potential competitors as well as those with whom we already compete.

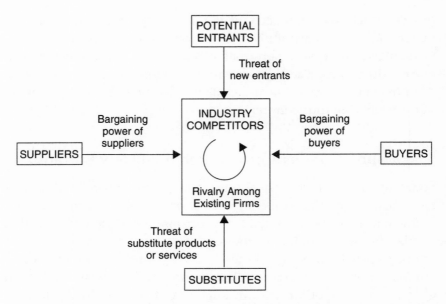

Figure 6–2. Forces Driving Industry Competition
SOURCE: Reprinted with the permission of The Free Press, a Division of Macmillan, Inc., New York, from *Competitive Strategy* by Michael E. Porter, p. 4. Copyright © 1980 by The Free Press.

DEFINING AN INDUSTRY IN "VERTICAL" TERMS

A narrow perspective on the supply side views competition as taking place between raw material suppliers, manufacturers, distribution organizations, or retailers *operating at the same level* in the vertical chain.

We might argue therefore if we were looking at, say, the textile industry, that a synthetics producer such as Du Pont competes directly with another major synthetics producer such as Celanese, and that printing and dyeing houses compete head on with other printing and dying houses, while branded clothing manufacturers like Benetton compete directly with Esprit or "The Gap."

This notion of competition, however, overlooks the fact that strong vertical arrangements between the members of the vertical chain may have important benefits at the end of the chain in terms of the final offering to the customer. These benefits may take the form of a superior product offering, on any one or more of the dimensions described in Chapter 3, or in terms of costs and hence price/value relationships. These two alternative perspectives on competition may be diagrammed as shown in Figure 6–3.

In fact, we must make an important distinction between the value-added chain *within* a particular company, and the value-added chain in the *vertical business system* that connects a variety of companies as we pass from raw materials through manufacturing and distribution to the final customers. Both vertical systems are important if we are to understand the nature of competition from a supply side perspective. *Within* the firm, we are talking about the value contributed by the various functions of the enterprise as the product or service is created. This may include purchasing, design, R&D, manufacturing, physical distribution, and marketing activities. The business system *external* to the firm may include a wide variety of organizations, owned, controlled, or totally independent, which in one way or another contribute to the product or service consumed by the customer at the end of the chain. Figure 6–4 makes this distinction clear.

The Nature of Vertical Relationships

The legal relationship between two companies doing business together in a vertical chain is not necessarily indicative of the degree

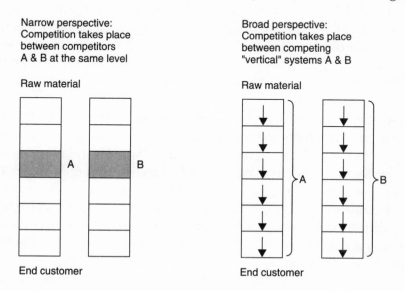

Figure 6–3. Two Perspectives on Competition

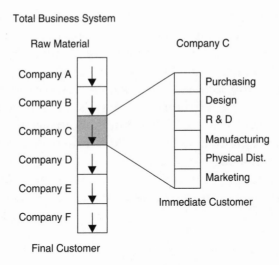

Figure 6–4. Value-added Chains

of coordination and integration that actually takes place between them. Two companies may, for example, operate at arm's length legally but be closely tied together in their business practices. "Just-in-time" delivery practices among two totally independent business entities would be one such example.

Legally, the spectrum of relationships runs from total independence, to alliance partnerships, to some degree of equity participation, to outright ownership. The latter is of course the result when a company integrates backwards into "upstream" supply operations, or forwards into "downstream" manufacturing, distribution, or service operations.

As far as the actual *working* relationship is concerned, this may run from something approaching antagonistic at one extreme to tightly integrated and cooperative at the other. The relationship, for example, between large food manufacturers and retail food chains is growing less cooperative—since large retail chains have developed substantial buying power and hence can fight fiercely for margins, allowances, and their own private brands. Their power is often exercised in shelf space decisions—which totally exclude all but top brands from display.

At the other end of the spectrum, cooperative working relationships may take a wide variety of forms. Customers may, for example, be instrumental in the product development processes of their suppliers—or, conversely, suppliers may reach forward to assist downstream companies to do a better job of marketing *their* products. The advent of information technology has presented many opportunities for companies to provide more information to each other about upstream and downstream operations—with resulting big advances in logistics, services, stock levels, and overall cost and quality from the perspective of the eventual customer.

Another related trend is the convergence of customers on single or limited supply sources as opposed to multiple sources of supply. Both customers and suppliers see more benefits in developing an integrated response to downstream market needs than they do in trying to negotiate better prices by keeping several alternative suppliers competitive with one another.

In practice, proclamations of the desire to work more closely with suppliers may not reflect actual working relationships. The "Big Three" U.S. automakers, facing severe global competition, were apparently convinced to look for closer "partnership" relationships with suppliers.[6] Believing that they needed higher quality, lower costs, and more innovation, they promised suppliers long-term contracts in return for ideas on improved product design and guaranteed annual price cuts. A corollary was an overall reduction in the number of suppliers. But with tougher times, these hoped-for closer relationships were dashed as automakers reverted to traditional lowest cost bids to try to get their own costs down, and to meet Japanese competitors. European automakers are not in much better shape.[7] According to a study by two leading consulting companies, the European car industry suffers a big disadvantage relative to the Japanese car industry because of fundamental differences at the supplier level and in the relationships between suppliers and manufacturers. Japanese manufacturers benefit substantially from higher labor productivity, higher quality, higher stock turns, faster delivery cycles, faster design and development cycles, higher design and development productivity, more variety, and in many cases, lower product costs. Behind these advantages are the close relationships which the Japanese manufacturers and suppliers have together. In other words, the Japanese automobile industry is *de-*

fined differently than either the U.S. or European industry with respect to the vertical relationships among firms in the value-added chain.

INDUSTRY TYPOLOGIES

On the incorrect assumption that firms competing in the same industry were defined similarly, a lot of the attention of microeconomists has traditionally been focused on three factors: concentration, barriers to entry and exit, and product differentiation among suppliers. Industries have therefore been defined principally by whether they were monopolistic, oligopolistic, or more fragmented—the so-called "structure" being presumed to have substantial impact on the conduct or behavior of competing firms, and on industry "performance"—as measured by such factors as innovativeness and profitability. Barriers to entry were presumed to reinforce monopolistic tendencies in concentrated industries, as was product differentiation.

Michael Porter[8] expanded this thinking substantially by postulating that an industry could only be understood by recognizing the pressures exerted by upstream suppliers or downstream customers on the profitability of companies at any particular stage of the chain, and by understanding the competition of immediate substitutes as well as potential new entrants for any segment of business activity.

The view of an "industry" as a series of overlays of companies differently defined in both horizontal and vertical dimensions results in a different industry typology: At one end of the spectrum are industries where most competitors are narrowly defined both horizontally and vertically, that is, they enjoy few synergies beyond their particular individual business area, nor do they have close upstream or downstream working relationships. At the other end of the spectrum are industries where most competitors are broadly defined horizontally and vertically, that is, they enjoy substantial synergies beyond their individual business area, and they have close upstream and downstream relationships. In fact there are few of the former type, and a growing number of the latter type—as it becomes more and more apparent that synergistic relationships horizontally and vertically play an important part in assembling the distinctive competence necessary to win in the marketplace.

The food industry, for example, has seen a wave of "horizontal" acquisitions and mergers aimed at broadening participation in the sector as a whole. One important benefit is the acquisition of brands with broad customer appeal; but another key reason is that broad line suppliers increase their bargaining power vis-à-vis distribution chains. In the textile industry, by contrast, subsectors of the overall industry are being redefined by a growing number of vertical arrangements connecting upstream design and manufacturing to downstream retailing. If anything, the "horizontal" dimensions of these subindustries are being narrowed as companies focus on well-defined customer segments and try to integrate the corporate vertical business system to serve them.

Nevertheless, the bulk of industries cannot be defined at one or other end of this spectrum and in fact are made up of diverse overlays—some competitors narrowly defined and others broadly defined horizontally or vertically. Each competitor is thus seeking to create value and manage costs in a somewhat different way, and defining his own business uniquely as the starting point.

Under these circumstances, traditional measures of supplier concentration, product differentiation among competitors, and market share become extremely difficult to formulate, let alone quantify. And the effects of high or low share of a particular segment of the market may tell only a very partial story because quality and cost positions are related to vertical or horizontal synergies on the *supply* side, not market share in a particular segment of overall demand.

"Generic" Company Strategies

Such broadly based industry definitions lead us logically to ask whether there are not some "generic" approaches to business definition at the individual company level. When talking about generic strategies, it is all too easy to fall into the trap of oversimplifying—and defining strategy by placing the company somewhere on a map defined by cost position on the one hand and perceived value on the other. But it is what lies *behind* high perceived value or low delivered cost that is important. The way the business is defined horizontally and vertically is a key ingredient for this, since it fundamentally affects how value is created and costs are accumulated. It is to each of these subjects that we now turn.

CHAPTER 7

THE COMPANY
AND ITS COMPETITORS:
VISIBLE DIFFERENCES

I n the previous chapter, the idea of a competitive *space* was introduced. This space has to be defined broadly enough, horizontally and vertically, to provide insight into the manifold ways that competences and resources—internal and external to a company and its competitors—are brought to bear to create value for the customer. In this chapter and the next, the focus is on the *occupants* of this space. In comparing and contrasting a company with its competitors, what specifically should we be evaluating if our objective is to look for points of distinction?

Just as we can draw a "customer satisfaction iceberg" to show how many ways there are beyond the physical product itself to influence customer satisfaction, we may draw a "competitor differentiation iceberg" to represent the many ways that one competitor may be distinguished from another. And like the customer satisfaction iceberg, a large proportion of these ways are "below the water line," hidden from immediate view, as shown in Figure 7–1.

Performance is perhaps the most "visible" feature distinguishing one competitor from another. But behind performance is an approach to the market which can also be described, if not measured, for each competitor. And behind the market approach is the basic definition of the business chosen by the competitor—on both horizontal and vertical dimensions.[1]

But while such descriptions of a company or its competitors are necessary, they are not sufficient. Beneath these "visible" differences are differences in the resources and competences that compet-

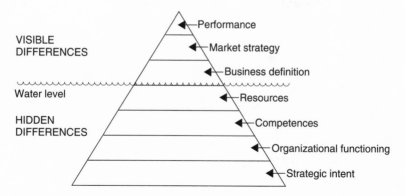

Figure 7–1. The Competitors Differentiation Iceberg

itors bring to bear on their activities. Resources and competences are much harder to assess for two reasons. First they are more *hidden* from view—and even for our own organization, they may be more difficult to evaluate. Secondly, resources and competences have little or no meaning in the abstract. They take on meaning when described in relation to customer needs that have to be met or exceeded. Only then is it possible to tell whether apparent strengths are *relevant* strengths, or whether weaknesses may be debilitating. To use a human analogy, having enormous biceps may be good for lifting 500-pound weights; it may be irrelevant for passing exams in chemistry; and it may even be dysfunctional for running a 100-yard dash.

Hidden strengths may be internal to the business itself, for example Nestle's purchasing capability with respect to cocoa beans in its chocolate business; or they may have their origins in corporate synergies, such as Nestle's overall brand image and distribution strength, or in vertical relationships such as assured supplies of low-cost and high-quality raw materials. Hidden strength may also be derived from the political-economic environment in which the firm operates, that is, Nestle may do better than Hershey in the chocolate business precisely because of its Swiss origins: while Swiss cows may not actually laugh, they have every reason to if one looks at their quality of life on Swiss pastures![2]

Differences in resources and competences may rest on a wide variety of possible organizational differences. Tom Peters preaches that organization is at the root of most corporate success and failure, and while giving "strategy" all due recognition, he argues that organization functioning—in particular entrepreneurial leadership in organization—is a decisive factor.[3]

Lastly, G. Hamel and C.K. Pralahad have highlighted the importance of "strategic intent" in shaping long-term corporate success or failure.[4] This has been included here at the very bottom of the "iceberg," to emphasize both its primordial role as well as its "hidden" nature.

While visible differences are therefore important in understanding the relative standing of companies in a marketplace, hidden differences are often even more important. We may, by analogy, watch *how* an army fights, but we can only gain real insight into the capacities of the protagonists if we know how they are trained, what their preparedness is, how well they are endowed with materiel, how well they are supplied, and of fundamental importance, how they function organizationally, and what their basic strategic intent is. Honda beats General Motors in the marketplace not simply because it has cars that have higher customer appeal, but because it has underlying competences in engine technology and design, superior resources to put behind these competences, and a well-oiled organization to formulate and carry out its long-term strategic intentions.

In the remainder of this chapter we shall concentrate on the "visible" differences, that is, on performance differences, differences in market strategy, and differences in the way the business is defined. In Chapter 8 we shall look at those differences that are buried within the organization itself: resources and competences, organizational functioning, and strategic intent.

PERFORMANCE

The *most* visible sign of a company's strength or weakness is its performance. Competitors differ substantially in terms of how well they perform, and it is the natural starting point of any attempt to compare one competitor with another—just as a doctor takes the temperature and pulse rate as measurable signs of bodily health. Performance measures fall into two broad categories: financial performance can be measured by various income statement and balance sheet items or ratios between them; market performance is usually measured by sales, market share, and growth data.

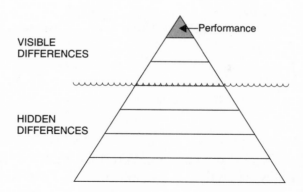

Performance cannot, of course, be assessed by any single measure taken alone. Comparisons of profitability expressed as a percentage of sales, assets, or equity may take on a different complexion when looked at in conjunction with changes in balance sheet items. Two companies may generate similar operating profits but one may invest these profits in working capital, facilities and equipment needed to grow, while a second may not. Cash flow outcomes will be very different. Indeed, some very profitable companies flirt constantly with illiquidity to try to manage the challenges of growth, while others use their strong operating performance in one business to invest in another. A more complete analysis, even of performance alone, requires an understanding not only of profit levels, but how profits are used—which in turn requires an understanding of tradeoffs between cash flow and market performance as measured by market share and growth.

Also, we must remember that financial and market performance give an indication of how well the company is *currently* serving its customers; it may tell little about its *future* potential to do so. One of the problems with using financial or market performance as a sign of strength or weakness is, in fact, that it often masks *inner* decay. How many managers have been tempted to cut future investments to sweeten current profitability? There are often, in fact, stages of getting into trouble—as shown in Figure 7–2.

In the best of times ("glory"), *both* the financial results and the underlying "fundamentals" of the business are positive. When the glory fades into what may pass as "good times," the fundamentals may have become negative, while positive financial results persist.

Figure 7–2. Stages of Getting into Trouble

This is a dangerous time for most companies because there is no sense of crisis. Real problems remain hidden from view. Disaster strikes eventually when financial results turn down as the underlying problems finally make their effects felt. By this time it is often too late to take avoiding action.

In other words, while financial performance is *one* sign of strength or weakness, it is only that—a sign. Good managers, like good doctors, look below the surface for the underlying factors which ultimately determine business health. As a senior executive at Bank of America is supposed to have said, "We grew fat and happy in the 1970s, sitting on top of a hill making money."[5]

MARKET STRATEGY

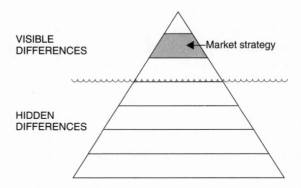

A good competitive comparison must include, in addition to performance, a description of what each competitor's approach is to the markets in which it operates. We can of course describe separately its products, services, distribution, promotion, and pricing. And in any case we should avoid the pitfall, as Chapter 3 made clear, of evaluating the product (or service) *in isolation* of other aspects of customer satisfaction. But of far greater value to our understanding is usually to take an overall *integrated* view of how these various elements of the "marketing mix" relate to one another and to the overall market strategy. To do this we have to consider not only the "part-to-part" integration between one functional activity and another, but also the "part-to-whole" integration between that functional activity and the overall market strategy. Part-to-part integration means, for example, that advertising and promotion strategy must be consistent with distribution strategy. It would make little sense to opt for highly selective distribution and at the same time to engage in large-scale mass media advertising aimed at stimulating impulse purchasing at convenient locations. Part-to-whole integration means that *both* advertising strategy and distribution strategy must be consistent with the overall market strategy and with the chosen positioning of the firm.

I prefer to define market strategy even more broadly than in terms of the well-known 4Ps of the marketing mix—product, "place" (distribution), promotion and price. In fact, *any* functional activity that contributes to the achievement of the company's program in the marketplace needs to be included. We can distinguish in this way between a market*ing* strategy and a market strategy. The former is limited to marketing elements of the overall approach; the latter includes manufacturing, logistics, research and development, engineering, and even human resource and administrative approaches if these underpin a unique market position. In fact, bringing the "back office" functions of manufacturing, engineering, and R&D into line with overall market needs is often even more critical—and even more difficult—than bringing market*ing* elements such as distribution, promotion, or advertising into line, simply because the individuals working in these functions tend to be more isolated than marketing people from contact with the customer.

The part-to-part, part-to-whole concept is just as important when we use this broader definition of market strategy as when we use the narrower one. Marketing and manufacturing must, for example, be harmonized to meet customer needs, implying close working relationships between the two—as is also the case between marketing and engineering or engineering and manufacturing. *All* functions have to be managed in a way that is consistent with the overall defined market strategy segment-by-segment. This proves to be very difficult in some companies where functional executives believe that they should retain a degree of independent decision-making authority—and do not like to dance to the tune of those product or segment managers charged with overall "program" responsibility.

Market strategies often vary dramatically among different competitors. Sometimes this results from conscious choices to attack different segments having different needs; sometimes it results from the belief that there is more than one way to skin a cat; more often than not it results from the fact that companies have very different underlying resources and competences and historically they develop certain ways of approaching the market which build on and exploit these competences. While there is an almost infinite variety of possible market strategies, three broad typologies provide a helpful way to think about and characterize one or other approach used. Each of these was outlined in Chapter 4; here we shall look at them in more detail.

High Perceived Value Versus Low Delivered Cost

Mercedes, Porsche, and Jaguar, and even more strikingly Rolls Royce, might be described as high perceived value competitors in the automobile industry. Toyota, Ford, and Volkswagen, and even more strikingly the now discontinued Citroen "Deux-Chevaux" might be described as competing on low delivered cost. And in other industries too, it is usually possible to array competitors somewhere along these two broad axes as shown in Figure 7–3. The advent of cars like Lexus and Audi, however, reveal that there are opportunities to *combine* high perceived value with low delivered cost approaches to the market.

In the men's and women's fashion industry, the entry of exclusive brands such as Dior, Yves St. Laurent, and Armani into broader markets at affordable prices is analogous. Such strategies may originate either through the persistent trading up of a lower-cost product into higher quality brackets (as Japanese manufacturers have often done) or through persistent efforts to achieve a better cost position from products initially positioned at the quality end of the spectrum (as European fashion houses have done)—see Figure 7–4.

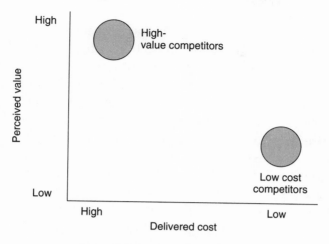

Figure 7–3. Market Strategy Matrix

Push Versus Pull

This concept is an old "workhorse" of marketing—yet it is potentially as useful today as ever. "Push" marketing means that most of the marketing activity goes through the channels of distribution. In particular, it typically implies that the customer relies heavily on the point of sale for pre- and postpurchase information, reassurance, and service. "Push" products usually require substantial trade

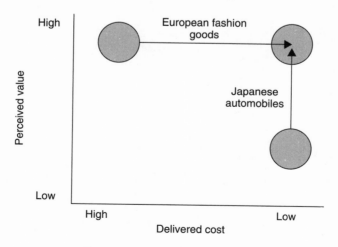

Figure 7–4. Market Strategy Matrix

margins to pay for the costs of such trade services. "Pull" marketing, by contrast, emphasizes communication directly with the customer, typically via the media, so that sufficient brand recognition is created to induce the final customer to "pull" the product through the distribution channels. "Pull" products are characterized by lower trade margins with a higher proportion of the marketing dollars being spent in the media than in the trade. Nescafé is a "pull" product; Savile Row suits are "push" products.

Figure 7–5 illustrates the fundamental difference between "push" and "pull." "Push" and "pull" marketing does not exist only in the consumer goods sector. When an industrial goods manufacturer goes "around" his immediate customer and either sells, promotes, or develops applications for his product with business entities further downstream, this is also "pull" marketing. Such is the case with engineered plastics manufacturers who develop applications with end users even though they sell plastic resins directly to intermediate plastic molders.

New developments in retailing which offer wide choice with *some* degree of point-of-sale service (for example Benetton stores) are blurring the lines between push and pull—just as the lines between high perceived value and low delivered cost strategies are being blurred. Nevertheless, the concept continues to offer a holistic way to capture broad differences in marketing approach among competitors in the same markets. L'Oréal markets pull products; its major German rival Wella sells mostly through hairdressing salons,

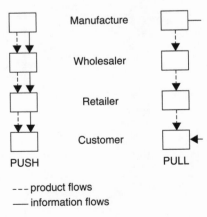

--- product flows
—— information flows

Figure 7–5. Push Versus Pull Strategies

and concentrates on push. Wella goes as far as to operate a school for hairdressers in Darmstadt, Germany, to support its in-store merchandising activities.

The concept of push versus pull can be useful for describing not only the status quo but *changes* in the market. Many products which begin their life as push products, end them as pull products. This happens as customers gain experience with purchase and use and therefore need proportionately less help at the point of sale, and as lower prices and broader markets suggest more efficient but less personalized forms of communication and reassurance. Frequently the brand provides the reassurance previously provided by the reputation of the outlet. As push transforms to pull, products originally found in specialty outlets—like watches, stereo systems, and fashion items—begin to appear in mass merchandising outlets.

Product Features Versus Service Intensity

A third useful way to contrast market strategies is along the dimension of service intensity. Manufacturing companies, as we saw in Chapter 3, have increasingly turned to service to differentiate their offerings from those of their competitors. This is in part a reaction to much faster competitive imitation, shorter life cycles, and increasing difficulties in achieving sustainable competitive advantage in the product itself. It also results from the growing realization that customers have been "underserved" in the past, and that real opportunities exist in this area—even for so-called "industrial" products—to improve customer satisfaction.

But it is the *degree* of attention to product features versus customer service that often differentiates one competitor from another in the marketplace. These may not always be alternative approaches to the same market but rather a response to different segments or sub-segments—one group of customers preferring to spend their money on the latest technical features; and another preferring to spend it on one or more dimensions of service. And as we have seen above for the traditional dichotomies of high perceived value/low delivered cost and pull/push, new aggressive competitors are increasingly appearing who try to do both with excellence, that is, to stay on the leading edge of *both* product technology and customer service.

This dichotomy is apparent if we compare large OEM computer manufacturers such as IBM or DEC with their smaller competitors (who are usually also their suppliers). These smaller companies invest heavily to stay on the leading edge of only one or a few hardware or software technologies. The larger producers have, by contrast, much more developed customer relations, sales, and service activities. But it is just as apparent in the automobile industry that the Japanese Lexus is not only an outstandingly engineered car, but that the company has "engineered" through its dealer network a very high level of customer service. This service extends from prepurchase, through purchase, to postpurchase. In fact Lexus owners appear to have just as many stories to tell about previously unheard-of (in this industry) services and service levels as they do about the car itself.

BUSINESS DEFINITION[6]

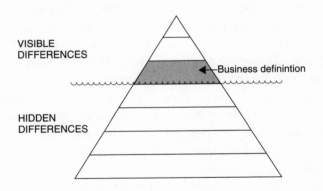

Behind a winning market strategy and successful performance in the marketplace usually lies a distinctive definition of the business. Competitive contrasts and comparisons on this dimension show substantial dispersion, just as we have seen already with performance and market strategy. In fact competition seldom takes place among equals; it takes place, even at the visible level, between businesses doing different things in different ways—and achieving differing results in the process.

Some of these differences have been described in the previous chapter—where it was shown how an "industry definition" depends on the "overlay" of the several firms that compete for a segment of the market. The horizontal and vertical dimensions of business definition are both important to understand, as we have also seen. In this section, I shall go further and consider the following questions: What role does business definition play as a differentiating element of business strategy? How does the question of definition vary with organizational level? And what factors should be considered in choosing a definition of the business so that strong financial and market performance will result?

"Horizontal" Business Definition

Choices with respect to customer groups, functions, and technologies play a central role in business strategy in two ways: Increased *scope* of participation provides opportunities for resource *efficiencies* which do not exist for more narrowly defined competitors; while increased *internal differentiation* among the approaches used to attack individual segments and subsegments increases *effectiveness*. General Motors took the lead from Ford in the 1920s partly because it achieved many of the same resource *efficiencies* as Ford through its broad overall participation in the car market, but it also achieved superior *effectiveness* in key customer segments by differentiating its product offering five ways: into five price/value segments represented respectively by Chevrolet, Oldsmobile, Buick, Pontiac, and Cadillac. Ford, meanwhile, persisted with its relatively undifferentiated "Any color you want as long as it's black" Model T approach. Three alternative strategies for defining a business "horizontally" are (1) focused, (2) differentiated, and (3) undifferentiated.

Focused Strategy

A company may focus on a particular customer group (for example, a geographical segment), customer function, or specific technology. Focus implies a basis for segmentation along one or more of these three dimensions, narrow scope involving only one or a few chosen segments, and differentiation from competitors through careful tailoring of the offering to the specific needs of the targeted segment(s). Bang and Olufsen's definition of the high fidelity consumer electronics business is an example of focus. Focus is achieved via targeting audiophiles, by concentrating on the latest technology, and by exceptional design—all at prices that result in the self-selection of a small but well-defined target audience.

Differentiated Strategy

This results when a company combines broad scope with differentiation across any or all of the three dimensions. By tailoring the offering to the specific needs of each segment, a company automatically increases its chance for competitive superiority. Whether or not *competitive* differentiation also results is purely a function of the extent to which competitors have also tailored their offerings to the same specific segment. As in the case of a focused strategy, the crucial aspect of a differentiated strategy is often the basis on which customer groups, customer functions, or technologies are segmented. One differentiated strategy may prove superior to another because its basis for segmentation more clearly highlights significant differences in customer requirements. Nestlé provides an outstanding example of differentiated strategy in the way it manages its coffee business—more than sixty different flavors are used worldwide, each requiring different manufacturing processes, research and development approaches, and specific packaging and marketing programs.

Undifferentiated Strategy

This strategy combines broad scope across any or all of the three dimensions with an undifferentiated approach to each segment. Standardized global marketing is in fact a recognition of the fact that, for some products at least, broad global participation does not necessarily imply a different approach country-by-country. In fact the resource efficiencies gained by pursuing a relatively similar approach everywhere substantially outweigh the benefits in terms of effectiveness of tailoring the offering market-by-market.

Scope and differentiation can be considered at several levels of aggregation. The higher the level of aggregation, the more the definition is likely to appear as focused or differentiated; the lower the level of aggregation, the more the definition is likely to appear as broad and undifferentiated. One measure of how differentiated or focused a business is can be derived from an assessment of the lowest level at which the definition can still be considered as focused or differentiated. The lower the level, the more the business can be said to be emphasizing effectiveness as opposed to efficiency; the higher the level the more the reverse will be true.

Horizontal business definition takes on a somewhat different *meaning* at different levels. I shall use the term "corporate level" to denote choices that might be made by corporate-level management; "business level" to denote choices that might be made by business-level management; and "program level" to denote choices that might be made by a product or market manager *within* an individual business. At the *corporate* level, we are apt to talk about questions of business definition or redefinition in terms of "diversification strategy"; at the individual business (or division) level business definition is conventionally expressed in terms of product/market strategy choices; and at the level of segments of the individual business, we are apt to talk of "positioning" choices.

Horizontal business definition is seldom given the attention it deserves as a central feature of managerial choice—choice which will certainly have a significant impact on many other aspects of the way a company conducts it business. Business definition is often the net result of a long series of partly coordinated and partly uncoordinated historical decisions which leave a company with a particular shape and size—just as a fifty-year-old human being wakes up one morning to discover that years of dubious eating and drinking habits have left behind a physical definition which has been acquired rather than deliberately selected.

Businesses grow and change on the horizontal dimension as companies migrate towards new opportunities in customer, function, or technology segments, as they diversify through internal growth or acquisition, or divest themselves of less attractive undertakings. Many factors influence these choices, formally or informally: changes in customer buying behavior; resource availability, internal competences, cost behavior, and of course internal managerial decision-making processes.

Vertical Business Definition

Choices with respect to participation in the vertical business chain also "visibly" differentiate one competitor from another in the same market.

As explained in the previous chapter, differences can take legal forms as well as managerial forms. At the risk of oversimplification, there are two extremes. On one extreme is a competitor who buys on an "arm's length" basis from many competing suppliers on a sealed bid basis and sells at arm's length to the next enterprise level, on a completely nonexclusive basis. At the other extreme is a competitor who coordinates and integrates every step in the vertical chain to ensure that the *end customer* gets the best possible level of customer satisfaction at the lowest possible price. This may or may not involve vertical integration upstream or downstream. Nowadays information technology is doing more to help the integration of vertical partners than equity participation!

We shall now turn from the "visible" differences to those "below the water line", i.e. those buried within the organization itself.

CHAPTER 8

THE COMPANY
AND ITS COMPETITORS:
HIDDEN DIFFERENCES

RESOURCES AND COMPETENCES

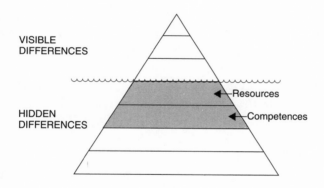

Resources and competences are not the same, although the distinction is seldom made clear. Resources are any form of wherewithal that can be harnessed to purposeful customer-satisfying activity. Resources may take financial form, human form, or physical form in the sense of land, facilities, or equipment. They are what economists like to call "factors of production," although resources are needed and used to accomplish *every* form of functional activity—not only production in the narrow sense of the word. Financial and physical resources show up on a company's balance sheet and in this respect they are tangible and measurable; human resources, it has been argued, *should* show up in a company's balance sheet given their relative importance, but the difficulty of putting a financial value on an individual rules this out.

Competences, on the other hand, are much less tangible, let alone measurable. They are not shown on any balance sheets, and are well hidden and often not recognized—on the inside as well as on the outside of firms. Competences are capabilities or "know-how." Competences do not exist in the absence of people. When a company's employees walk out of the door, its competences go with them. But competences extend well beyond the capabilities of *individuals.* A company may build competence in a specific area of activity through a team—a team drawn from within a particular department, or one that crosses departmental lines. Competence may be built (and equally well dissipated) over time, and mechanisms may be needed to ensure that competence is passed on—outlasting individuals or even specifically identifiable teams.

Competence is associated with *doing* something. Competence usually grows with its application. When a competence is simply "held in inventory" it often decays. Finally, competence is multidimensional in character. An individual who demonstrates exceptional competence in mathematics draws on a wide variety of individual talents, skills, and previous experiences when his competence is put to the test. So it is with a corporate competence, which generally describes an *aggregate* set of capabilities, specific skills, and experiences.

Competences can cover all aspects of a corporation's activities. They may reside within the four walls of the firm or be embedded in the relationships or activities which the firm engages in with others—either horizontal and/or vertical partners. Competences can be technical or organizational in nature, and can be found in purchasing, manufacturing, research, engineering, sales, marketing, logistics, administration, finance, or in management.

Distinctive competences are competences that distinguish a firm from its competitors. They are unique to that particular organization. *Core competences* are those competences that are the mainspring of the company's success. When a company has a distinctive core competence and applies it uniquely to the satisfaction of a distinct customer need, it is bound to succeed.

The discussion of resources and competences and how they affect success or failure in the marketplace may be divided into five broad categories:

1. Internal resources and competences (i.e., internal to the specific business unit)

2. External resources and competences (i.e., those resulting from alliances or other similar arrangements)

3. Corporate synergies

4. Vertical synergies

5. Country context factors

In many successful firms today, internal resources and competences are dwarfed by those that derive from alliances, synergies, and vertical relationships with others—as well as from making shrewd choices with respect to geographic locations that provide the firm with a rich variety of infrastructure benefits. Core competences therefore are not only to be found internally. They may just as well derive from the four other important sources. Unless they are under the company's control, however, there is always the risk that other parties may one day withdraw them, or strike a harder bargain for their continued exploitation.

Let us look at these five categories of resources and competences one by one. We must always bear in mind, as stated earlier, that resources and competences can never be looked at in the abstract; they can only be evaluated properly when the nature of the task to which these resources and competences are to be applied is known. The question then is not *whether* a competitor has the needed resources and competences; the question is whether he has *superior* resources and the *special* competences required to undertake the activities on which the achievement of customer satisfaction—and thus competitive advantage—rests.

"Internal" Resources and Competences

Always with an eye to the market, and to the specific needs of target segments, we must evaluate first what is available *within the business unit itself.* Are there special design capabilities? Manufacturing process techniques? Purchasing arrangements? Total quality capabilities? Logistics systems? Or marketing experience? And are there any capabilities or special competences that cut across several functions—for example a capability to introduce new products speedily, which depends on the way design, engineering, production, and marketing work *together?* And what is the scale and quality of the resources—human, financial, and physical—that can be put behind these capabilities? If they do not exist, can they be built, or if there are endemic weaknesses, can they be redressed?

A useful way to evaluate the inventory of resources and competences is to draw the "business system," which shows how each functional activity within the firm adds its share of the total value added. Figure 8–1 depicts the business system for a typical manufacturer. It is then a relatively straightforward matter to assess how costs are accumulated at each step along the way, and where specific competences and/or resources can be brought to bear. The comparison of this internal business system for each of the major competitors often reveals substantial differences in value added, in cost breakdown, and in competences and resources which can be exploited.

"External" Resources and Competences

Japan's NEC is reported[1] to have entered into more than a hundred alliances with others to support its position in semiconductors.[1] The goal was evidently to acquire technologies quickly and effectively in areas where it was not necessary for NEC itself to make the necessary technology investments. Likewise, two of the computer industry's biggest rivals, Apple and IBM, joined forces to develop new hybrid personal computers.[2] Apple's user friendly Macintosh system will be integrated into IBM's product line while IBM will provide Apple with advanced high-speed microprocessors. They will work together on new generations of high-powered "multime-

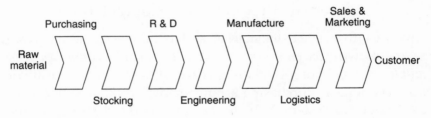

Figure 8–1.

dia" hardware and software. And in countless other industries, competition is marked by an increasingly complex patchwork of collaborative alliances whose purpose is to provide partners with resources and competences they do not have or cannot develop quickly enough or effectively enough themselves. Such alliances cover every imaginable functional area from technology and R&D to manufacturing, to marketing and distribution.

Companies enter such alliances because to stay at the leading edge in a particular market segment now demands an array of competences and resources that goes beyond the capabilities of any single firm. Acquiring competences and resources via alliances also provides flexibility that "internal" solutions can never provide: as market requirements change and new competence and resources are needed, new partnerships can be sought—and old ones abandoned!

Corporate Synergies

In the last decade, leading companies in the United States and Europe have moved further down the path of creating decentralized business units. Starting two decades or more ago with the transformation from functional to divisional forms, many leading organizations have now subdivided further—giving preference to the presumed benefits of entrepreneurial decentralized management over the decision-making processes inherent in matrix forms or more centralized units. "Globalization" has, on the geographic dimension at least, reversed this process. But within more powerful worldwide product units, decentralization along other dimensions—typically product or market segments or subsegments—continues unabated. As an example, ABB, one of the world's leading global corporations, is a strong proponent of decentralization, and claims some five hundred separate "business units"!

Corporate synergy has suffered as a result. Resource efficiencies which depend on broad participation in a number of related areas often cannot be exploited; and competences that may span several different activities get insufficient nourishment. The pendulum is likely, of course, to swing back. Good companies will find their own unique equilibria between the entrepreneurial benefits of decentralization and the benefits of recognizing and exploiting corporate synergies. These equilibria are certainly going to be found at different points for different products and markets, but they are likely overall to result in less, not more, decentralization.

I want to explore here the types of synergy that may be available. All corporations exhibit the potential for their exploitation; only some succeed in taking advantage of them. Nestlé certainly could not enjoy the same success that it enjoys in frozen peas if it did not also market a line of frozen beans. And its overall success in frozen vegetables is related to its commitment to other frozen products. Even the frozen products category benefits from its broader commitment to consumer foods. In fact Nestlé's acquisition of Rowntree, Britain's leading confectionery manufacturer, was fundamentally driven by the belief that Rowntree had outstanding brands—such as KitKat, Polo, McKintosh, and After Eight—which could be marketed much more extensively through Nestlé's worldwide marketing network.

Effective Versus Efficient Corporate Strategies

A business strategy may result in high financial and market performance for one of two reasons: either it is more *efficient*—efficiency in this sense being a measure of relative costs and prices—or it is more *effective*—effectiveness being a measure of how well the offering meets customer needs. A *focused* strategy on the market side can usually be said to emphasize effectiveness as opposed to efficiency. It relies on customizing the physical product and market strategy to the needs of a particular customer/function/technology segment. An *undifferentiated* strategy, by contrast, emphasizes efficiency as opposed to effectiveness. It relies on standardizing the product and/or marketing strategy across customer groups, customer functions, or technologies. The advantages of such an approach, as we shall see in the next chapter, are the potential scale economies or "experience" effects associated with higher volumes of standardized products. A *differentiated* strategy seeks the best of both worlds. Efficiency is achieved via broad scope, and effectiveness is achieved via differentiation.

But these strategic classifications are essentially demand-side ones. If we take a supply-side perspective, it is evident that segment focus, as Nestlé does with each of its frozen food product lines, can still be combined with the benefits of corporate synergy *across* product lines. These synergies may occur in R&D, engineering, manufacturing, physical distribution, sales, distribution, branding, or indeed any function or resource area.

Synergies do not result automatically simply because a company *participates* in several related product or market areas. They have to be nurtured and exploited. Many mergers and acquisitions have failed to produce the very synergies that were their prime motivation because the two organizations were either unwilling or unable to take the steps needed to move from vision to reality.

"Corporate" synergies can be derived at each successive organizational level, once their potential is recognized, as shown in Figure 8–2. These synergies may criss-cross organizational levels as well as involve *multiple* units at the same level. Because of the organizational difficulties of realizing such complex synergistic relationships, most organizations fall far short of realizing the full potential of such opportunities. Instead, they behave like football teams where each player is intent on trying to reach the scoring area and kick in the goal himself rather than relying on passing the ball and using the synergies of teamwork.

Synergy results when two or more activities, at whatever organizational level, share a common resource. The result can be either increased efficiency—in the sense of lower costs—or increased effectiveness—in the sense of increased competence—which translates into higher customer benefits and increased satisfaction (see Figure 8–3). Alternatively, synergy can result when a single new ac-

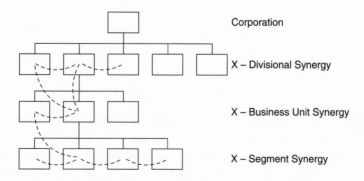

Figure 8–2. Synergy at Different Organizational Levels

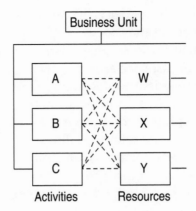

Figure 8–3.

tivity draws on resources which are "attached" to other already existing activities (see Figure 8–4).

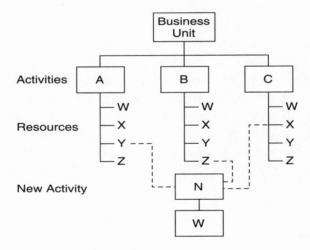

Figure 8–4.

Vertical Synergies

Synergistic relationships between upstream and downstream companies in the vertical business system can result in lower costs or quality improvements or both. As long as they are passed on, they benefit each successive chain member, and eventually the end customer. But like corporate synergies, realization requires management, and many companies fail to take advantage of the enormous potential that often exists for orchestrating the whole business system as effectively as possible. What Benetton has done for the fashion industry could well be repeated in many other sectors if only the vision and leadership existed to break with conventional industry wisdom.

Vertical synergy takes three distinct forms: The first form is improved coordination or competence building between suppliers and their *immediate* customers or vice versa. The second form is a variant of the "pull" strategies described earlier in this chapter. An upstream (or downstream) business entity works with another entity *beyond* its immediate customer (or supplier) to improve overall effectiveness. This can take the form of improvements in logistical flows, information flows, products, or even the provision of managerial assistance. The third form usually involves the application of information technology throughout several successive steps of the business system, as Benetton has done, to dramatically redefine product, service or delivery standards. Just-in-time practices at each stage of a vertical chain involving many successive members can sometimes change delivery times from months to even days! But, as with Benetton, the benefits may not be confined to time improvements. They may result in better quality, wider choices, lower costs, and faster introduction of new products or services.

Country Context

A special report on France in *Time Magazine* highlighted the country's propensity for "grands projets."[3] These range from I. M. Pei's pyramidal transformation of the Louvre and the contemporary Grande Arche at La Défense, to its TGV (Train à Grande Vitesse), to its network of nuclear power stations, to Minitel videotext units in nearly six million homes, to Versailles, and even back to its chain of cathedrals—a constant reminder "that France was the birthplace of the Gothic movement, the defining architecture of European civilization." Analogous distinctions can be made on the "software" side of France's infrastructure. A chain of elite "grandes écoles" are the educational counterpart of the chain of nuclear power stations. France stands out in many other areas also—its art, its design capabilities, its cuisine, its "Cartesian" philosophies, its extensive coastlines, its mixture of Latin and Norman cultures. The list is long, as it is for other developed nations.

What does all this mean for firms that do their business, for example, from a French base and how does this, if at all, influence their distinctiveness? And what of other countries less well endowed, or differently endowed than France, and what of their firms, and their distinctions? Turning it around the other way, why do some countries consistently provide the home base for some successful industries (e.g., German cars), when other countries are home base for others (e.g., Swiss chocolate)? Michael Porter[4] points to four main factors influencing an industry's (and therefore a firm's) competitiveness, each having its origins in one aspect or another of the local geographic environment. These are:

1. *Factor conditions*—the nation's position in the factors of production, such as skilled labor or infrastructure, necessary to compete in a given industry.

2. *Demand conditions*—the nature of home demand for the industry's product or service, in particular how discriminating are domestic consumers and how tough are their demands for quality.

3. *Related and supporting industries*—the presence or absence in

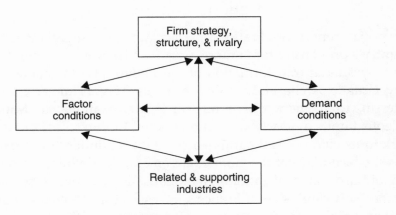

Figure 8–5. Determinants of National Advantage
Adapted from Michael E. Porter, *The Competitive Advantage of Nations* (New York: Free Press, 1989).

the nation of supporting industries and related industries that are internationally competitive.

4. *Firm strategy, structure, and rivalry*—the conditions in the nation governing how companies are created, organized and managed, and the nature of domestic rivalry.

Porter has diagramed these four "determinants of national advantage" into the diamond pattern shown in Figure 8–5. And as he points out, "the 'diamond' is a mutually reinforcing system. The effect of one determinant is contingent on the state of others."

ORGANIZATIONAL FUNCTIONING

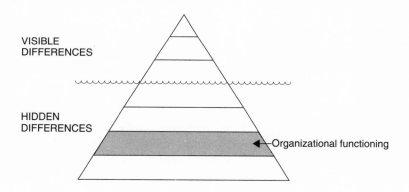

At the base of our "iceberg" are the underlying organizational processes and "strategic intentions" that determine even the way competences are built and resources strengthened. When we make competitive comparisons, and attempt to understand the origins of competitive distinction, we discover that these characteristics are among the most influential and at the same time the most difficult to observe and assess. No attempt will be made here to provide more than a superficial treatment of how organizational functioning can affect competitive distinction in the marketplace, but several factors nevertheless stand out.

The vast majority of "Western" organizations are in a process of transformation that is affecting organizational structures, decision-making processes, and leadership practices. These transformations are being made in response to growing international competition and the impact of new technology—but also in response to the recognition that giving managers responsibility and the freedom to exercise initiative increases their motivation and energy. Parenthetically, Eastern Europe and the ex-USSR are experiencing the same sort of organizational changes at the political level that Western Europe and North America face at the company level. *Eventually,* these changes in the political economic system will be paralleled by a similar evolution of forms and processes within enterprises.

Let me describe two stereotypes.[5] "Old" organizations were common in less competitive times. Many still exist, but will die unless they change. "New" organizations are relatively rare, but many firms are trying to change in this direction. The new organizations have a much higher chance of succeeding in today's business environment of ferocious competition, rapid change, instability, and global scope. The new organization totally differs in structure, form, processes, and vitality from its predecessor. Changing an organization from "old" to "new" is one of management's greatest challenges.

The old organizations depended for success on a durable competitive advantage in a defined market, or localized and restricted competition. The new organizations, by contrast, acknowledge that their product or service superiority will be short-term due to global competition and rapid technological change. Constant innovation and renewal are essential to maintaining uniqueness.

With a durable advantage, an old organization's people had well-defined jobs. Their task was learning to do their jobs better— roughly like rowing a boat, or learning to march in step. Because neither markets nor customer demands changed much, there was very little real competition. If an organization could learn to do its defined tasks well, it could usually succeed.

Old organizations had well-defined boxes on their organization charts, and everybody knew exactly what each box meant. The organizations did not like people to do things outside of their boxes, because when people marched out of step it upset others trying to march in step. Consequently, these organizations enforced discipline through hierarchy and "top-down" management. Senior management set the rules, and the rest obeyed.

The result, all too often, was a not-too-subtle interdiction of both initiative and personal responsibility. People did what they were supposed to do within the safety of their boxes, but not much more. Punishments for unsuccessful initiatives tended to outweigh rewards for successful ones, so initiatives were rare, and unsuccessful initiatives tended to become someone else's property. Responsibility was either collectivized and laid on the doorstep of a committee, or shifted onto another department or individual.

The old organizations are breaking down because if everybody is doing a well-defined task and job requirements change, people do not know what to do any more—nor do their bosses. And today's fast-moving, competitive markets will not let you hide this kind of ignorance inside your organization.

In new organizations, "changing" the business is much more important than "running" the business. In the old organization, as chief executive or senior manager, you inherited the business, ran it like a custodian, and then passed it to someone else to run. In the new organization, you inherit it, you change it as much as you can to conform to the new, evolving competition, and you hand it over to someone else to change again. If the old organization was like a rowboat, the modern organization is more like a fleet of small battle craft, each sailing against part of an enemy fleet, fighting its own battles, but within an overall strategy.

As well as using decentralized structures to focus on different business lines and market segments, the new organizations tend to have these attributes;

- *Market-driven.* New organizations must respond quickly and flexibly to changing market needs and competitive initiatives. A market-driven firm not only has a greater awareness of, and focus on, the customer at the point of sale or service, but is also more responsive to customers throughout its organization. Market-driven enterprises find ways to connect manufacturing, R&D, and human resource management to the marketplace.
- *Entrepreneurial.* The risk-averse, bureaucratic organizational climate found in all too many old-style firms cannot suffice for the new, decentralized, market-driven companies. They need an entrepreneurial climate to actively encourage initiative further down the organization both by those responsible for major sectors of activity, and also by those whose cooperation

will determine whether those initiatives are successfully implemented. Increasingly, the competitive environment demands teamwork across functions as well as between functional heads and unit heads. The whole team must participate in conceiving and implementing initiatives like just-in-time manufacturing, global marketing, or strategy-based information systems. An entrepreneurial climate encourages people to embrace change as a way of life, and carries not only a "bias toward action" but a bias toward individual responsibility.

- *Horizontal decision making.* This contrasts with the hierarchy of the "old" organization. Responsibility is no longer necessarily tied to authority over the resources needed to do the job. Business segment managers, or "program managers" as they are often called, must negotiate the allocation of major organizational resources like manufacturing, sales, and R&D with their peers in functional management. These new, much more complex forms of negotiated decision making cannot happen in a hierarchical and/or bureaucratic organization.

Most organizations find themselves currently somewhere *between* the "old" and the "new," and recognition is growing that Tom Peters is probably right—the pursuit of excellence involves a high quotient of organizational as well as strategic change in most companies.[6]

STRATEGIC INTENT

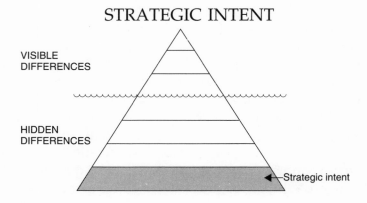

The concept of "strategic intent" is not new—but recognition of its overriding importance in achieving competitive distinction is!

The first step in the direction of recognizing the importance of strategic intent was taken in the 1970s with the notion that each business unit in a corporate "portfolio" of business might have a different strategic "role."[7] Not all units and subunits need to or can grow at the same rate; not all units and subunits need produce the same level of profitability; and not all must contribute equally to cash flow objectives.

This concept of the organization as a collection of units and subunits having different objectives was at the very root of "strategic market planning"—and the term "portfolio" was commonly used to describe such a collection. Differences were expressed in terms of whether a unit was a net source of a user of cash, as well as goals for growth, market share, net income, and return on investment. This was in contrast to earlier practices which emphasized primarily sales, net income, and return on investment as major measures of performance.

Part of the metamorphosis in planning was due to the fact that many firms confronted limited cash resources in the late 1960s and early 1970s. In the period after World War II, many firms had been able to finance growth by some combination of internally generated funds and increased borrowing. In the more competitive markets of the late 1960s and 1970s, profit margins shrank, decreasing internally generated cash resources. At the same time debt-to-equity ratios climbed to levels where further borrowing was difficult.

"Portfolio" planning in practice leads to important shifts in relative position in the marketplace. In one situation, two large corporations, one a highly diversified company with its core competence in electrical/electronic engineering, and the other a less diversified chemicals company, competed for one high-grade materials business. Because the chemicals company defined materials as a growth opportunity worthy of substantial investment, while the diversified engineering company saw it as a source of badly needed cash, the latter suffered substantial loss of market position.

The more recent concept of "strategic intent" goes much further than the idea of a "portfolio role" for an individual business. Companies may indeed differ in the role they each assign to two competing business units as did the companies described above, but when two companies have different strategic intentions, even more may be at stake. Hamel and Pralahad, for example, ascribe the overtaking of many large U.S. companies by their Japanese competitors in a wide variety of key industrial sectors to fundamental differences in strategic intent.[8]

Simply put, the strategic intent of many leading Japanese firms is a ten-to-twenty-year quest to win in the worldwide marketplace. It is characterized by such words as "resolution," "stamina," "ambition," and "inventiveness." It focuses the organization on tomorrow's opportunities. It commits the organization to a step-by-step plan to achieve the strategic intent and to meet each successive "challenge" successfully. The essence of strategic intent, according to Hamel and Pralahad, "lies in creating tomorrow's competitive advantages faster than competitors mimic the ones you possess today."[9]

Many possibilities for competitive distinction have been suggested in this and the previous chapter—ranging from successful financial and market performance, to better products and marketing programs, to superior definition of the business, to some of the more underlying factors such as competences, resources, organizational processes, and basic strategic intent. In the next two chapters, we turn from distinctiveness in terms of these qualities to distinctiveness on the cost side. Doing things better is one thing; doing things cheaper is another; doing things better *and* cheaper is unbeatable.

THE COST PERSPECTIVE

CHAPTER 9

THE DYNAMICS OF COSTS

Costs play a central role in ensuring short-term and long-term company health. When costs get out of hand relative to revenues, it may in fact threaten a company's very survival; and even when costs appear to be under control, failure to understand the strategic implications of costs may lead to insufficient margins to make needed investments in the company's future. The underlying equation between costs, cash flow from current operations, and cash flow needed to build and retain a leading market position is often more a product of wishful thinking than rigorous analysis.

Sound management of costs starts with a sound understanding of cost behavior. Senior management cannot rely on accounting principles only, nor solely on the accounting profession, to achieve this understanding. There are, in fact, a few important principles of cost measurement, cost assignment, and cost behavior which are more closely related to marketing and operations management concepts than they are to accounting. And herein lies a fundamental problem in many organizations: finance and accounting staff are not sufficiently familiar with market strategy concepts and decision processes to provide the right data in the right format; while marketing and operations line management have too little experience in "pushing the numbers" to define precisely what cost data they need.

This chapter is intended to provide a "general management" view of costs and their management—useful for the "numbers pushers" and the "non-numbers pushers" alike. It starts with some *basic principles* of cost measurement, cost assignment, and cost reporting. It goes on to explain what lies *behind competitor cost differences* in terms of three major phenomena: scale effects, technology change, and experience effects.

COSTS—SOME BASIC PRINCIPLES

Costs are usually accumulated initially "by nature." This means, for example, that salaries, wages, and social security costs are accumulated under the heading "personnel"; purchased parts, materials, and components are accumulated under the heading "raw materials"; and executive air fares and hotel bills may be accumulated under the heading "travel."

The next step, for many organizations, already causes some difficulty. It is to *reassign* these "by nature" costs to specific functional departments or so-called "cost centers." A manufacturing plant may be one such cost center; and in all likelihood it will comprise several cost subcenters; physical sales and marketing activities may be another group; and R&D a third. Often concerns about "allocation" are unjustified at this stage of the process, because the costs "by nature" can be *directly* attributed to one cost center or another— since the costs are, in fact, accumulated there. There is, for example, no issue of allocation in assigning manufacturing personnel costs to a manufacturing cost center, as long as they work exclusively within that cost center.

Allocation problems arise only when a cost is *shared* by several different cost centers. For example, the salary of the vice-president of manufacturing cannot be easily divided between several cost subcenters within the manufacturing department. It is even more difficult to allocate the sizeable depreciation cost of the building that houses, say, the plant and part of the general administration offices of the company.

Such allocation problems present accountants with two broad alternatives: on the one hand they can choose some reasonable basis for allocating such costs; alternatively they may decide to exclude them from cost center accounts completely and consider them in a totally separate "general overhead" account. In practice a mixture of both alternatives is often used—some overhead items being allocated where there is a sensible basis for doing so; and others being excluded at that particular level of cost accumulation. Senior management is usually well-advised to enquire what is and what is not included in the various cost center accounts, however, and when overhead items that cannot be charged directly are included, what basis of allocation has been used.

From Cost Centers to Activity Centers

More difficult, from the viewpoint of assigning or allocating costs, is the problem of their distribution to specific activities. From a managerial viewpoint, costs can, and should, be controlled "by nature" and according to the cost center they are charged to. But management also needs to know the costs of specific products in order to assess profit margins and, if possible, overall profitability; management might also like to assess the margins and profits available in certain segments of the market; and ultimately they will be interested in the profitability of a particular "line of business" combining several products and markets, or at the next hierarchical level, the profitability of each major division, country, or "strategic business unit."

The definition of activity centers to which costs should be reassigned is intimately related to market segmentation, and through it to the internal structure of the organization itself. As we shall see in Chapter 14, market segmentation choices have to be directly reflected in organizational structure so that management responsibility is clearly assigned. This not only means responsibility for each of the major resource/functional departments of the organization but also for activities in each major market or market segment—however these are defined. The implication is that accounting and control systems, to be effective, must follow the same structural definition. As market segmentation schemes evolve and are mirrored by organizational redesign, activity centers for cost accounting purposes must be redefined also. This tight link between market segmentation, organizational design, and activity centers for cost accounting purposes is often overlooked.

The reassignment of costs to activity centers may take place in *one step* directly from accounts "by nature" to an activity center (without being first assigned to a functional cost center as described earlier), or in *two steps*, first to a functional cost center and then second to an activity center. In the direct process there are more opportunities for confusion about allocations than there are in the process of reassigning costs from "by nature" accounts to cost centers. Many categories of cost cannot be assigned directly and exclusively to one activity or another because they are shared by several activities. Such is the case, for example, for a manufacturing plant that produces a variety of products or even product lines under one roof. Although direct labor costs and direct material costs may be relatively easy to assign, many categories of "overhead" costs must either be allocated or excluded at that particular level of aggregation. Again management is well-advised to become fully familiar with the basis for such choices before using such data.

The increased emphasis on market segmentation and subsegmentation as competition becomes fiercer, and the many creative possibilities for cutting up the market cake are putting new demands on accounting and control staff to develop useful cost data. Finer segmentation implies finer definition of organizational responsibilities and finer reporting. The corollary is that more and more cost items are indeed shared costs—and the question of allocation becomes more and more troublesome. A fine line has to be found between allocations that have little rationale, and the exclusion of overhead costs altogether from narrowly defined activities. The former route provides management with little useful information; the latter risks the exclusion of so many costs that little is left on which to base sound judgments.

This effect of progressively finer segmentation on organization and therefore on the allocation of costs to activity centers is illustrated by the three figures below. Figure 9–1 shows the easiest situation, one in which all costs can be directly attributed to each "line of business" because each functional resource is itself decentralized to that activity (as shown for line of business A). Figure 9–2 shows a similar segmentation into three lines of business, but in this case all the functional resources of the division are centralized and *shared* by the three "lines of business." Costs must also be shared, or excluded.

Figure 9–3 shows the effect of functional decentralization, as in

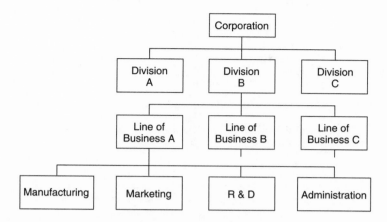

Figure 9–1. Functions Decentralized

Figure 9–1, but in this case there is further segmentation of activities. The company has divided "line of business" A into two main
segments: A and B. The problem of allocation evident in Figure 9–2
is reproduced but at one level further down. Successively finer segmentation inevitably produces such allocation problems if management is interested (as it should be) in assessing segment-by-segment
performance.

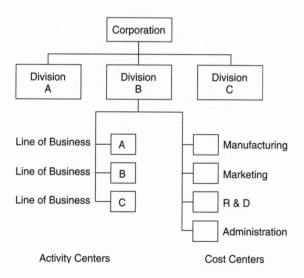

Figure 9–2. Functions Centralized

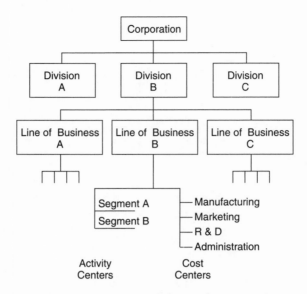

Figure 9–3. Functions Decentralized to Lines of Business;
Centralized with Respect to Segments

Fixed and Variable Costs

Managers can only develop an intuitive understanding of the "economics" of their business if they recognize its underlying "cost structure" in terms of the breakdown of fixed and variable costs. An understanding of cost structure provides the basis for answering a whole series of "what if" questions—such as "What if sales were to increase by 20 percent as a result of a new $2 million advertising campaign?" or "What if sales were to decrease by 10 percent if we raised prices by 15 percent?" Quite often it is easier to pose the question in the reverse sense: "What would we *need* to sell additionally to cover the cost of this or that new investment?" or "What could we afford to lose in terms of volume if prices were raised by a certain amount?"

The importance of cost structure is dramatically illustrated in Figure 9–4, which contrasts two products with very difficult ratios of fixed to variable costs. Product A with very low variable costs relative to fixed costs "contributes" a large proportion of the revenue from each unit sold to the fixed costs. To "break even," enough units would have, in fact, to be sold to allow *total* contribution (unit

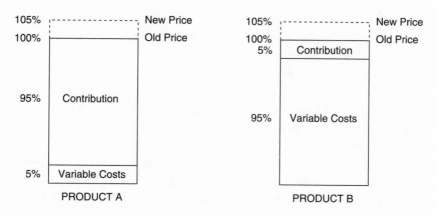

Figure 9–4.

contribution multiplied by units sold) to meet all the fixed costs. Product B, by contrast, has a very high ratio of variable costs to fixed costs. Each unit sold contributes substantially less than a unit of product A. To break even, a much higher volume would be required to cover the same total amount of fixed costs—or an incremental new investment.

But the real difference between A and B shows up when we consider a price increase or decrease. A 5 percent price increase, say, in product A increases unit contribution by just over 10 percent, but a 5 percent price increase in product B virtually doubles its unit contribution! Similarly, a 5 percent price decrease in A has only a small effect on contribution; a 5 percent price decrease in B makes the business nonviable, since there is no contribution remaining to cover any fixed costs.

Which costs are fixed and which variable? Theoretically speaking, any costs that vary directly and proportionately with the level of activity are variable; any costs that remain totally unaffected by the level of business activity are fixed. Thus raw material purchases are variable; while a one-time R&D investment or the cost of an advertising campaign can for all intents and purposes be regarded as fixed. Practically speaking, however, many costs are harder to classify. What about direct labor costs, for example? If the workforce cannot be immediately adjusted in size in response to a falloff or increase in demand, or if adjustments can only be made through attrition, direct labor costs may be "semivariable"—they vary, but not proportionately. Indirect labor, that is, staff and supervisory personnel, may be even more "sticky"—and hence more fixed—in such adjustment processes.

Time obviously plays an important role in classifying costs as variable, semivariable or fixed; a cost that may be fixed for one decision where the time horizon of adjustment is short may be semivariable or even completely variable for a decision where the adjustment time horizon is long. A different classification of fixed and variable costs would be necessary, for example, for the decision to invest in a short-term sales promotion campaign than for a decision to build a completely new manufacturing facility. In the former, many more of the costs are fixed.

Deciding on fixed and variable costs categories is often a matter of common sense and sound managerial judgement. Few general rules are useful. Of more importance than making precise distinctions is to do it at all! When such classifications are made as a matter of course, as long as the basis is reasonable, it is easy to assess the effects of volume change on the financial health of a business; when not, top management is limited to a static as opposed to a dynamic view of its business. This can be illustrated most clearly by contrasting the following two presentations of a company's income statement. Both show net profitability, but only income statement B, expressed in terms of variable costs and contribution, can be used to assess the effects of a *change* in the revenue assumptions.

Income Statement A		Income Statement B	
	Revenues		Revenues
−	Cost of Cost Sold	−	Variable Costs
=	Gross margin	=	Contribution
−	Expenses	−	Fixed Costs
=	Gross Profit	=	Gross Profit
−	Taxes	−	Taxes
=	Net Profit	=	Net Profit

Costs in the Value-Added Chain

In Chapter 6, the distinction was made between the value-added chain "within" a particular company, and the value-added chain in the vertical business system that connects raw material suppliers to manufacturers to distributors to, eventually, the final end customer. As value is added through these chains, so are costs. It is a useful exercise therefore to split up costs according to the step in each chain at which they are accumulated and to compare, where possible, cost and value additions. Too high costs at the end of the line can often be attributed to one stage or another where costs substantially exceed value additions. These become high priorities for management attention.

Such analyses must be undertaken in two steps: the first step is to develop a clear picture of the *internal* value added chain, by breaking down internal operations into each of the main functions where value is accumulated. Direct costs can then be assigned as shown in Figure 9–5. This not only gives an indication of cost versus value added at each stage, it enables management to identify clearly where the major elements of cost in the internal business system truly lie—and where there may be real leverage for cost reductions if costs are out of line. Too often the faulty assumption is made that direct labor costs in manufacturing are the culprit for too high costs in aggregate. But in increasingly automated manufacturing plants, direct labor may be 10 percent or less of total costs so that a 10 percent reduction in direct labor still only results in a 1 percent reduction overall! Such an internal stepwise evaluation of costs often clearly reveals that leverage points for cost reduction are not in labor at all, but in other areas such as improved raw materials purchasing arrangements, cutting the cost of inventories throughout the business system, or in *managerial* overheads!

Having performed such an *internal* cost analysis, attention has to be turned to the *external* business system—and an analogous exer-

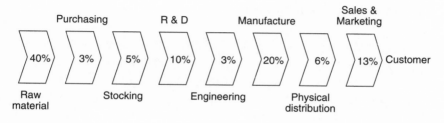

Figure 9–5.

cise undertaken to assess value and costs added by each member of the vertical chain. Such an analysis often points up the fact that leverage points for cost reduction lie *beyond* the organizational boundaries of one particular firm. Leverage points may well exist upstream in terms of improving raw materials acquisition costs, intermediate processing costs, or in key components costs, or downstream in physical distribution and marketing. Just-in-time inventory has had a major impact not only on dramatically shortening the cycle time between order placement and final delivery, but on squeezing out inventory carrying costs at key points in the overall business system.

BEHIND COMPETITOR COST DIFFERENCES

With these basic principles of costs in mind, we shall now turn to the broader question of how and why costs differ between one competitor and another. Managers often express disbelief when one competitor or another cuts prices to "unheard of" levels or when a new competitor enters the market with a very low price. Such actions are often explained away as "dumping,"[1] "unprofitable" buying of market share, or short-term desperation moves to get some business. In fact the competitor may have achieved a permanent and substantially lower cost position as a springboard for such actions—and even if prices are not cut, the lower cost position provides the opportunity for substantially better margins and therefore for future competitive investments in R&D and/or marketing.

There are three different ways in which a corporation may systematically improve costs:

- through better utilization of capacity
- through improved process technologies
- through experience effects

These possibilities apply not only to manufacturing operations but to every single step in the value-added chain, that is, to "inbound" raw materials acquisition procedures, to R&D and engineering activities, and to "outbound" functions such as physical distribution, sales, and marketing. Often it is indeed in these nonmanufacturing functions that the largest opportunities exist to affect costs. It may well be, for example, that a modernized manufacturing plant is working at or near capacity but that R&D costs or sales and marketing costs are far too high because capacity utilization in these activities is far below the optimum.

It is also often the case that upstream or downstream members of the vertical business system are working with too high cost structures even though our own costs are highly competitive. This suggests that analysis of the three major factors influencing costs should be applied not only to our own particular level in the overall business system, but to upstream and downstream entities as well. Uncompetitive prices to end customers may have their origins in capacity, process, experience, or overhead problems at other upstream or downstream stages.

So what are these three ways in which costs may be improved? I shall take capacity utilization, process technology, and "experience" effects one at a time:

Capacity Utilization Effects

I shall use a manufacturing plant as an example of these effects, but it should be remembered, as noted above, that these phenomena apply equally well to *all* functional resources that contribute to the final product value.

The impact of capacity utilization on costs depends mainly on the proportion of fixed and variable costs in the overall cost structure. When fixed costs are large, then there are substantial unit cost improvements from working at or near capacity. This is one reason why high fixed cost businesses like steel making or hotel accommodation are characterized by price cutting and special promotion aimed at getting as high a throughput of the capacity as possible. When variable costs are a substantial portion of the total costs, capacity utilization improvements have a smaller effect on unit costs. This is shown in Figures 9–6 (p. 144) and 9–7 (p. 145).

It is important to note that whatever the cost structure of the business, unit costs tend to rise again once some optimum capacity utilization point is passed. What may be normally referred to as 100 percent capacity utilization may in fact combine the utilization of some parts of the plant operating at 90 percent with other parts already working at 110 percent. As capacity becomes constrained in

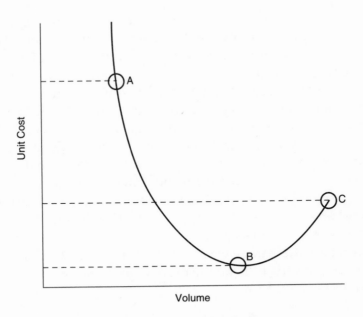

Figure 9–6. High Fixed Cost Business

one or more of these areas, even though other parts of the plant are not yet working at full capacity, attempts to increase aggregate capacity utilization further usually imply some extra costs to unblock these early constraints. These may range from overtime payment to extra staff to special shifts, or may just mean inefficiencies from running "hot."

Competitors may have different costs simply because they are operating at different points on the capacity utilization curve, and these differences may be large in high fixed cost industries—as shown in Figure 9–8 (p. 146).

Competitor A, for example, may be a new entrant in the market; lacking market share and volume, it may be operating at the lowest capacity utilization with the highest unit costs. Competitors B and D may have similar unit costs but for different reasons—B operating somewhat below full capacity, while D is operating above full capacity. Competitor C, in this example, exhibits the best cost position—in manufacturing at least. It should not be forgotten that having the best capacity utilization in the manufacturing plant may not ensure the best cost position overall. Competitor C may have just built a new warehouse, and, anticipating substantial future growth,

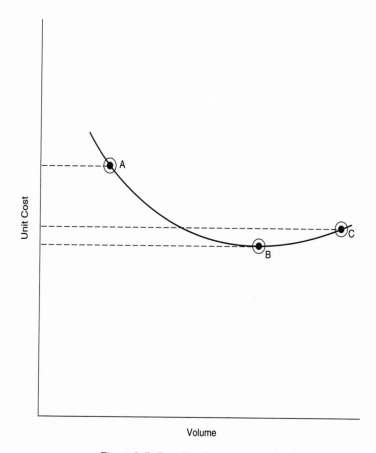

Figure 9–7. Low Fixed Cost Business

may be operating it at only 50 percent of capacity initially. This puts competitor C in competitor A's position with respect to unit distribution costs. Thus having low unit costs overall means keeping capacity utilization in balance for each and every functional resource in the internal value-added chain.

Process Technology Effects

The capacity utilization phenomena described above have so far assumed that each and every competitor uses the same process technology, and that this remains a constant. In fact, processes are constantly being improved—in all aspects of business operations, not

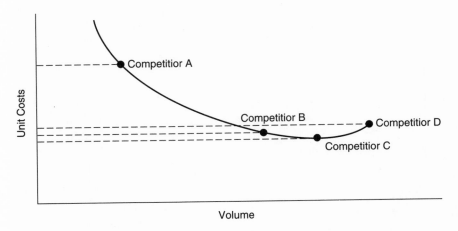

Figure 9–8. Costs and Capacity Utilization

just in manufacturing. When a company constructs new capacity, the odds are that it will use superior process technology to that in plants already in existence, and at the same level of throughput, achieve lower costs. This is shown in the Figure 9–9.

In this illustration, competitor B is working at optimum capacity but in an outdated plant. Competitor D has the best cost position by operating at capacity in a modernized plant. In fact, even competi-

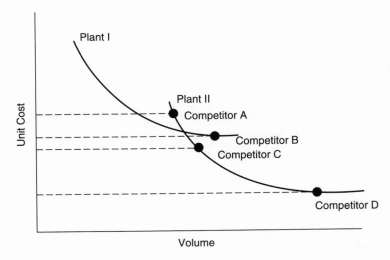

Figure 9–9. Costs and Process Technology

tor C, who has not yet reached full capacity with a modernized plant, has a better cost position than competitor B. Competitor A, as a newcomer or low share competitor, has the worst cost position, but nevertheless has the potential to match the cost leader.

As markets and process technologies evolve, new plant configurations offer better and better possibilities for reducing costs. Thus the *long run* cost behavior of an industry may be represented by an "envelope" connecting the lowest points of a series of overlapping cost curves—each one representing a particular class of process technology. This is shown in Figure 9–10.

Economists call this the "long-run average cost curve." It is important for managers to understand this phenomenon conceptually rather than in precise numerical terms because it often helps to explain the wide differences in pricing strategies and investment capabilities of different competitors. Competitor B may, for example, be able to derive a substantial cost advantage over competitor A, in spite of operating at substantially lower capacity utilization, simply by using far superior process technology. No matter how well competitor A does, it will not be possible to match competitor B's costs.

Managers often mix up the two effects of capacity utilization ratios and the underlying process on which capacity utilization rests. Both are discussed under the overall heading of "capacity" or

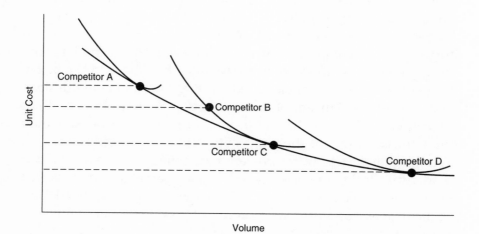

Figure 9–10. Long-Run Cost Curve

"spreading of fixed costs." It is important not only to separate these two effects as illustrated above, but to do so for each and every step in the value-added chain. Only then does it become possible to understand some of the possible underlying reasons for major cost advantage or disadvantage. Too often, the whole question of cost differences among competitors is oversimplified by "static" estimates of costs at one point in time, for one type of process technology. To know that our product costs are $50 per unit while our competitor's costs are approximately $60 per unit tells us little of any value. What is important is how costs can change, and can be managed, as we and our competitors pass from one level of capacity utilization to another, and from one process technology to another.

Experience Effects

The experience effect, whereby costs fall with *cumulative* production, is measurable and predictable: it has been observed in a wide range of products including automobiles, semiconductors, petrochemicals, long-distance telephone service, synthetic fibers, airline transportation, life insurance administration, and crushed limestone, to mention a few.[2] Note that this list ranges from high-technology to low-technology products, service to manufacturing industries, consumer to industrial products, new to mature products, and process to assembly-oriented products, indicating the wide range of applicability.

The phenomenon is age-old. For example, in the eighteenth century U.S. clockmaking was by and large a handcraft, and its products could only be afforded by the wealthy. But about 1800 it began to change: as experience increased, producers found better designs and more efficient means of manufacture. In Boston, Simon Willard produced shelf clocks that were similar to but less expensive than the tall case clocks of the eighteenth century. In Connecticut, Eli Terry began to use water-powered machinery to make wooden works for clocks and use assembly-line methods and unskilled labor to assemble them. In the 1830s inexpensive parts enabled Connecticut clockworkers to mass produce brass shelf clocks with simple mechanisms. With their extremely low prices, they quickly dominated the international market. By 1840, what had formerly been a luxury had become accessible to a large number of American families. In 1860, Chauncy Jerome, a pioneer clock manufacturer, wrote: "The business of manufacture of them has become so systematized of late that it has brought the prices exceedingly low and it has long been the astonishment of the whole world how they could be made so cheap and yet be so good."[3]

However, it is only comparatively recently that this phenomenon has been carefully measured and quantified; at first it was thought to apply only to the *labor* portion of *manufacturing* costs. Perhaps the earliest quantification was in 1925, when the commander of the Wright-Patterson Air Force Base observed that the number of direct labor hours required to assemble a plane decreased as the total number of aircraft assembled increased. The relationship between labor costs and cumulative production became an important quantitative planning tool, known as the *learning curve.*

In the 1960s evidence mounted that the phenomenon was broader. Personnel from the Boston Consulting Group and others showed that each time cumulative volume of a product doubled, total value-added costs—including administration, sales, marketing, distribution, and the like in addition to manufacturing—fell by a constant and predictable percentage. In addition, the costs of purchased items usually fell as suppliers reduced prices as *their* costs fell, due also to the experience effect. The relationship between costs and experience was called the *experience curve.*[4]

An experience curve is plotted with the cumulative units produced on the horizontal axis, and cost per unit on the vertical axis. An "85 percent" experience curve is shown in Figure 9–11. The "85 percent" means that every time experience doubles, costs per unit drop to 85 percent of the original level. It is known as the *learning rate.* Stated differently, costs per unit decrease 15 percent for every doubling of cumulative production. For example, the cost of the twentieth unit produced is about 85 percent of the cost of the tenth unit.

An experience curve appears as a straight line when plotted on double log paper (logarithmic scale for both the horizontal and vertical axes). To determine the learning rate of an experience curve we measure the ratio of costs for any two points having a ratio of experience of 2 to 1.

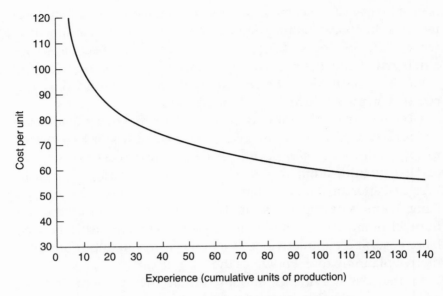

Figure 9–11. A typical Experience Curve (85%)

Sources of the Experience Effect

The experience effect has a variety of sources; to capitalize on it requires knowledge of why it occurs. Sources of the experience effect are outlined below:

1. *Labor efficiency.* Labor's contribution to the experience effect, portrayed by the learning curve, has already been mentioned. As workers repeat a particular production task, they become more dexterous and learn improvements and short-cuts which increase their collective efficiency. The greater the number of worker-paced operations, the greater the amount of learning that can accrue with experience.

   This learning effect goes beyond the labor directly involved in manufacturing. Maintenance personnel, supervisors, and persons in other line and staff manufacturing positions also increase their productivity, as do people in marketing, sales, administration, and other functions.

2. *Work specialization and methods improvements.* Specialization increases worker proficiency at a given task. Consider what

happens when two workers, who formerly did both parts of a two-stage operation, each specialize in a single stage. Each worker now handles twice as many items and accumulates experience twice as fast on the more specialized task. Redesign of work operations (methods) can also result in greater efficiency.

3. *New production processes.* Process innovations and improvements can be an important source of cost reductions, especially in capital-intensive industries. The low-labor-content semiconductor industry, for instance, achieves experience curves of 70 percent to 80 percent from improved production technology by devoting a large percentage of its research and development to process improvements. Similar process improvements have been observed in refineries, nuclear power plants, and steel mills, to mention but a few.

4. *Getting better performance from production equipment.* When first designed, a piece of production equipment may have a conservatively rated output. Experience may reveal innovative ways of increasing its output. For instance, capacity of a fluid catalytic cracking unit typically "grows" by about 50 percent over a ten-year period.[5]

5. *Changes in the resource mix.* As experience accumulates, a producer can often incorporate different or less expensive resources in the operation. For instance, less skilled workers can replace skilled workers or automation can replace labor.

6. *Product standardization.* Standardization allows the replication of tasks necessary for worker learning. Production of the Ford Model T, for example, followed a strategy of deliberate standardization; as a result, from 1909 to 1923 its price was repeatedly reduced, following an 85 percent experience curve.[6] Even when flexibility and/or a wider product line are important marketing considerations, standardization can be achieved by modularization. For example, by making just a few types of engines, transmissions, chassis, seats, body styles, and so on, an auto manufacturer can achieve experi-

ence effects due to specialization in each part. These in turn can be assembled into a wide variety of models.

7. *Product redesign.* As experience is gained with a product, both the manufacturer and customers gain a clear understanding of its performance requirements. This understanding allows the product to be redesigned to conserve material, allows greater efficiency in manufacture, and substitutes less costly materials and resources, while at the same time improving performance on relevant dimensions. The change from wooden to brass works of clocks in the early 1800s is a good example; so are the new designs and substitution of plastic, synthetic fiber, and rubber for leather in ski boots.

The above list of sources dramatizes the observation that cost reductions due to experience do not occur by natural inclination; they are the result of substantial, concerted effort and pressure to lower costs. In fact, left unmanaged, costs rise. Thus, experience does not *cause* reductions but rather provides an opportunity that alert managements can exploit.[7] Consequently strategies resulting from market planning should explicitly address *how* cost reductions are to be achieved.

Gaining full efficiency benefits from experience requires high quality and stability in the workforce. Otherwise, productivity gains are diminished from slow learning by marginal workers, and as new workers are brought up to proficiency. The compensation plan of the firm and employee relations policies can also have an important influence on its experience curves.[8]

The list of reasons for the experience effect raises perplexing questions on the difference between experience and scale effects. For instance, isn't it true that work specialization and project standardization, mentioned in the experience list, become possible because of the *size* of an operation? Therefore, aren't they each really scale effects? The answer is that they are probably both.

The confusion arises because growth in experience usually coincides with growth in size of an operation. We consider the experience effect to arise primarily due to ingenuity, cleverness, skill, and dexterity derived from experience as embodied in the adages "practice makes perfect" or "experience is the best teacher." On the other hand, scale effect comes from capitalizing on the size of an operation.

There are those who would include scale as part of, or as a reason for, the experience effect.[9] But there are important examples where firms with low experience use scale to achieve significant cost advantages over firms with far greater experience. The Japanese steel industry has done so to its more experienced U.S. counterpart. So scale effect can exist independently of experience effect. Likewise experience effects can exist independently of scale effects; for example, you tie your shoes much faster now than when you were younger.

Usually the overlap between the two effects is so great that it is difficult (and not too important) to separate them. This is the practice we will adopt from here on (while remaining alert for those exceptions where scale effect can be achieved alone, such as in high fixed-cost, capital-intensive industries.)

Shared Experience

Additional complications and strategic opportunities arise when there is shared experience. Shared experience can occur when two or more products share a common resource or activity in a similar manner. For instance, the same assembly operation may produce high-torque motors for oil exploration and low-torque motors for conveyors. Or tape drives and disk drives may share the same computer marketing organization. Or foam and cellulose insulation may be sold through the same distribution channel. The key is that they use the common resource or activity in a similar manner so that any economies learned from dealing with one product can be applied to the rest. Thus shared experience is important because costs of one product are reduced additionally due to experience accumulated in dealing with the other products.

One of the most common manifestations of shared experience occurs when two or more products share a common component, as when several automobile models use the same transmission or several petrochemical products derive from the same intermediate product. However, it can occur when the products serve different customer groups (the motor example), customer functions (the computer example), or use different technologies (the insulation example).

Opportunities for shared experience must be carefully sought, analyzed, and exploited to gain cost advantage over competition, especially in diversified companies. By focusing new product efforts where shared experience plays a major role, a firm can build diversity into a strength. Likewise, the impact of reducing shared experience when a product is dropped must also be analyzed. Shared experience is an important special case of the need to analyze cost components separately—but one providing significant strategic opportunities. It is to these strategic opportunities that we now turn.

CHAPTER 10

MANAGING COSTS FOR COMPETITIVE ADVANTAGE

$\mathbf{A}$s noted already, increased scale, new process technology, and experience provide an *opportunity* for cost reduction rather than *causing* costs to fall. To actually exploit the opportunities requires the implementation of explicit, well-thought-out cost reduction efforts.

The starting points of cost reduction are cost *measurement*, cost *reporting*, and cost *control*. This raises three key questions: What precisely should be measured? With what frequency? And against what should it be compared?

Managers often drown in cost (as well as other) information, but have little useful data when it actually comes to managing costs and making decisions where costs are an important factor. Choices of what to measure and how to report it are therefore critical. Of particular importance is that the managers who are to use the data have a substantial hand in determining what they will receive, and how it will be presented.

The preceding chapter provided many guidelines about *what* should be measured; but so far little has been said about what it should be compared with for cost management purposes. Too often, cost comparisons are limited to comparisons with equivalent data for past periods—either last month, last quarter, or last year. This may provide a sense of the degree of improvement, but little more.

Costs can be managed more aggressively only if actual costs are compared with some desired levels. These can take one of three forms: *budgeted levels, competitive levels,* or *targeted levels.* The three figures may or may not be identical. In some cases, a targeted level of cost may be a considerable "stretch" beyond what is actually budgeted for. This could happen for example when a company undertakes a major "overhead value analysis" program during the course of the year, or when it tries to move rapidly down the experience or scale curve by substantially building volume. Competitors' costs may be lower or higher than either budgeted or targeted cost levels, depending on the particular competitive position in a product area or particular market segment, and the strategic objectives which the company has set. In practice, all three comparisons are useful on each of the major components of cost, and all three provide important inputs to improved cost management.

So-called standard costs are a way of simplifying such cost comparisons, by using estimated figures routinely for budgeting each of the major cost subcategories and as the basis for comparison with actual data when costs are actually incurred.

Finally, it should be said again that the secret of sound cost management is to give considerable attention to the *variation* of costs with volume, process technology changes, and experience. "Static" costs calculated at a single point in time are much less revealing to management than a thorough understanding and familiarity with cost "dynamics." Only then can the effects of volume, processes, and experience be properly factored into managerial decision making.

ASSESSING COSTS IN PRACTICE

The concepts described in the previous chapter look deceptively simple; their application requires considerable ingenuity, judgment, and care. Products and markets must be defined bearing in mind difficult tradeoffs between narrow and broad definition, and between market versus production-oriented definitions. Cost data is frequently difficult to obtain from the accounting system, and corrections must be made for inflation. "Static" data at one particular point in time is usually much easier to find than "dynamic" data which shows cost changes not only with time, but with volume and experience. Each major component of cost must be analyzed separately when either scale, process technology, or experience has a different effect on each. And opportunities for "shared" effects must be sought out, analyzed, and exploited. Furthermore, data must cover a sufficient time period to overcome the effects of short-run cost fluctuations.

Similar analyses of competitive costs and market positions will be needed, but competitive data will be even more difficult to acquire than internal data. In all cases, incomplete data is better than none, but considerable effort to collect, refine, and check data is usually justified.

There is a fine ethical line to tread when it comes to collecting competitive cost data. What sources can we use? Certainly data that can be considered to be in the "public domain" is beyond question; but what about data that is collected from an ex-employee of a competitor, acting as a "consultant." Is it different whether his or her employment dates back six months or six years? A good practice in such cases is to set clear internal policies about what is and what is not acceptable, and where the line lies between "competitive analysis" and "industrial espionage." Since this "line" is often a gray area rather than a clear divide between black and white, *open* discussion case-by-case of how policies should be applied in the specific situation may be valuable in creating a body of precedent. A useful "rule of thumb" in making reasonable choices is to use only data sources that will later stand up to "public scrutiny"—as one executive put it: "I like to use approaches (to getting competitive data) which I would be proud to tell my children about."

Defining the Unit of Analysis

An important decision that is a prerequisite for good cost analysis is determining its purview.[1] Should costs be analyzed for a market segment? For individual products? For a product line? For a business as a whole? The answer is particularly important if market share is being used to make judgments about experience relative to competitors. A company may have a large share of a small market segment, yet have considerably less experience than a larger competitor who has a smaller overall share of a much broader market.

There are risks both of defining the unit of analysis too broadly and too narrowly. If it is defined too broadly, then important *specialized* experience advantages might be missed. For instance, the grinding wheel industry produces hundreds of thousands of different types of wheels, each particularly suited for certain industrial applications. Production of a *given type* of wheel requires development and control of a "recipe" consisting of quantity, type and size of abrasive, bonding agents, fillers, wetting agents, and so forth; the timing of adding these to the "mix"; baking times and temperatures; finishing techniques; and so on. Likewise, a firm can gain important experience advantages in the selling and servicing of wheels for a particular application or a particular industry. Experience advantages on a given type of wheel can yield important cost advantages. Here the unit of analysis should be the type of wheel or the application; if it were simply "grinding wheels," significant cost advantages due to specialization would be missed. Important supporting evidence is that while the U.S. grinding industry is dominated by three producers, many small, specialized companies are very successful.

In other situations, defining the unit of analysis too narrowly can cause problems, such as missing important shared experience or volume effects. Related to this is the difficulty of isolating costs applicable to the unit of analysis, when a resource (such as a sales force or R&D) is shared with other potential units of analysis.

Thus, flexibility and art are required to balance conflicting needs in defining the unit of analysis. Sometimes it is wise to repeat a cost analysis using several different definitions; sometimes it is wise to use a different unit of analysis for estimating a competitor's costs than that used to estimate your own. (This is particularly true when one competitor pursues a "specialized" strategy and another challenges you on a much broader market).

And sometimes it is wise to analyze experience effects for different resources separately, as a prelude to defining the unit of analysis. This will be especially true when resources are shared by several products. A manufacturing plant may, for example, make pumps for oil drilling and marine applications; at the same time, one sales force may sell pumps and motors to oil companies, while another sells pumps, motors, and controls to marine buyers. In such a case, costs must be estimated for selling and manufacturing separately, taking into account the fact that two types of pump share the manufacturing resource, while some pumps, motors, and controls share the sales resource. This analysis will reveal the potential for cost improvement in each resource and the relative contribution of each resource to the cost of each product. This information in turn can often be used to group products into units of analysis.

STRATEGIC IMPLICATIONS OF COSTS

Some of the more fundamental strategic implications relating cost position to strategic choices will be taken up in Chapters 11 and 12. Here I shall refer only to two important relationships: the relationship of fixed/variable *cost structure* to profitability; and the relationship between market leadership strategies and cost behavior.

Fixed/Variable Cost Structures and Profitability

In the previous chapter, the relationship between change in contribution margin and price change for high and low variable cost businesses was explained. However, the sensitivity of contribution margin to price is really only half of the story. Strategically, we need to understand not only what happens *internally to costs* as prices change volume up or down, but also what happens *externally to demand*, as prices change. The *combination* of these internal and external effects has important strategic implications.

On the demand side, demand may be extremely sensitive to price as in the case of commodity products such as standard rolled steel or, say, basic chemicals, or it may be almost insensitive to price as in the case of luxury goods such as high-priced fashion items or fine wines. Many complex industrial products in which there are sharp technological, service, or quality differences are also relatively "price inelastic."

The combination of "contribution sensitivity" and "demand sensitivity" then has the following overall strategic implications:

		Demand Sensitivity	
		High	Low
% Variable Costs	High	?	Profits sensitive to price increases
	Low	Profits sensitive to price decreases and volume	?

In the top, right-hand cell, where variable costs are a substantial proportion of the existing price and where demand is relatively inelastic, big gains in profits can be made by increasing prices. Why? Small price increases mean large contribution increases and with inelastic demand, these gains more than compensate any volume losses. Such is the case with products like high-priced delicatessen items which have high (variable) raw materials costs, but which are such specialty items that they are still purchased even at very high prices.

In the bottom left-hand cell, by contrast, where variable costs are a small proportion of the price, and where demand is relatively elastic, big gains in profits can be made by decreasing prices. Why? Price decreases, even substantial ones, do not have such a deleterious effect on contribution margins, yet volume increases from price cuts are large—large enough to more than compensate for the loss in unit contribution margins. A classic example of a business like this is the hotel industry. Variable costs are a small percentage of price—effectively only the cost of changing the sheets and replacing the towels (if it is done at all!). Yet demand is quite sensitive to the price of the room—especially nonbusiness tourist demand. Hence we see the practice of very substantial price discounting of room prices on weekend "specials" and on off-season periods.

Care has to be taken with these overall "strategic" generalizations in two particular respects. First, one should never *assume* that a strategic action is correct simply by the position of a business in one cell or another. Obviously many others factors play a role, both strategically and in the process of implementation. All that can be said is that such an analysis may indicate the *options* that are certainly worth exploring further. Secondly, demand sensitivity is itself a result of two quite different responses. The first is the response of the *customer* to a price increase or decrease; the second is the response of *competitors* to our price increase or decrease. If our price reductions are immediately matched by those of a competitor, the *net* effect on our demand may be small—limited only to whatever proportional share we take of the *overall* demand movement. If, on the other hand, our price change is a unilateral one, and not matched by competition, the net effect on our demand may be much more substantial.

Costs and Market Leadership

In industries where a significant portion of total cost can be reduced due to scale or experience, important cost advantages can usually be achieved by pursuing a strategy geared to accumulating scale and/or experience faster than competitors. (Such a strategy will ultimately require that the firm acquire the largest market share relative to competition.)

To see this, consider a three-firm industry where each competitor is moving down the same experience curve and firm A leads firm B which in turn leads firm C in experience. This situation is shown in Figure 10–1.

Firm A has a significant cost advantage over B and a major edge on C. The difference in cost can spell the difference between profit and loss; if industry price is falling with experience, as assumed in Figure 10–1, then A will have a substantial profit, B a much smaller profit, and C a loss. In the extreme, if firm A pursued an aggressive strategy, cutting prices in proportion to cost reductions, it could easily drive out smaller, inefficient competitors such as C. Or, it

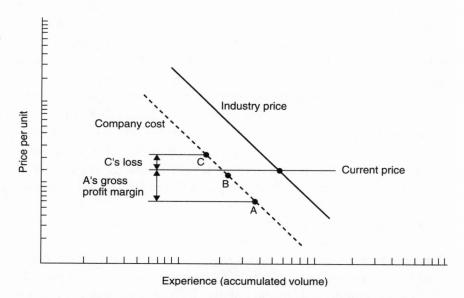

Figure 10–1. Profitability Advantages of Greater Experience (Market Share)
SOURCE: "Adapted from "The Experience Curve-Reviewed: I. The Concept" (Boston: The Boston Consulting Group, 1973). Perspectives. No. 124.

could reduce its prices more slowly to improve its own margin, but it will thereby improve the margin of its competitors, too. This will improve their financial health and may encourage them to improve their own performance by increasing their experience (and consequently market share) relative to the leader.

The dominant producer can greatly influence industry profitability. The rate of decline of competitors' costs must at least keep pace with the leader if they are to maintain profitability. If their costs decrease more slowly, either because they are pursuing cost reductions less aggressively or are growing more slowly than the leader, then their profits will eventually disappear, thus eliminating them from the market. In situations such as the foregoing ones, the advantage of being the leader is obvious. Leadership is usually best seized at the start when experience doubles quickly.

The best course of action for a producer depends on a number of factors, one of the most important being the market growth rate. In fast-growing markets, experience can be gained by taking a disproportionate share of new sales, thereby avoiding taking sales away from competitors (which would be vigorously resisted). Therefore, with high rates of growth, aggressive action may be called for. But share-gaining tactics are usually costly in the short run, due to reduced margins from lower prices, added advertising and market expense, new product development costs, and the like. This means that if it lacks the resources (product, financial, and other) for leadership and in particular if it is opposed by a very aggressive competitor, a firm may find it wise to abandon the market entirely or focus on a segment it can dominate. On the other hand, in no-growth or slowly growing markets it is hard to take share from competitors and the time it takes to acquire superior experience is usually too long and the cost too great to favor aggressive strategies.

In stable competitive markets, usually the firm with the largest share of market has the greatest experience and it is often the case that each firm's experience is roughly proportional to market share. A notable exception occurs when a late entrant to a market quickly obtains a commanding market share. It may have less experience than some early entrants.

Before embarking on an experience-based strategy, especially a share-increasing one, it is essential to calculate explicitly the required time and investment to see whether the target is feasible and desirable. These pro forma projections must extend over many years. For instance, consider a firm with 6 percent of a market that is growing at an 8 percent real growth rate and whose leader has a 24 percent share.

To catch up with the leader's share, our firm would have to grow at a 26 percent growth rate for nine years, if the leader held its share by growing at the 8 percent industry rate. That means expanding at over three times the industry rate for nine years, and that sales and capacity would have to expand by 640 percent!

These numbers raise important questions, some of which are: Can the expansion be financed? What strategy will achieve such a large share gain? From which competitor(s) will the share come? Will the smaller ones be squeezed out by an aggressive strategy? What competitive reactions can be expected? Will the market be worth leading nine years from now?

The importance of doing these calculations and heeding their implications was underscored by the withdrawal of RCA, Xerox, and GE from the mainframe computer business; all three firms experienced multimillion dollar losses in computers.[2] An appropriate set of calculations, done at the outset, might have dissuaded these companies from even entering this market.

The example also shows that good information about the market, its growth, market shares, and competitors' experience or costs is essential. Without knowledge of how fast a market is actually growing, a firm may be unaware that competitors are rapidly gaining share. Or it may be in a poor position to assess the probable effects of proposed market actions. On the other hand, a fully informed company is equipped to make successful strategic decisions at the expense of less-informed competitors.

It is clear that when experience and scale are significant cost factors, being the leader is advantageous and being a distant follower is a serious handicap. However, since no firm has the resources to lead in all markets, it must decide which market to attempt to lead, in which to hold a viable nonleadership share (as firm B does in Figure 10–1), and which to abandon.

The selection of a competitive strategy based on cost reduction due to experience or scale often involves a fundamental choice. It is the selection of cost-price *efficiency* over non-cost-price marketing *effectiveness.* However, when the market is more concerned with product and service features and up-to-date technology, a firm pursuing efficiency can find itself offering a low-priced product that few customers want. Thus two basic questions arise: (1) when should an efficiency strategy be used, and (2) if it is, how far can it be pushed before running into dangers of losing effectiveness. For instance, Hewlett-Packard (HP) has been outstandingly profitable using an "effectiveness" strategy against successful "efficiency"-oriented companies such as Texas Instruments (TI) in calculators, and Digital Equipment Corporation in small computers.[3] These companies aggressively used "experience curve pricing" to achieve an early market share and a subsequent strong competitive cost position. In contrast, HP maintained its prices, concentrating on developing products so advanced that customers were willing to pay a premium for them. The low-share, high-quality strategy worked well for them.[4]

Whether to pursue an efficiency strategy depends on answers to questions such as:

1. Does the industry offer significant cost advantages from experience or scale (as in semiconductors or chemicals)?

2. Are there significant market segments that will reward competitors with low prices?

3. Is the firm well-equipped (financially, managerially, technologically, etc.) for, or already geared up for, strategies relying heavily on having the lowest cost (as TI was in the above example)?

If the answer is "yes" to all these questions, then "efficiency" strategies should probably be pursued.

Once it decides to pursue an "efficiency" strategy, a firm must guard against going so far that it loses effectiveness, primarily through inability to respond to changes. For instance, experience-based strategies frequently require a highly specialized workforce, facilities, and organization, making it difficult to respond to changes in consumer demand, to respond to competitors' innovations, or to imitate them. In addition, large-scale plants are vulnerable to changes in process technology, and the heavy cost of operation below capacity.

For example, Ford's Model T automobile ultimately suffered the consequences of inflexibility due to over-emphasizing "efficiency."[5] As noted earlier, Ford followed a classic experience-based strategy; over time it slashed its product line to a single model (the Model T), built modern plants, pushed division of labor, introduced the continuous assembly line, obtained economies in purchased parts through high-volume, backward-integrated, increased mechanization and cut prices as costs fell. The lower prices increased Ford's share of a growing market to a high of 55 percent by 1921.

In the meantime, as we have seen, consumer demand began shifting to heavier, closed-body cars and to more comfort. Ford's chief rival, General Motors, had the flexibility to respond quickly with new designs. Ford responded by adding features to its existing standard design. While the features softened the inroads of GM, the basic Model T design, upon which Ford's "efficiency" strategy was based, inadequately met the market's new performance standards. To make matters worse, the turmoil in production due to constant design changes slowed experience-based efficiency gains. Finally Ford was forced, at enormous cost, to close for a whole year beginning May 1927 while it retooled to introduce its Model A. Hence experience or scale-based *efficiency* was carried too far and thus it ultimately limited *effectiveness* to meet consumer needs, to innovate, and to respond.

The previous eight chapters have laid the necessary foundations for understanding strategies, both for the present and for the future. We now turn specifically to what we mean by "dual strategies" and how each can be conceived and implemented. I shall begin with strategies for making the very best of competences and resources already in hand.

PART III
DUAL STRATEGIES

CHAPTER 11

MASTERING THE PRESENT

The phrase "they really have their act together" nicely captures the essence of what this chapter is all about. It invokes an image of excellence today, and of harmony—harmony in the sense that the people involved know what they are doing; harmony in the sense that the various "players" are working together in a well orchestrated team; and harmony in the sense that there is a close match between what is being done and what is required.

Walk into an outstanding restaurant and without even consulting the menu, you know instinctively whether they have their act together. A sense of quiet organization prevails. The maître d'hôtel has his eyes everywhere, and everybody seems to know exactly what his own role is in providing you with not only outstanding food, but outstanding service in an outstanding ambience.

Large companies may have more problems getting their act together than small restaurants but, when they do, we recognize it just as well. Swissair and Singapore Airlines have their act together in the way they currently run their airline business; IKEA has its act together in the furniture business; and McDonalds in the fast food business. Each appear to have a "success formula" for doing business, a formula that works, and that they adhere to strictly.

"Having their act together" says little or nothing, of course, about the ability of the organization to succeed in the future. On a different stage, before a different audience, with different choreography and a different script, there is no guarantee that today's excellence can be maintained. Running the current "show" and preparing for future shows are not one and the same thing.

Yet excellence today requires just as much "vision" as excellence tomorrow. The idea of a "success formula," to which all excellent organizations appear to adhere closely, itself represents a clear vision—a vision of how the business has to be run today. This meaning of vision is often hard to grasp at first, because we intuitively associate vision with the future. But good managers have a clear vision of how their businesses have to be run today to achieve excellence, and they devote very considerable time and energy to bringing reality into line with this vision.

For the best managers, even this "present vision" is a moving target. Like fanatic mountaineers, they scale one peak, only to set their sights on others—even higher and more challenging. "Only the best is good enough"[1] is their call to arms—where "best" is being continuously redefined as they leapfrog continuously between more and more refined visions of what can be achieved today, and higher and higher achievements.

What then is the secret of those organizations—and individuals—who have their act together? Is it the clarity of their vision? Is it their recipe for success? Is it their ability to turn the vision into reality? And how much does it depend on personal determination and commitment? The answer is that it is all of these—and more. The starting point for all of the above is the pinpointing of a clear segment of opportunity where *current* resources and competences can be most effectively deployed. The words "pinpointing current opportunities" aptly describe what lies behind every successful performance—be it in show business, the restaurant business, or corporate business; "pinpointing" means to take careful aim—and fire into the target!

In a business setting, it is a process of narrowing in on a specific *market* target, and going all out to satisfy customers in that segment. This target should be one that takes the greatest advantage of the firm's current resources and competences, and at the same time sidesteps, or ever better, completely avoids head-on competition.

Pinpointing today's customers with a well-defined offering is not a one-time process, but a *continuous* process of searching for better and better ways to define the company's participation in its markets. It should be never ending. Even when competitive challenges are few, standing still for very long is to sow the first seeds of failure.

Pinpointing today's customers should be considered as a *learning process,* by which understanding of the market and its opportunities and possibilities are progressively narrowed and refined.

Pinpointing today's customers is an *interactive* process. It has to be reviewed in its totality as well as developed in a step-by-step fashion.

Pinpointing today's customers is also an *explicit* process. It requires explicit statements of target markets, the "success formula," functional programs to achieve this success, and actionable implementation steps.

Finally, pinpointing today's customers is a *team* process led by general management. It cannot be carried out only by planning staff—since it lies at the very heart of current business success. In fact, for many companies, it is here that the bigger battle for long-term market superiority will be won or lost, because in the absence of strong performance today, neither the funds nor the market momentum will be created to win in the future.

The *time horizon* for such a process is necessarily short—usually a year or less—because it deals primarily with exploiting competences and resources that are already in hand. This of course does not exclude *minor* modifications in the short term. Some weaknesses can be overcome and others minimized, and certain strengths can be further reinforced. But this is a totally different process than managing the fundamental changes needed to compete successfully in the future.

There are several things that this process is *not.* It is certainly not centered on short-term (or long-term for that matter) forecasting and budgeting. It is not "operational" planning—although it includes some operational plans; rather, it is *short-term* but *strategic* in nature.

The changes that do result from this process are *not* just marginal improvements on the capabilities side of the matrix; they are much more likely to be on clarifying and sharpening up the definition of the target market, and all that this implies for the strategic approach needed.

An explicitly defined methodology will now be suggested for deciding how best to do this. It is an approach that results in a progressively sharper and sharper definition of where the current opportunities lie, and how they can be exploited. Although it appears to be stepwise, the reader must constantly be aware of the need to "go round again" as assumptions are clarified and new insights gained from the analysis itself.

The output from such an exercise should rarely be a single "best" solution. It is a methodology for creating as well as evaluating strategic options—and like so many managerial phenomena, the questions raised in working through the process are often as important as the specific answers.

A METHODOLOGY FOR PINPOINTING CURRENT OPPORTUNITIES

Three main steps are required in the process of pinpointing current opportunities:

1. Dividing the market into segments

2. Identifying segments that potentially seem most attractive *to our company*

3. Formulating a detailed strategic approach to each—and pinpointing final choices on *where* and *how* the company will compete today

This three-part process progressively sharpens the focus as we proceed from a view of the whole market in Step One, to identification of apparently high potential segments in Step Two, to final choices in Step Three, where detailed programs are worked out and evaluated financially. Steps One and Two are analytical in nature; Step 3 moves from analysis to decisions.

Sometimes it transpires after passing through this whole cycle once that *none* of the options that have been considered are attractive enough to give the green light to. An option is then to redo the analysis, making different assumptions and perhaps different judgments about approaches or levels of commitment needed to succeed. The proposed methodology in this sense is holistic and circular rather than discrete and sequential.

We shall now consider each of these steps in turn, and "walk through" the various substeps required to use the methodology in practice.

Step One—Dividing the Market into Segments

Chapters 3 and 4 of this book are devoted to this topic, and should be reread carefully at this point if the ideas have not been thoroughly internalized. Only the main points will be repeated here.

Two related judgments have to be made. First, how to break up the market; and second, to what degree of disaggregation to carry the analysis. In both, it is important to find the balance between simplicity and creativity. Many companies are content to view their markets as a "matrix" of product-market "cells," each representing a particular product sold to a particular class of customer or use. Such an approach is shown for example in Figure 11–1 below, for the global shipbuilding market.

This seemingly straightforward approach may satisfy the criterion of simplicity, but may fail the second criterion of creativity. As explained in Chapters 3 and 4, we are looking for ways to divide the market that distance us not only from competition, but from competitors' *thinking;* and we are always looking for ways that will give us a sustainable basis for excellence, in the customer's eyes, as well as competitive advantage. As pointed out in Chapter 4, art as well as science plays an important part in dividing up markets to accomplish these two objectives.

Step one is a crucial one, since every subsequent decision follows from this first step. Both the way we divide up the market and the degree to which we disaggregate the segments are themselves vital parts of the overall strategic decision-making process. It behooves management therefore to spend considerable time and effort on this step, and to include as many alternative ways to look at segmentation as possible. There is usually no shortage of possibilities. The limiting factors are only the insight, imagination, and rigor that management applies to the task.

Step Two—Identifying Potentially Attractive Segments

This requires five distinct substeps, the outcomes of which finally have to be weighed and balanced in an overall evaluation.

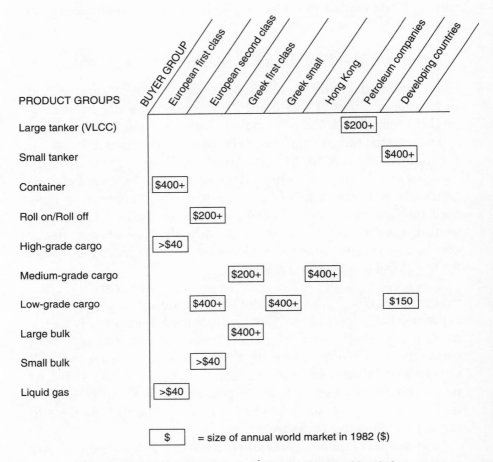

$\boxed{\$}$ = size of annual world market in 1982 ($)

Figure 11–1. Product-Market Matrix for the Global Shipbuilding Industry
Reproduced with permission of The Free Press, a Division of Macmillan, Inc., New York, from
Market Driven Strategy, p. 106. by George S. Day. Copyright © 1990 by George S. Day.

The five sub-steps require, respectively, a *segment-by-segment* assessment of:

1. Current performance ("how *are* we doing")

2. Market attractiveness (what *could* be done)

3. "Fit" of our competences to key success requirements, versus the "fit" of competitors (what *can* be done)

4. Management's interests (what do we *want* to do)

5. Other (than management) stakeholders' interests (what *should* be done)

We shall take these one at a time.

1. Assessing Current Performance

In Chapter 5, suggestions were made for evaluating company and competitive performance for a "line of business." What is needed here is to see "how we are doing" on a more disaggregated segment-by-segment basis. This type of evaluation is often considerably more difficult to obtain—and the more the definition of segments departs from the conventional, and the finer the segmentation employed, the more difficult the task becomes. It is quite usual to find, for example, that performance data are easier to come by for individual products than they are for any kind of breakdown by market segment.

This is no excuse for not trying to get *some* data on performance, along the lines required. Several measures of performance are usually better than one, and four main yardsticks taken together, provide management with a good composite picture. These are:

–profitability (gross margins, contribution margins or, even better, return on sales or return on investment)

–cash flow

–growth (in units and revenues)

–market share

Piecing together such data is like piecing together a jigsaw puzzle—in which several important pieces may be missing. Nevertheless, to the trained eye, even partially completed pictures can tell a great deal about a company's performance segment-by-segment.

Ideally, also, we would like to understand the *trajectory* of these various performance measures over time. To the extent possible, therefore, we try to assemble data on the past as well as on the present, and with all the usual reservations about forecasting, extrapolate this at least into the next few periods.

If, of course, this is a *new* undertaking, and the company has no history of doing business so far, performance assessment is impossible. In such a case, we may try to assess how existing and potential competitors are currently doing—just to provide an initial *quantification* of segment-by-segment attractiveness.

2. *Assessing Market Attractiveness*

Market segments differ substantially in terms of their attractiveness. And often, even though a particular market may be perceived as relatively unattractive overall, certain segments within it may be highly attractive. Such has been the case with very high priced watches within the watch industry, four-wheel drive cars in the automobile industry, facsimile machines in the office equipment market, and a host of others. Markets and segments of markets can also change dramatically in their attractiveness over time, as life cycles run their course, and as external forces reshape customer demand.

Before we can assess attractiveness, we have to decide what we mean by it. I use the term here in a special sense to mean the *inherent* attractiveness independent of whether or not one competitor or another is well equipped to exploit the particular set of opportunities presented. It is, for example, usually reasonable to assume that high-growth markets are *per se* more attractive than stable or declining markets, and that differentiated product markets are more attractive than commodity markets. Whether a potentially attractive segment is attractive for a particular company is quite another question—depending on the "fit" between their specific competences and resources and market requirements.

Nevertheless we must always remember to *specify* what measure of attractiveness we are interested in. Growth markets, for example, may be attractive in terms of potential financial returns, but unattractive from a cash flow perspective—since profits have to be reinvested in expanded physical facilities, equipment, and working capital.

Many factors may be viewed as contributing to market attractiveness. They are often grouped under five major headings: market factors; competition; financial and economic factors; technological factors; and sociopolitical factors. A typical list is shown below:

Factors Contributing to Market Attractiveness[2]

Market Factors
Size (dollars, units, or both)
Size of key segments
Growth rate per year:
  Total
  Segments
Diversity of market
Sensitivity to price, service features, and external factors
Cyclicality
Seasonality
Bargaining power of upstram suppliers
Bargaining power of downstream suppliers

Financial and Economic Factors
Contribution margins
Leveraging factors, such as economies of scale and experience
Barriers to entry or exit (both financial and non-financial)
Capacity utilization

Technological Factors
Maturity and volatility
Complexity
Differentiation
Patents and copyrights
Manufacturing process technology required

Competition
Types of competitors
Degree of concentration
Changes in type and mix
Entries and exits
Changes in share
Substitution by new technology
Degrees and types of integration

Sociopolitical Factors in Your Environment
Social attitudes and trends
Laws and government agency regulations
Influence with pressure groups & government representatives
Human factors, such as unionization and community acceptance

But using such "laundry lists" to assess attractiveness presents three underlying problems:

–The factors that impact on attractiveness have to be identified by the analyst.

–The strength and direction of the relationship between a particular factor and attractiveness has to be assessed judgmentally.

–Overall assessments of attractiveness depend on some implicit or explicit "weighting" of the different factors involved.

The so-called PIMS (Profit Impact of Market Strategy) project circumvented some of these difficulties by using empirical evidence from a large number of different businesses in a large number of different industries, to assess correlations between various measures of attractiveness and profitability.[3] A computer "regression model" showed how each factor related to results and weighted the factors according to their relative importance in the total equation. Long- and short-term industry growth rates, stage in the product life cycle, degree of vertical integration, and product differentiation consistently appeared on the top of the PIMS lists—across a wide variety of industries.

One of the most useful ways to think conceptually about market attractiveness is that proposed by Michael Porter. According to Porter, the attractiveness of an "industry" depends on five competitive forces: (1) the threat of new entrants, (2) the threat of substitute products and services, (3) the bargaining power of suppliers, (4) the bargaining power of buyers, and (5) the rivalry among existing competitors.[4]

When all five forces are "favorable," a market or segment can be considered as attractive in terms of the opportunity for long-run sustained profitability. The threat of new entrants or substitute products would limit such opportunities. So would powerful suppliers or buyers who could negotiate a better deal for themselves at the company's expense. And fierce internal rivalry in the existing market usually erodes profitability, even though at the same time it hones the underlying competitiveness of participating firms—and may actually improve their chances in other less demanding markets.

I recommend a composite of quantitative and qualitative approaches to the assessment of attractiveness. Having decided which segments or clusters of segments we wish to evaluate, judgment is needed to decide which factors are likely to have a major impact on present and future profitability and on present and future cash flow, and on how each factor should be weighted. Factors that are singled out as relevant in one segment may be less relevant for another—and would therefore be given less weight or totally ignored. And some factors that are of high importance today may dwindle in importance tomorrow. It is not wise or necessary to try to quantify and weight every input—only to arrive at a misleading, though numerically impeccable, conclusion.

In assessing the attractiveness of segments, it is particularly important, whichever approach is used, to consider how things might *change*—and what the forces for change are. Even in making decisions for today, the possible impact of such forces must be considered. They can range from technology change, to political change, to economic change, to social change, and their effect can be immediate and sweeping—positive and negative.

We do not have to "overdo" this analysis of attractiveness, however. While relative attractiveness is one important consideration in decisions about where to aim and where to commit resources, it is seldom a dominant consideration at this stage of what is an iterative process.

3. Assessing "Fit"

The assessment of fit of *our* competences and resources against market requirements, and the fit of competitors' competences and resources, is an important indicator of attractiveness of a segment *to us*. In the foregoing substep, we asked what *could* be done, that is, by any unspecified organization; in this substep, we ask the question "what *can* be done," that is, by our own company, given our strengths and weaknesses relative to those of our competitors, and relative to what is needed in this particular segment. In asking what *could* be done, we are essentially looking *out* at the market; in asking what *can* be done, we are looking *in* at the firm, and its capabilities.

To assess fit in practice, we have to have to go through an important analytical process—transforming the description of key customer needs segment by segment into a description of what has to be provided by a firm to satisfy these needs. Internal capabilities can then be compared with these so called "critical success factors" to assess where we and our competitors have particular advantages or disadvantages.

The transformation process from needs to critical success factors requires not only good judgment but a thorough managerial understanding of how a firm can meet particular needs. To do this it is helpful to define an "intermediate" concept which we call the "basis for competition." Thus we go through the following sequence in our analytical thinking:

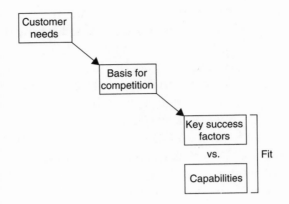

Let us suppose for example that key needs in a particular segment of the high fidelity music reproduction business are distinguishably better sound, "value," and "trouble free" operation. The basis for competition might then be sound quality, price, and guarantees as well as service; and key success factors might be acoustical engineering skills, costs, and manufacturing quality. For this segment we would therefore have to go through the following thought process. These key success factors can then be compared with company capabilities to assess fit.

Customer needs	Basis for competition	Key success factors
• distinguishably better sound	• sound quality	• acoustical engineering skills
		• Electronic engineering skills
• value	• price	• costs
• trouble free	• guaranteed service	• manufacturing quality
		• service arrangements

Making *explicit* the distinction between needs, the basis for competition, and key success factors is important. Too often, it is glossed over with the result that management lacks a careful assessment of the capabilities that will be needed to succeed in a particular segment. It is hard enough to make an objective assessment of one's own and competitors' capabilities; to set these against a poorly defined yardstick of what is going to be needed only compounds superficiality.

An evaluation of competences and resources too often ends up in a long list of general strengths and weaknesses, without reference to key success factors. This is a worthless exercise. Strengths and weaknesses, as pointed out before, cannot be evaluated in the abstract; they can only be evaluated in relation to the specific requirements of a defined segment of opportunity.

To be complete, an evaluation of capabilities includes not only those competences and resources that are likely to create superior customer value, but also those factors that may create cost advantages, such as scale, technology, and experience effects. And, as we have seen in Chapter 8, satisfying customer needs in a particular segment depends not only on "internal" competences and resources specific to that particular segment of activity, but also on the exploitation of "external" competences and resources. These may reside in other business units or divisions in the corporate entity, or outside. They may be directly owned, or result from business alliances or even arm's length relationships. They may be "horizontally" related to the main activity—as are, for example, technology, manufacturing, and sales capabilities, or "vertically" related as are special purchasing arrangements or downstream relationships with distribution channels. *All* existing competences and resources, whereever they reside, inside or outside of the firm, must figure in the evaluation of fit.

This assessment of the fit between key success factors by segment and *current* resources and competences is a crucial step in the whole process of deciding how to pinpoint *today*'s markets. While looking "out" and assessing segment attractiveness is important, looking "in" and checking the capabilities to meet key success requirements is even more important. It often receives too little attention in the overall managerial equation. So-called opportunity based planning frequently overrides so-called resource based planning. The result, later, is often mediocrity and market followership because the company brings no *distinctive* competences to the party. Minor weaknesses can, of course, be overcome, and strengths may be moderately reinforced, but *today*'s strategies are bound, by and large, by whatever the firm currently has available in the way of resources and capabilities.

Some critics have claimed that such analyses of "fit" are limited in their usefulness—either because the outputs have greater validity in relatively stable and predictable markets[5], or because they distract management from broader issues of long-term strategic intent.[6] But if the objective of the exercise is to assess *today's* possibilities for connecting with customers, these criticisms seem unfounded. On the contrary, it is an essential step in the whole exercise.

4. Assessing Management's Interests

What "could be done" and what "can be done" are largely academic unless there is a champion inside the organization to actually make it happen! Too often, the approach used to analyze and pinpoint current opportunities is much too "technocratic." It uses "left brain" rather than "right brain" perspectives—focusing on the rational, objective parts of the problem as opposed to the less rational, subjective issue of what management *wants* to do.

The question should be asked from the very beginning: "Is there anyone in the organization for whom this undertaking represents a personal passion?" It is not too strong to say that when there is such a committed champion, the chances of success are frequently high *even* if the underlying fit between competences and requirements is not immediately obvious. Committed individuals *make* things happen, and create strengths and redefine standards even where these were lacking before. On the other hand, even when the underlying needed competences and resources are abundant, the absence of passionate commitment is more than likely to doom the result from the start.

The German philosopher Hegel put it as follows:

So müssen wir überhaupt sagen, dass nichts Grosses in der Welt ohne Leidenschaft vollbracht geworden ist.[7]

5. Assessing Other Stakeholder' Interests

There is still another dimension, and an increasingly important one, for management to consider—namely what *should* be done. Societal, ecological, and ethical considerations fall into this category, as they affect employees, other stakeholders such as the immediate community, or the public at large.

As an example, Time Warner's issue, in 1992, of Ice-T's "Cop-Killer" song in its album "Body Count" may have satisfied some managers' objectives, but it certainly did not satisfy other company stakeholders. According to one newspaper account,

> Despite glowing reports about healthy profits, the announcement of a 4:1 stock split, and the success of the movie "Batman Returns," Time Warner's Annual General Meeting was interrupted over and over again as people on the floor brought up the 'Cop-Killer' issue.[8]

This may be an extreme case, but it exemplifies a broad category of societal, ecological, and ethical, to say nothing of legal, issues. And even where these broader issues are not at stake, the question is increasingly being asked about how far companies *should* go in satisfying customer needs—if in so doing general standards degenerate.

One can of course ask "by whose standards?" This author happens to believe strongly that managers have responsibilities to *set* standards, not just cater to customer needs. But how far should this go? Refusal to market drugs? alcoholic beverages? cigarettes? pornographic "literature"? violence on TV? tabloid newspapers? junk food? "disposable" items in certain categories? disposable items generally? coffee "to go" in a plastic cup? Should managers or consumers be the final arbiters of taste—to say nothing of designers, engineers, retailers, advertisers, publishers, government officials, special interest groups, lobbyists, and so on. What we probably can all agree on is that managers cannot be pure "technocrats" in such complex debates and decision processes—and should recognize a broad range of stakeholder interests.

Putting the Step Two Analyses Together

The assessment of performance tells us where we stand today; the subsequent four steps help us to understand why—and suggest where we should focus in the immediate future. As we look to what to do, the question of how to *balance* what *could* be done, with what *can* be done, with what *should* be done, and with what we *want* to do becomes paramount. Here there are no formulas to help us. Good managers can reach very different conclusions, using exactly the same inputs. Nevertheless certain imbalances should be watched out for.

First, the old adage about "the eyes being bigger than the stomach" has its analogy in management practice; market place opportunities are sometimes pursued that exceed the firm's capacity to take advantage of. In Chapter 2, reference was made to Shering's failed bid to enter applications in the central nervous system pharmaceutical business—where the company did not appreciate all of the abilities needed to successfully compete in that particular segment. Schering's experience is far from unique. Many firms extend or diversify activities into areas where they have little *distinctive* competence vis-à-vis competitors—with predictably mediocre results.

Secondly, "resource-based" strategies, *even* when supported by a passionate management champion, may not fare well unless they also incorporate a sound dose of customer orientation into formulation and implementation. Many "brilliantly engineered" products, having their origins in the laboratory, fail in the marketplace precisely because R&D focuses more on what can be done than on what is required.

To avoid imbalance, it may be useful to depict the four forces that impinge on decisions regarding the attractiveness of a particular segment in the following way:

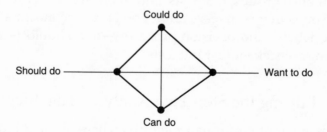

If it seems that one or another dimension is getting shortchanged— or at the other extreme, getting the lion's share of attention at the expense of others—further reflection, and discussion, is probably needed.

Once that it seems that the various inputs are each being given appropriate attention, several outcomes are still possible with respect to the "fit" between requirements on the one hand and capabilities on the other. Here we must introduce a new concept—the difference between "qualifying" requirements, that is, those that are required to even participate competitively and "determining" requirements, that is, those that are needed to *win*. Both are "critical success factors" in the sense that a competitor cannot do without them, but "determining" requirements are those that truly make the competitive difference.

A useful way to consider "fit" is then to use a chart like the one below:

Success Factors

		Qualifying	Determining
	Strengths	In the game	Leverage to win the business
Capabilities	Weaknesses	Invest resources to become "me too"	Invest resources to compete for leadership of the business

It is usually better to lead from strength, but sometimes specific weaknesses can be overcome—even in the short term.

Not surprisingly, these analyses often reveal a substantial lack of consensus among responsible managers. The exercise is a useful one just because it surfaces differences of opinion. These differences may be rooted in the absence of objective data, they may be rooted in wishful thinking about the *real* levels of competence and resources which the company can bring to bear; and often they are rooted in only a vague understanding and conceptualization of customer needs, the basis of competition, and key success factors segment by segment. Making these factors explicit, through a broadly participative process involving each key level and responsibility within the overall managerial term, is a vital part of organizational learning about existing market opportunities, the company's current capabilities, other stakeholder expectations, and management's *own* views about what it wants to do.

Step Three—Positioning and Strategy Formulation

Step Three moves us from analysis to decisions for each of those segments that appears to be highly attractive—and is itself an iterative, holistic process in the sense that each decision is in some way dependent on others. Methodologically the following sequence of substeps is recommended, but finally everything must be internally consistent with no clear starting or ending point:

1. Choose the precise "positioning"

2. Decide on the "strategic thrust"

3. Set objectives and levels of commitment

4. Develop functional plans internally and resource plans externally

5. Lay out specific actions required

6. Calculate financial implications and risks

Only when the iterative sequence of substeps is complete and internally consistent can a final budget be prepared. Each of these substeps will now be considered in turn.

I. Positioning

Creatively dividing the overall market cake into segments as in Step One is one thing; positioning *within* a segment is quite another. Many managers confuse the two. The first step requires a relatively "coarse" segmentation aimed at differentiating the company's approach in one part of the market from its approach to another; the second step—positioning—requires a much finer segmentation aimed at differentiating the company's approach from that of its competitors.

Positioning emphasizes points of sustainable competitive advantage—and it identifies customer segments or subsegments with needs that are distinct and that can be served in a differentiated fashion. Quite often, as we have seen in Chapters 3 and 4, the "fine" segmentation on which positioning choices are based is related to nonproduct aspects of customer satisfaction—needs for service, information, reassurance, convenience, delivery, and the like. In some cases, positioning differences relate solely to the *way* the product or service is presented to the customer; for example, the only obvious difference between two apparently similar health food products may be that one is marketed via food stores and the other through pharmacies and drug stores. But this "positioning," especially if supported by a clear marketing communications strategy, is enough to sharply differentiate the two offerings in the minds of consumers. Marketing communications in the form of advertising, sales promotion, and branding are often important tools, as in the example above, to reinforce positioning choices.

Quite frequently, the company's own managers believe that they know instinctively how their offering is differentiated from that of competitors. And, although they may have a tendency to exaggerate quality differences in their own favor, their basis of differentiation is nevertheless correct. What they fail to recognize is that *customers* have a much inferior understanding of how one competitor differs from another, and for that matter even of the *terms* on which two offerings might be compared. An important part of positioning strategy is often therefore to communicate not only the relative qualities to consumers, but to communicate also the very frame of reference on which the customer should make her judgments. When well done, this has a strong multiplicative effect on the positioning statement itself.

Relatively undifferentiated products often *depend* for their success on well thought out and clearly communicated positioning choices. Such is the case with the "head on" competition between such brands as Marlboro and Camel, or Coca Cola and Pepsi Cola. But more differentiated consumer products, and many industrial products and services, also require clear positioning. Without it, the customer has no way of knowing which of the many, many product attributes and differences are the critical ones which should make him decide in favor of one competitor and not another, and why this is more appropriate for him than for another customer with different needs and characteristics.

2. *Deciding on the Overall Strategic Thrust*

In Chapter 7, we reviewed some broad typologies of market strategy such as "push" versus "pull"; "high perceived value" versus "low delivered cost"; and "product" versus "service" intensive approaches. The reader was also cautioned not to ignore strategies that combine the best elements of each extreme, for example strategies which provide both high perceived value and low prices, or strategies that emphasize both product and service quality.

Such an overall description can be useful in highlighting the main *strategic thrust* of a market strategy. It is often a useful "shorthand" for communicating the main points of emphasis—and it should be directly related to "key success factors" in a segment given a particular choice.

It is usually enough to pick out the three or four critical elements of a market strategy to communicate throughout the organization those things that have to be constantly smothered with attention. In the case of a "push" strategy, this may be personal selling to wholesale and retail channels, excellent merchandising materials, and trade margins and incentives; in the case of a "pull" strategy, it may be the quality and quantity of advertising, relationships with mass merchandisers, and achievement of shelf space. In other situations, the main strategic thrusts may be quite different, for example speed of new product development, service quality, or rapid delivery.

Whatever the situation, the main point to remember is that not *everything* can be done, or has to be done, with excellence. But those three or four things that create the real competitive differentiation, and on which one wants to meet and even exceed customers expectations, have to be the constant focus of management's attention.

3. Deciding on Commitments and Objectives

Positioning choices and the interrelated question of overall strategic thrust cannot be separated from the objectives that are set for the particular segment of opportunity, and the financial commitments that have to be made to achieve these objectives.

A useful way to depict choices of objectives for a particular segment of opportunity is to use a so-called portfolio chart.[9] The four quadrants of the chart represent the familiar "cash cows," "stars," "question marks," and "dogs." A company may then choose one of four main strategies.

1. To *build market share*—usually while the overall market is still growing—by moving from "question mark" to "star status."

This often requires infusion of cash from sources outside that particular business segment—for example, from other existing "cash cows."

2. To *hold market share* in anticipation of slowing market growth—which eventually means that "stars" are transformed automatically into "cash cows." Holding market share neither produces nor uses substantial amounts of cash.

3. To *"harvest"* the activity—by purposely allowing market share to decline in order to maximize short-term earnings and cash flow (from operations, lowered fixed investments, and lowered investments in working capital).

4. To *withdraw*—when the activity in a segment has less than the critical share for viability, and overwhelming short run sacrifices would be required to catch up.

Selection from these four basic strategies requires much judgment—in addition to the analysis presented in Step Two. For the most part, portfolio analysis is simply a useful way to *portray* the options at hand, rather than to aid the decision-making process itself. "Success sequences" and "disaster sequences" can, however, be clearly identified as shown in Figure 11–2.[10] Other more elaborate methods for conceptualizing and displaying objectives and financial commitments are also often used. They will not be tackled here, but the technically minded reader can find them described fully in many recent strategic management texts.[11]

Strategic Windows of Opportunity[12]—When changes in a market are only incremental, firms may successfully adapt themselves to the new situation by modifying the scope of their participation, refocusing on some segments at the expense of others, and modifying current marketing or other functional programs. Sometimes, however, market changes are so far reaching that the competence of the firm to continue to compete effectively is called into question. Or, conversely, chance sometimes intervenes on the positive side, giving the firm a unique opportunity to deploy its competences. It is in such situations that the concept of a "strategic window" is applicable.

The term "strategic window" is used here to focus attention on

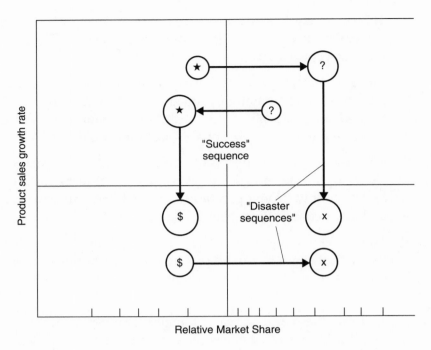

Figure 11–2.
SOURCE: Derek F. Abell and John S. Hammond, *Strategic Marketing Planning*, ©
1979, p. 180. Prentice Hall, Englewood Cliffs, New Jersey.

the fact that there are only limited periods during which the "fit"
between the key requirements of a market and the particular competencies of a firm competing in the market is at an optimum. Investment in a product line or market area should be timed to coin-
cide with periods in which such a strategic window is open.
Conversely, disinvestment should be contemplated if what was
once a good fit has been eroded that is, if changes in market requirements outstrip the firm's capability to adapt itself to them.

Resource allocation decisions of this nature all require a careful
assessment of the future evolution of the market involved and an
accurate appraisal of the firm's capability to successfully meet key
market requirements. The strategic window concept encourages the
analysis of these questions in a dynamic rather than a static framework, and forces management to be as specific as they can about
patterns of market evolution and the firm's capability to adapt to

them in the short term. Adaptation in the long term is the subject of Chapter 12.

In setting objectives and making commitments, two additional and related points must be borne in mind.

First, the process that has been described tends to be bottom-up in nature. It is derived from the detailed perspective of managers who are familiar with the "ins and outs" of the business, who know where the business currently stands, and who have been actively involved in devising positioning strategies and the overall strategic thrust needed. Top management, at the division or even corporate level, may bring an entirely different perspective to such choices. Theirs is the perspective of overall divisional or corporate *expectations,* rather than segment *possibilities.*

Quite often in the planning process, these two perspectives are found to differ substantially. Sometimes managers working from the bottom up see opportunities for the company that are hidden from top management's immediate view. And when exploitation of these opportunities requires substantial amounts of "up-front" investment, the "information gap" has to be closed before real commitment can be obtained. And sometimes, quite the reverse happens: top management pushes for performance levels that lower-level managers know, based on their close familiarity with the business, cannot be achieved. The "negotiation" that usually ensues in bringing together top management expectations and lower-level management insight, is an important part of every planning process and will be discussed more fully in Chapter 15.

Second, long-term objectives and short-term objectives may not always point in the same direction. This may happen because of a downturn in the market or short-term problems that require cuts in discretionary spending. If these areas of spending are critical to long-term success, such as expenditures on R&D projects, long-term new product development, marketing campaigns aimed at reinforcing brand image and position, or expenditures on human resources, difficult trade-offs may have to be made. This is one of the important areas of overlap and relationship between the "planning for today," covered in this chapter, and the "planning for tomorrow," covered in Chapter 13. A complete review of how the two perspectives and two horizons have to be dovetailed is contained in

Chapter 15, where planning systems which reflect the dual nature of planning are discussed.

4. *Deriving Functional Plans and Resource Plans*

I have used the word "deriving" to describe this process because short-term functional plans must be *contingent* on the broader strategic choices made with respect to positioning, the strategic thrust, and overall commitments and objectives.

Short-term functional plans differ substantially in this respect from longer-term "future-oriented" functional plans, as we shall see in subsequent chapters. When it comes to how to *use* existing functional capabilities and resources, the functional players in the business orchestra must strictly follow the "score" and look to the conductor—usually a segment or division general manager—to understand what needs to be done. As we shall see in Chapter 13, this is not at all the case with respect to *building* functional capabilities and resources. Here the functional managers have a much more intimate knowledge of what the future possibilities are, and this has to be combined with a vision of the future to determine the way forward.

A plan must be derived for each function, reflecting the specific tasks of that function with respect to the overall strategic thrust. In Chapter 7, this was referred to as "part-to-whole integration." Chapter 7 also cited the need to attend to "part-to-part" integration, that is, the harmonious relationship of each function to each of the other functions. Diagrammatically we may then represent a segment strategy as shown in Figure 11–3.

The fact that not all functions are completely dedicated to a particular segment of activity is not relevant in this picture; the main point is that *whatever* the degree to which a function participates in the accomplishment of overall segment objectives, this function must develop *contingent* plans to fulfill these objectives.

What *is* important is that each function, within the context of its role in the overall strategy, strives constantly for improvement on those factors that are critical to success in that segment. Here is where major room exists for functional initiative—in the short term as well as in the long term. If, for example, a critical success factor in one market is "reliability," this implies not only superior manufac-

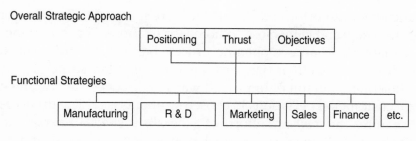

Figure 11–3.

turing, but also superior product design, superior materials and components purchasing "upstream," superior care of the product in the physical distribution process, superior service and guarantees, and superior advertising and promotion designed to reinforce the consumer's perception of reliability. While segment management and general management can specify the need for such levels of reliability, only the functional executives involved are likely to come up with the creative ways to make it actually happen.

All that has been said about internal functions can also be said about external resources—whether they be "corporate" resources, or resources owned and managed by horizontally related or vertically related partner firms. All must be directed towards the strategic ends that have been determined.

"Total quality management" is the catchall term often given to programs that aim at bringing functional and resource activities in line with strategic ends, and that aim at a steady upgrading of standards in each of these areas. Too often TQM programs are seen as something separate and independent of the overall strategic process described here. This is a mistake because a company should only have one main beacon of excellence before it—not competing inputs from several different sources.

Benchmarking is an extremely useful approach to ensure that the highest standards are being reached in the process of functional and resource planning. Benchmarking looks for "best practices" in each separate activity or subactivity, and then sets out to bring standards up to this level. In searching for best practices, the net has to be cast widely. They may be found in other divisions or units within the same enterprise, in competitors within the same sector of activity, or in firms completely outside of our own industry—where similar functions are performed but in a different context. They may be found geographically close to home, or offshore. Benchmarking is for many firms an eye-opening process because they discover for the first time that their standards are not "the" standards.

Relentless pursuit of improved ways to discover, satisfy, and *exceed* customer expectations in chosen segments is critical to success. It requires the *combined* efforts of generalists, specialists, and partners in related organizations. Just as in an orchestra, while the conductor needs to have a deep familiarity with how to play the various instruments in order to conduct the whole orchestra, few conductors are instrumental virtuosos. And even if they master one instrument with excellence, none can master the whole array of instruments that make up the complete orchestra. Conducting is one thing; individual playing brilliance is another. The two together are needed to achieve the highest standards of concert—and business—performance.

5. Action Planning

Formulating functional and resource plans is one thing; implementing them is another. Specific actions required for successful implementation will, of course, be more or less effective in producing the desired results, depending on overall organizational factors such as structure, the appropriateness of the company's management systems, company culture, overall organizational vitality, and leadership. These general "contextual" variables can of course be changed in the medium to long term, but in the short-term picture they are relatively fixed. Like competences and resources, these organizational factors form the "backdrops" within which short-term plans have to be implemented.

Implementation, short-term, therefore boils down to identifying the specific *actions* needed to carry through today's plans, denominating those responsible for carrying out the actions, and setting timetables for their successful completion.

While considerably less glamorous, at least conceptually, implementation is, after all, at the very heart of strategy. Without it, nothing is accomplished. It tends to be grossly underestimated as part of the overall strategic process. Specifying the discrete actions needed to implement a strategic program in a segment is a time-consuming and rigorous undertaking. Being explicit about what has to be done, by whom, and by which date, is an important discipline. It is a large step on the way to accomplishing the visions which otherwise may remain cerebral or only slightly better, committed to planning documents filed away until the next planning period.

Action steps usually relate to each internal function and external resource involved in carrying through the total program. In many cases, they require *coordinated* action between internal functions or between internal functions and external resources.

Action statements provide direction to subordinate levels of management activity, and should become the basis for individual objective setting, performance measurement, and in some cases, compensation or other forms of reward.

Communication plays a particularly important role in sound implementation. Good communication starts with broad participation in the planning process itself. This does not necessarily mean that every executive from the president to the lowest new management recruit has to be involved in every aspect of the process, at every step along the way. But it *does* mean that participation is important in all of those questions that the individual can directly influence in the subsequent implementation stages, and in all of those questions that *have* an effect, directly or indirectly, on the individual's work.

Participation does not necessarily mean sharing in the final decision. Participation can take many forms from mere "presence," to being explicitly informed, to active participation in discussions, to being requested to give advice or counsel, to being asked to represent a position, to actually making the decision itself.

When participation in the strategy formulation process is neither possible (for example, for reasons of time or geographic distance), nor perhaps desirable (for example, for reasons of secrecy), clear communication is even more necessary to let everybody involved in implementation know what has been decided, and what their specific roles are in carrying it through. Organizations in which the key participants all "sing the same song," even if the song is not perfectly attuned to market needs, usually have a higher chance of success than those where some singers are off-key or even sing different songs! The former kind of organization usually learns its way to the right result; the latter can be incapacitated with internal friction, lack of clear direction, and general disharmony.

Managers sometimes ask whether the very explicit and formalized strategic process outlined here is really putting the cart before the horse. There is a belief among some that strategy *starts* with implementation, and that by a continuous process of trial and error, strategies emerge *post facto*. The truth is probably somewhere between these two extremes, but in this author's opinion, the key elements of strategy, functional plans, and actions, have to be made explicit. As the old proverb so aptly says:

"If you don't know where you are going, any road will take you there."

6. *Calculating the Financial Implications and Risks*

The financial implications of a short-term strategy should be assessed *during the process itself*, as options are considered, modified, elaborated, or rejected. Financial analysis should attempt to capture the main financial consequences of various alternatives, and not be so carefully computed that there is only time to consider the consequences of *one* championed proposal. Having even a rough idea of the financial consequences at hand is one of the most important yardsticks that business unit management and top management can use to debate the pros and cons of various options. Today, simple spreadsheet analysis has largely replaced the proverbial "back of the envelope," but the underlying intention is the same—namely the presentation of the essential financial consequences, so that several broad possibilities can be evaluated for each high potential segment.

These "interim" financial analyses usually must cover three essential points:

1. Projections of costs, revenues, and hence contribution margins and profits. As noted in Chapters 9 and 10, working on a "contribution" basis is infinitely preferable, at this stage, to the assessment of cost of goods sold and gross margins. It allows the effects of different volume assumptions to be quickly reflected in the calculation of profitability.

2. Projections of various investment and liability items to see the effect of a strategy on the balance sheet as well as on the income statement.

3. Projections of cash flow—and particularly cash requirements if the strategy is investment intensive.

Once these checks are made and the strategy has been refined through a process of several iterations of substeps 1 to 5, two tasks remain.

First, a series of "what if" questions must be asked. The world of competitive markets is, above all, unpredictable. What if our revenue assumptions are off by 10 percent, 20 percent, 50 percent? What if we do not achieve the cost levels that have been projected? What if our main competitor introduces a dramatically different new product in the course of the year? What if there is another major oil crisis? What if our main alliance partner terminates his agreement with us?

Of course, it is very easy to get bogged down in "what if" questions. Rapid computing and easy-to-do spreadsheet analysis tempt us to look at every possible permutation and combination of events and their consequences. This is a mistake. "Analysis paralysis" then sets in and drives out action. What *is* required is to develop an intuitive understanding of the factors that might truly make a real difference to effective accomplishment of our plans, and to understand the magnitude of the variations in performance if these events were actually to occur.

Second, and *lastly* in the financial qualification of strategy, a *budget* must be prepared. Budget preparation is not only the final task, but also the easiest, relatively speaking. Curiously, it takes on a complicated life of its own in many companies. Precision to several decimal points, complex allocation schemes, and unfounded forecasts and projections of costs, revenues, and investments can drown out rigorous strategic analysis. Budget preparation too early in the strategic process not only rules out the consideration of important strategic options but puts strategic decision making in the wrong office—in the accounting department instead of the office of the general manager.

SOME EXAMPLES IN PRACTICE

To complete this chapter, we shall review three examples of companies that faced the task of pinpointing their current opportunities to better master the present. These companies all faced the same challenge: in addition to thinking about the future, what could they do now to make the *current* business as successful as possible? All of these examples are more than a decade old, yet the issues are as alive today as they were then.

Scott-Air Corporation[13] is a disguised but real U.S. based organization competing in the central air conditioning market with giants such as Carrier, General Electric, and Sears. Scott confronted two main problems: its 4 percent market share was considered too small to be an effective competitor; and this share of the business meant that Scott was operating at only about 30 percent of its full manufacturing capacity. With high costs and no clear competitive distinction except some superior heat-pump technology, Scott's future was cloudy. A positive aspect was, however, Scott's corporate management investment philosophy. *If* a satisfactory strategy could be formulated, corporate funds could be made available—albeit at a very high rate of return.

An analysis of Scott's market revealed diverse possibilities for segmentation: by geographic region, since air conditioning usage patterns vary widely with climate; by type of product, the main ones being year-round heating and cooling units versus cooling only; and by end-user market. This latter breakdown showed substantial differences in needs, in the bases for competition, and in key success factors in four segments: new private construction, renovation and remodeling (R&R), replacement, and "commercial." Scott had established a much stronger position in the R&R and replacement segments than it had in either new construction or commercial buildings. Scott's main competitors, General Electric and Carrier, together accounted for nearly 35 percent of the new construction business.

Scott's management wondered how and whether the company could lower costs to compete effectively, and build its share in what was a rapidly developing overall market. In trying to pinpoint its current opportunities, two points became very clear: first, there was no way that Scott, with a small share and substantially lower total "experience," could compete with GE, Carrier, or any other majors on cost; secondly, pricing and customer relations with large developers were key success factors for competing in the new construction business. Scott's only hope was to build on its areas of strength—namely to focus much more explicitly on the R&R and replacement business. In these segments "push," through distributors and dealers, is the key to success.

This strategic conclusion led to a whole series of decisions regarding functional policies and actions, as well as policies and actions relating the firm with its channels of distribution. Scott's dealer network needed a complete overhaul, with some ineffective dealers needing to be dropped and new dealers added; merchandising needed improvement, particularly with respect to putting field inventories in place in dealer storerooms, and sales efforts needed to be redefined to provide a "sell through" rather than "sell to" competence. Costs needed to be lowered, but since price in these chosen segments was not a determining key success factor—dealer reputation being much more important—Scott could live with its inherently higher cost structure.

This case nicely demonstrates that without making *fundamental* changes in its inventory of capabilities, but rather by better pinpointing its current opportunities, Scott had a chance of carving out a respectable position in the overall central air conditioning business. What was needed was to recognize existing strengths and weaknesses relative to requirements in each segment, and aim specifically for those segments where existing strengths could be deployed. With this decision made, weaknesses could be minimized and areas of strength further reinforced.

The second example involves a company which we shall also refer to by its disguised name "Tex-Fiber Industries.[14] Tex-Fiber, together with two other major competitors, controlled some 65 percent of the world's "petroloid products" (also a disguised term) business. However, it came in a fairly distant second to "Standard American," the world market leader who had 35 percent of the business, compared with Tex-Fiber's 20 percent.

The segmentation exercise in this case also revealed many different ways to cut the market cake—by product, market, customer type, and specialty versus commodity business, to name but a few.

But it was apparent in this industry that competitors had very different competitive positions along two main dimensions: in different world geographic markets, and in three main areas of business—the commodity-like "oils" business; the "petro-rubbers" business, and the speciality FAS (foams, adhesives, and sealants) business.

Tex-Fiber had the strongest position in the specialty end of the business in the United States, and was weaker internationally and in the high-volume, low-price commodity ends of the business where its competitor held in apparently impregnable position. Of particular importance in this case is that Tex-Fiber's *corporate* management was demanding that the division produce cash returns for reinvestment elsewhere in the textile business (Tex-Fiber Petroloids Division was a relative anomaly in that it dealt with chemicals in a large diversified company dealing otherwise exclusively with textile activities). Its main competitor Standard American had, by contrast, 76 percent of its *total* corporate business in petroloids, and was reported to be considering large future investments, rather than divestments, in this sector.

Tex-Fiber's options were obviously limited. It is easy to rule out head-to-head competition in large-volume international markets. But what is less obvious, without going step-by-step through the methodology suggested in this chapter, is whether Tex-Fiber could find a niche in the overall market that would at the same time allow it to satisfy its corporate owners' needs for cash, while maintaining or even building on its position in an area of strength. The FAS segment, and speciality segments of both petro rubbers and even oils do in fact provide such a competitive niche, both in the United States as well as selective European markets. Tex-Fiber's problem was not so much changing, as *identifying* where its current "fit" was the most effective, and then focusing all of its attention on these areas.

The third example is an undisguised one. Gould Graphics was a division of a larger high technology manufacturing company.[15] The Graphics Division developed, in its laboratories, a new high-speed computer printing device using technology that had originated in a quite different area—medical recording devices.

Like many "technology driven" companies, Gould developed

the new printing device without initially making a very thorough investigation of potential markets. The product was actually well on the way to prototype testing before the first serious market investigation was undertaken. Management, spurred on by Gould's engineers, were convinced that high-speed computer printers would satisfy important so far unsatisfied needs, and that buyers would "beat a path to their door" once the new technology was introduced.

The truth turned out to be very different. In fact, although Gould's new printer had some clear strengths, it also had important weaknesses in each and every segment where it was to be introduced. Some were correctable with relatively minor design modifications; others were more intractable. Gould's problem turned out not to be so much a technical one as one of pinpointing exactly where its product might fit best in a very complex "patchwork" of segments and subsegments—and redressing weaknesses and reinforcing strengths to allow it to target these.

That is the nature of pinpointing current opportunities. *Every* company faces similar challenges in trying to perform well in the present. But mastering the present, while necessary, is not sufficient. The future has to be looked after too. This is the equally daunting challenge to which we turn in the two chapters that follow.

CHAPTER 12

AGENDAS FOR CHANGE

$\mathbf{H}_{\bullet}$ G. Wells said of Gladstone, Britain's charismatic late nine-teenth-century Liberal Prime Minister:

> Gladstone did not remain set in a course of pure conservatism, he presently began to realize the strength of the stream upon which things were being carried forward; his intelligence . . . set itself to grasp the real forms of the torrents of change about him.[1]

This is a quite different mode of enquiry than that described in Chapter 11, where we were trying to see how best to exploit capabilities already in hand. Gladstone was presumably trying to define the shape of things to come—by comprehending the essential features of the far-reaching political, social, technological, and economic changes that were swirling around him at the time. But presumably also, this was no idle "crystal ball" gazing—his need to comprehend derived from his need to act—to lay the right foundations for Britain's future.

The present planning described in Chapter 11 is necessary but not sufficient—just as for Gladstone being concerned with Britain's current opportunities was presumably necessary but not sufficient. Companies that brilliantly pinpoint today's opportunities can, and do, fail catastrophically if they are not getting ready for tomorrow at the same time. Success today produces the cash flow and momentum to enable preparation for the future; making the *right* preparations for the future maximizes the chances for future success when the time comes.

Scientists still ponder the reasons for the extinction of the dinosaur. Was there a climate change to which it did not adapt? Was there a massive and sudden crisis in the form of a meteorite striking the earth? Or did it just become too ponderous to survive? Analogously we may ask why some of yesterday's great corporations now face extinction also—are these dinosaurs of the business world doomed to the same fate? And what might they have done in terms of laying the proper foundations to avoid it?

In the 1960s, A&P was one of America's oldest, and certainly most prestigious, food retailer chains.[2] It had the largest market share; it was very profitable and it had an excellent balance sheet. Its *current* performance was incontestable. By the early 1970s, it was no longer the largest chain; it was barely profitable; and in spite of rescue by a German company, it had to close 40 percent of its stores. By the 1980s, A&P had ceased to be a significant force in food retailing.

A&P's underlying problem was that it failed to respond aggressively enough to new important trends in the food retailing industry—increased store sizes, discounting, the rise of "fast foods," and the importance of market share city-by-city and suburb-by-suburb.

The Swiss watch industry also came close to being a dinosaur. From a position of world leadership in the 1950s and 1960s, both market share and reputation slid dramatically. By the 1980s, the industry as a whole had become very unprofitable, and there were massive layoffs and plant closures.

The Swiss watch industry had basically refused to confront several basic changes—the shift from a cottage industry to mass production, the shift from jewelry store distribution to drugstores, supermarkets, and discounters, and the shift from mechanical movements to electronics. While others were making profits and market share gains, Swiss watchmakers were reassuring themselves that the new competitors didn't have a product worth worrying about: "If it wasn't sold through a jeweler, it just wasn't a watch!" Only with the introduction of Swatch has the situation finally been turned around.

A further example of failure to adapt is provided by a bank—and not just any bank! In fact, in the late 1970s, Bank of America was the world's largest bank. In addition, it was very profitable. Deposits gathered from nearly 1,000 California branches provided a cheap source of funds for worldwide lending. The stock was selling above $30.

By the late 1980s, Bank of America was no longer the world's largest—in fact it could not even be counted among the world's top ten. It suffered the largest loss ever for a U.S. bank, and its bond rating had been reduced. The stock was selling for only $14.

Bank of America responded to some of its new challenges—but too slowly. The Californian retail banking business had become highly competitive, with substantial "in-fighting" between foreign banks, savings and loans, out-of-state banks, and other new forms of financial institution who were entering the banking business. There was, in addition, a growing importance of electronic retail banking, and the application of advanced computer technology systems. Banking was becoming nationwide as deregulation allowed broadened competition.

While A&P, Swiss watchmakers, and Bank of America fared badly, other companies—even in the same industry segments— fared much better. In food retailing, well-situated "hypermarkets" were coming of age to accommodate the different shopping patterns of the suburban shopper on the one hand, while more focused specialty food chains were appearing on the other; in watches and in banking the lead was being taken by Japanese firms. But in many other industries, completely new domestic and foreign enterprises were springing up to replace the old dinosaurs—doing business in new ways to answer new needs. These newcomers, often seen initially as "upstarts" by established firms, simply defined their businesses differently! Swatch was one of these; Benetton, Apple, Sony, IKEA, and Canon were among many others. As Tom Peters suggests so aptly with the title of one of his recent books, some firms "thrive on chaos."[3] But as we see, others fall apart!

What distinguishes these two kinds of organization, and even more importantly from our point of view, what can we do to raise the chances of thriving rather than becoming another extinct species when confronted with substantial change?

That leadership and overall organizational flexibility play an important role, there can be no doubt—but are these enough? In times of change, some organizations seem to have more problems envisioning their future than others; and some, even with vision, cannot cope with the process of change itself.

In fact, we see in organizations all the ailments that affect the human eye. Twenty-twenty sight is a standard that few organizations achieve. Shortsightedness, that is, the ability to focus only on what is close at hand, is common. Long sight is rare, but even when present it can sometimes be lethal when it is not combined with a healthy respect for the present. Blurred vision is frequent both for near- and longer-term views; and many companies are apt to see the future through rose-colored glasses.

To bring things into focus in the long term as well as in the short term requires more than shrewd leadership and organizational flexibility. It requires *eyes* and *brains* at each organizational vantage point—people who like Gladstone can grasp the real forms of the torrents of change about them. Let us look in more depth therefore at the forms these changes take in practice, where they are registered within the organization, and how managements cope with them. As in Chapter 2, I draw heavily here on the experience of a number of leading multinationals who were the main subjects of study for this part of the book.

HOW SOME LARGE MULTINATIONALS VIEW THE FUTURE

Contrary to most conventional wisdom, and writing, about the subject, the top managers whom I studied were rarely worried about changes that might take place in the *future*. They could not worry much about these since they simply didn't know much about what might come along! What they were worried about were changes that had *already* taken place, to which the firm had not adapted, or changes *currently underway*, whose true form and impact were difficult to assess. In almost all cases, firms were also attempting to make a number of *internal* changes, not because of any specific external stimulus but because they knew that their current setup was far short of optimum. These three change agendas can be summarized as follows:

1. The "world" *changed;* we didn't yet and we must

2. The "world *is changing;* we must also change

3. We are *off base* in this or that area; we must improve

Only rarely is there in practice much attention to the fourth type of agenda—which conventional wisdom assumes is primordial:

4. The "world" *will change;* we must change to *prepare* for it.

All of these four agendas for change are felt at key organizational
vantage points—at the corporate level; at the division or business
unit level; at the segment level; and by each functional department.
Change is not the sole preserve of top management, nor indeed of
general management. In fact, since change appears to be as concerned with staying abreast or even just catching up with events as
it does with anticipating the future, it turns out to be everybody's
business. And lower-level "everybodys" are often more knowl-
edgeable about events that have transpired or are transpiring than
top management, who are often more isolated from the day-to-day
business. In this respect those companies that denominate the future as primarily a top management responsibility would seem
most prone to failure.

What then, for the multinationals that were studied in depth, are
the driving forces that cause change, and what do they specifically
concentrate on when it comes to change itself? While these companies varied substantially in the particularities of their industry and
general environment, and in the specifics of the challenges they confronted, there were some common threads in their responses. To a
greater or lesser degree, all of the companies were tackling three
main areas of change:

- organizational change
- redefinition of activities
- building capabilities for the future

These changes manifested themselves differently and varied in importance from company to company and from one organizational
level to another within a company. In some companies there appeared to be a strong interrelationship between the strategic redefinition of activities, the building of new capabilities and organizational change; in others this was less apparent.

Change at Nestlé

At Nestlé as we have seen in Chapter 2, the driving forces for
change were partly internal and partly external. An increasingly diversified product line was putting new demands on market management; some new products were getting insufficient attention; a

doubling in overall size in the previous decade was testing existing management structures; and pressures for region-wide and even global marketing integration were calling into question the traditionally decentralized powers of zone and market management.

Nestlé's organizational response, after much deliberation, was to rebalance the roles of functional, zone, market, and "business" (product line) management. Profit responsibility was retained in the individual country markets, but at the same time the responsibilities of "business" (product line) management at the center were broadened and augmented. Charged previously with mainly staff marketing responsibilities, product line management now began to take on responsibility for the total business plan and its implementation. One result was that central corporate functions would become more "demand-driven" than before, that is, driven by the requirements of each individual product or business area. Some Nestlé managers questioned whether these organizational changes, substantial as they were, went far enough. Reflecting on the option of giving product division management profit responsibility as well as enlarged management responsibilities, R. F. Domeniconi, Nestlé's executive vice president for finance, stated:

> One good reason would be that only one good person would be needed instead of two—we now need a person for both markets and products. But it is part of Nestlé's culture to evolve; not to make revolutionary changes.

Domeniconi also questioned whether the heavy emphasis or *structural* change was altogether appropriate. He noted:

> To get excellence, the greatest source of untapped resources is from middle management down. But people play the old games: knowledge is power; and initiatives get blocked. Although I don't believe that human beings are always good per se, in the last two decades people seem increasingly to want to do things individually. It means giving up some of our controls and using other checks and balances. We need management systems which encourage people using "natural inclinations" to go in the right direction.
>
> At Nestlé there is more concern for structure; the human processes are often thought to be more esoteric. The current power structure is anyway not impregnated with these ideas. Key top management is

more conventional, more structural in their thinking—although one
or two of our younger people think more this way. As a result we still
achieve some balance in our thinking.

In addition to organizational change, Nestlé continued to redefine
the overall corporate scope of its activities through merger and acquisition activity. Mergers and acquisitions had always been important to Nestlé—starting with the merger of Anglo-Swiss Condensed
Milk Co. and Farine Lacteé Henri Nestlé in 1905, brands such as
Cailler, Cross and Blackwell, Findus, Libby, Stouffer, L'Oréal (with
a monetary participation), Alcon, and Chambourcy were added
progressively over the next seventy years. But in the 1980s and early
1990s, Nestlé redoubled its M&A activity, resulting in the addition
of such brands as Carnation, Buitoni-Perugina, Rowntree, and Perrier. These acquisitions will certainly play a key role, in terms of
both brand reputation and internal resources and capabilities, in
carrying Nestlé into the next millennium.

A third leg of corporate level change may be placed under the
general heading of building corporate competences for the future.
One manifestation of this is Nestlé's overall approach to R&D. By
not breaking R&D into a series of smaller activities managed market-by-market or business-by-business, Nestlé retains a worldwide
overview. Technology developed for one product can easily be
used in another. Several "core technological competences" such as
freeze-drying, extrusion processes, and energy saving are therefore
retained at the corporate level. Nestlé managers pointed also, however, to the building of corporate *managerial* competences—including quality control procedures, information technology management, and reporting and control procedures.

Vertical relationships were also seen as an area of special competence. Although Nestlé eschews direct ownership of either upstream suppliers or downstream distribution, it builds very close
links with both. One manager remarked:

> We have hundreds of people around the world working with dairy
> farmers; we have been working on soya research in India for twenty-
> five years; via Findus we have a big influence on pea production, and
> cooperatives strictly follow our guidelines. Ownership is not the
> most important factor; it is the relationship that counts.

Several Nestlé managers, when asked to describe their vision of how they saw Nestlé's future distinctive competences, focused on the more general problem of how the company would maintain its competitive differentiation in the future. One remarked:

> The days when one could keep a technological or product advantage for several years are over! If you can keep it for one year you should be happy. So you have to forget about going slowly and deliberately into the market in a classic "roll-out." In reality you have to be different and quick, and prepare for the onslaught from competition. The timeframe is compressed. It is better to be there with something fast than to be 100 percent perfect. The challenge is to act. The corporation as a whole has to find ways to integrate its various processes and functional activities to speed up.
>
> We all have the same data bases; we all have similar resources; we all have the same kinds of people; even the leaders are more similar than they were in the past. So corporate differentiation has to come from our history, our corporate culture, and our vision of what is going on in the world.

All of these comments on corporate level change point to the same conclusion. At Nestlé there is a relatively clear consensus on what the challenges are. Many of these are already visible—at least in outline form. The goal is to achieve consensus on the corporation's responses. In terms of strategic definition of its business via acquisition and merger, Nestlé's vision and ability to realize it seem incontestable; in terms of organizational structure, the company is on the way to realizing an important evolutionary step; in terms of building tangible internal competences and external relationships, Nestlé's record is strong. Most of the outstanding questions raised by management concern not strategy, structure, or specific competences, but the much less tangible processes and culture change, which some feel will be the most important keys to the future.

Nestlé is also engaged in a myriad of change agendas below the level of corporate headquarters. These included both "organizational improvement" projects related to individual zones and markets, as well as projects aimed at improving specific aspects of operations. One of the largest was the "reconfiguration" of Nestlé's roughly three hundred European manufacturing plants to better service the needs of the new more integrated European market. Like the corporate level changes, these projects nearly all appeared to aim at adapting to changes that had either already occurred or were in the process of occurring, rather than anticipating as yet un-identified future changes.

Sometimes changes at the individual market or business level have been quite far-reaching—bearing little resemblance to the shorter-term "pinpointing of current opportunities." Such a change occurred in the Spanish market. After Franco's death, and the over-all turn in Spain's internal political economy, the decision was made to undertake a basic shift in Nestlé's practices in its Spanish market. The most basic change was described by Nestlé management as combining a shift from sales to marketing, the imbuing of a much greater "fighting spirit" into the organization, and an overall shift from a company run by faith to a company run by conviction."

One member of Nestlé's top management identified four ele-ments considered essential to the success of "change projects" tak-ing place beyond corporate headquarters:

–the *visible* commitment of top management

–a common language, and common thinking, of top manage-ment on the main issues

–involvement of key managers in the decision process itself

–clear transmission of the ideas further *down* the particular or-ganization involved.

The actual mechanisms used, whether it be a task force, project team, or individually led effort, were felt to be less important than the above.

Changes at Caterpillar

At Caterpillar, the main driving force for change was a change in its market—the declining relative importance of large earth-moving machines in contrast to smaller, lighter, and more versatile ma-chines for a wide variety of construction, municipal, and industrial uses. This shift in the market coincided with the entrance of new competitors—a principal one being Komatsu—redefining the nature of the business in accordance with the new requirements for less expensive, less robustly-engineered and more flexible solutions in many new segments. Caterpillar's traditional strengths—an exceptional dealer network, outstanding parts and service support, and well-engineered but relatively expensive products, all under the Caterpillar brand—were not necessarily seen as strengths in some of the new emerging markets.

Caterpillar responded in all three areas—organizational, strategic, and in building new competences; it combined responses at the corporate, regional, business unit, and dealer levels:

As pointed out in Chapter 2, Caterpillar had made a strategic decision to grow in traditional *and* new markets—but this still left two big unanswered questions: first, how to capitalize on Caterpillar's traditional strengths in new segments where the quality/cost tradeoffs were fundamentally different than in their existing business; and second, how to redesign distribution for such products as small machines and power systems, while retaining the strength of the existing dealer network. While the end may have been clear for Caterpillar, the path to achieve it was less so.

Organizational change to support this new strategy was taking place at corporate and regional levels. At the corporate level, thirteen profit centers corresponding to geographic and product or user segments were established. At the European region level (Caterpillar Overseas S.A.—COSA), the structural reorganization into profit centers representing key lines of business actually preceded headquarters changes. But according to Sig Ramseyer, managing director, although Caterpillar was *structurally* different than before the change, it still had not yet moved much to reduce levels of hierarchy, make changes in management, and focus on key strategic issues. Like Nestlé, it seems Caterpillar is relatively more adept at changing organizational structures than it is at changing organizational processes.

On the competence dimension, Caterpillar's primary emphasis appeared to be on changing its cost structure. Some $2 billion was being invested in new manufacturing technology with one of its main objectives being the reduction of costs. But distribution cost reduction, in parallel with the maintenance of product support and service levels, was also a key target.

At other levels, change at Caterpillar was no less dramatic. The dealer view, according to Ramseyer, was fairly straightforward:

> They want quality, timely products—and say they can look after the rest themselves. They complain when there is insufficient R&D, slowness, or quality problems. Often if the right product is not there for a segment, they "manufacture" it themselves via attachments, or they source it somewhere else.

According to Ramseyer, Caterpillar dealers were often in the vanguard of change:

> Dealers increasingly have young executives with new ideas, willing to think of new ways to do business. But they have to convince the "old guard" who still have important decision-making responsibility at the top.

Caterpillar's Power Systems Division provides a good example of the kinds of issues raised by change at the business unit level. At this level too, there were three main focuses—organizational change, strategic change, and competence building for the future. But in this case, strategic change was on the leading edge, and new competences were being envisioned to implement the new thrust. Organizational change was apparent, but not central.

The Power System's vision of its own future started with a vision of where the market as a whole appeared to be going. As J. A. Dörig, manager for the Power Systems business put it, "We have a clear vision of the near future; a half-clear vision of the medium term; and 'dreams to be clarified' for the long term."

Caterpillar had originally entered the engine business in the late 1960s—later creating the Power Systems Division for engines in the size range of 100–7000 HP. The engine industry was characterized by increasing consolidation and mergers, as was Caterpillar's diesel truck business where a lot of products were sold. Dörig's view in early 1991 was:

> The moment to get into the Euro-truck business is *now*—before truck mergers lead companies to build their own engine plants. Advanced

R&D for low emission city buses is another area. Our division can pilot some new approaches, for example in distribution, for the whole company, without putting everything at risk.

Dörig's strategic vision for the business was heavily influenced by the fact that Caterpillar's share was still small, in spite of technological leadership in some key areas. His strategic vision can be summarized as follows:

–concentration where Caterpillar had traditional strength— 250 HP engines and up

–a redefinition of the business. Dörig observed: "Customers increasingly want total solutions, ecologically friendly solutions, and lifetime 'bonuses,' including product guarantees. It is not enough for us to supply the engine and forget about it—we must look at the whole system."

–doubling of volume in the next five years, as in the preceding five years.

It is noteworthy that this strategic vision was not based on guesses about *future* changes in customer buying behavior; it was based on changes that were already evident and had apparently been evident for some time.

The strategic vision had broad implications for the resources and new competences that would be needed. A crucial feature was distribution, where Caterpillar was already encouraging its dealers to split out the engine business from the main Caterpillar dealerships. It also included a vision of the type of people that would be needed—the more complex and technical the business, the more the need for "professionalism" and skill training in engineering and product support services.

Dörig was also envisioning a different organizational approach. As he put it, "We are engineering a better, more focused organization—more flexible than hierarchical." But the details of this change apparently remained to be worked out—presumably still a "dream to be clarified."

Change at Schering

At Schering A. G., change was apparently internally driven. Its focus was mainly strategic, rather than organizational or competence building—although these would certainly follow.

Schering had traditionally operated with five major divisional activities, of which pharmaceuticals, representing 54 percent of the total sales, was by far the largest, followed by agrochemicals. In 1991, Schering decided it only had sufficient management and financial resources to compete in two areas, namely pharmaceuticals and agrochemicals, with an emphasis on the former. An attempt at a joint venture with Sandoz in agrochemicals failed when Sandoz set as a condition a parallel participation in the pharmaceutical area—an area where Schering believed it could go it alone.

Schering was further defined within pharmaceuticals as a niche player—concentrating on small markets with special medical needs, high R&D inputs, and high margins. Its main agenda for change appears to have been to reinforce this overall strategic niche positioning, and to decide specifically where and where not to compete in the future.

Change at Heineken

At Heineken, three main driving forces appear to have been at work in the early 1990s: first, the recognition of changing views and habits concerning alcohol consumption; second, the perception that the international beer business would be dominated by a few major international brands as beer suppliers increasingly consolidated; and third, an internal driver—the shift from a long history of family-dominated management to professional management by "outsiders."

These forces were resulting at Heineken in a strategic redefinition of the business, from a beverage company with an accent on beer, to a beer company with varying beer products. Furthermore, the new strategy called for brand leadership worldwide with a few key brands—Heineken ("the jewel in the crown"), Amstel, and Buckler (low alcohol beer).

But at Heineken, organizational change was taking the main share of management attention in late 1990 and early 1991. We have already described in Chapter 2 the changing nature of the management board's responsibilities in line with an increasingly centralized approach to global markets. But it also included a long list of other projects. Task forces were working, among other things, on:

–defining new relationships between operating companies and the center

–shaping the new central marketing function

–shaping the new production function

–shaping the new finance function

–building consistent internal data systems

–restructuring the cost accounting system

–developing a new European client relations structure

–improving internal communication

This list, which is only partial, gives a flavor for the organizational upheaval that Heineken had embarked on. Country managers were seen as critical to the change process—mainly because of their changing roles vis-à-vis headquarters. All communications concerning change had to pass through them, and the whole project was coordinated overall by Ray Van Schaik, Heineken's chief executive.

I shall not dwell in detail on change at the other six companies that were studied, although these were no less dramatic or interesting. Every one of these was engaged in a major process of change which entailed new organizational, strategic, and competence-building initiatives. In each case, however, the main focus of attention was somewhat different, and the form of the changes varied considerably. While some companies, like Nestlé, were further diversifying their portfolio of activities; others, more like Schering, were increasingly focusing on one or only a few core businesses. Some companies were increasing the role of the corporate center at the expense of country management, to recognize the importance of global markets and global marketing approaches; others, like Caterpillar, were decentralizing. Some were busy trying to build new technical capabilities; others were focusing more on human resources; some were concerned with internal resources, while others were busy entering alliances and other forms of close working relationships with suppliers and channels to secure external capabilities. All had active programs of change at various levels, including corporate, business, and country organizational levels.

Change at Sulzer

The Swiss machinery manufacturer Sulzer provides a particularly clear view of the three processes going on in parallel: a major redefinition and focusing of the corporate portfolio; a parallel organizational shift from a multiproduct industrial company with a large central staff to a "strategic holding"; and a clear focus on the building of a few key areas of corporate competence. None of the companies studied provided such a comprehensive view of how the three processes are actually closely related and integrated.

Changes in these three areas were not new at Sulzer. Starting in 1975, attempts had been to streamline the broadly diversified product portfolio, reduce current assets (particularly working capital), and overhaul the relatively "heavy" corporate decision-making apparatus. A long-term vision was in the first phases of formulation in the late 1980s, but a "raid" launched on Sulzer by an outsider distracted top management and delayed events by at least a year. The arrival of a new CEO, Fritz Fahrni, in 1987 provided the momentum for the changes to be concretized—and set into motion.

On the strategic side, the company considered three options to halt the long slide in overall profitability:

– "regrouping" of the business units

– further diversification with the eventual objective of becoming a "financial holding" company

– focusing on fewer business areas with some common key capabilities, and halting diversification completely for five to seven years

A combination of the first and third options was chosen, and Sulzer's existing twenty-seven product divisions were classified into three groups:

–"pillar businesses" (with high profit and strong market positions)

–growth businesses

–turnaround businesses

Turnaround businesses were given two to three years to return to profitability, and otherwise were divested. The longer-term objective was to expand from two to four "pillar" businesses and to have enough growth businesses to create several future pillars. By 1991, the twenty-seven product divisions had been reduced to fourteen major product groups.

The strategic changes described above were paralleled by a number of important organizational and process changes. These included:

1. Reduction in central staff to about 80–100 people (from more than 800 before). The corporate headquarters supported the business units in four major areas: human resource management, technology development, international marketing, and finance.

2. Enlargement of the decision-making powers of the president vis-à-vis the corporate executive management—a previously all-powerful internal "executive committee."

3. Reduction of decision-making responsibility on the country side of the matrix, coupled with augmentation of responsibilities on the product division/business unit side. As a result, Sulzer International, the company's international marketing arm, became more of a marketing service organization.

The third key area of corporate attention was on building "core skills" (as they were called at Sulzer headquarters) in the four areas where the corporation had decided to provide support to individual business units: technology/R&D (with a special focus on materials technology, vibration technology, fluid dynamics, and acoustics); human resources management; international marketing; and finance and administration. The "old" core skills of manufacturing and engineering, which had been heavily represented in the previous central staff, were decentralized to the divisional level. In each of the four core skill areas, corporate management increasingly took the lead in making investments above and beyond what each individual business might do.

Sulzer top management used both inside and outside sources to continually develop this long-term vision of required core competences at the center. On the outside these included relationships with local universities, individual contacts with experts, advisory groups, and many other mechanisms. To get business unit management to "buy in" to the process of corporate-level capability development Sulzer ran a series of seminars entitled "Tools Used at the Corporate Level," involving corporate- and business-level executives. Participants were expected to put themselves in the shoes of corporate management, and to take a broader view of Sulzer's capabilities and their development—reinforcing the concept of a "strategic holding" as opposed to simply a "financial holding."

In early 1991 Sulzer's president, Fritz Fahrni, commented on the change process at the divisional level as follows:

> Few divisions yet have a long-term vision of their business analogous to the long-term vision existing at the corporate level. But most if not all have a workable "mid-range" strategic plan.
>
> One factor promoting the need for future visions at the business level, above and beyond these mid-term plans, is the rising identification of employees with the individual businesses rather than Sulzer as a whole. This is coming about as we move to a more decentralized and global business environment.

Sulzer illustrates not only the three-legged process of getting ready for the future, but the parallel need—going under the label of "mid-range planning"—to have a strategic approach to the present as well.

CHAPTER 13

PREEMPTING THE FUTURE

The preceding chapter was largely descriptive in character—illustrating what large multinationals seem actually to be doing. But what can we conclude from these experiences which might provide the basis for a more generalizable approach? While a precise "methodology" of the kind suggested in Chapter 11 for pinpointing current opportunities is not as easy to define, some general analytical principles can nonetheless be formulated.

VISION

This frequently used word too often lacks precision when it comes to managing change. Does it mean a vision of the future business and competitive environment in which the firm will find itself? Or the future approaches the firm should follow? Or the way to go from where we are today to where we would like to be in the future? Does it apply to the situation one year from now, three to five years from now, or ten to twenty years from now? And how does the word "vision" differ, if at all, from the words "mission," "strategy," and "plan"?

The research underlying this section of the book suggests that managerial vision can be manifested in at least *five* different ways, and that the word "vision" takes on a somewhat different meaning as we look from different organizational vantage points.

1. A Vision of the Situation

As noted earlier, this vision results from blending three judgments:

    a. judgment about events that have *already transpired*, which *have resulted in a gap* between the firm's actual and desired position

b. judgment about events that are *currently unfolding,* which are *creating a gap* between the firm's actual and desired position

c. judgment about events that *may unfold* in the future, and which *would create a gap* between the firm's actual and desired position

Based on the ten companies studied, but also on previous experience with many others, visions of the situation into which the firm is headed are *heavily* influenced by recognition of past and present changes, and only lightly influenced by guesses about the future. This simply underlines the fact that most firms react to change rather than anticipating it. Competitive advantage, contrary to the conventional wisdom, seems to depend on who can react faster rather than who is the most farsighted. Obviously the two are not totally unrelated, since those who think ahead are also those who are best prepared to change when the time comes. But the weight seems to be as much on good hindsight as it does on good foresight. Nestlé's vision of its future situation was heavily influenced by its comprehension of the effects of *past* growth and diversification, and by the input of *current* changes going on in global markets; Caterpillar's vision of its situation was influenced by competitive changes towards smaller machines that had already been going on for a decade; and Heineken was apparently extrapolating trends that were already discernible.

A vision of the future situation is dependent on managements' ability to recognize and interpret *patterns*—and to relate what they are seeing to other analogous situations. This is not to say that history will repeat itself exactly, but it is always worthwhile to ask "What's similar, and what's different" in this situation relative to others.

The future situation can also best be understood if the underlying *driving forces* for change, and not only change itself, are identified. Many of these driving forces were reviewed in Chapter 5 under the heading "Markets in Motion." They range from technology change to overall shifts in the economic, political, and social context, to industry-specific drivers such as the blurring of industry boundaries, loss of competitive uniqueness, change in customer behavior, and the globalization of some product markets. Poor performance

itself can be a driving force for change, but by the time it is registered, the situation may be serious and changes long overdue.

2. Strategic Vision

Strategic vision takes a substantially different form at the corporate
level than it does at the individual business or country level.

At the *corporate* level, strategic vision appears to be concerned
mainly with the future shape of the corporate portfolio, and how it
is to be managed. How much corporate diversification should there
be? What relationships should there be among the various business
units, and what is the "raison d'être" of the corporation overall.
Should the resulting portfolio be managed as a "strategic holding"
of related or semirelated units (as Sulzer envisions it), as a more
tightly knit worldwide entity (as Heineken appears to be envisioning it), or more as a financial holding (as many other highly diversified companies envision themselves)?

These "high-level" decisions appear to be as much influenced by
managements' intuitive preference and judgments as they are by
concrete analyses. Whatever the process, however, it does produce
strikingly different outcomes and strikingly different visions of
strategic change. While Nestlé is, for example, aggressively diversifying its already impressive collection of leading brands, Sulzer is
narrowing and consolidating its portfolio. Heineken sees its future
linked to just three major brands marketed on a world scale:
Heineken, Amstel, and Buckler.

Some of the other companies studied have equally distinctive,
but contrasting, visions of their future corporate "shape." Swedish-
based Procordia, a highly diversified conglomerate in fields as diverse as food and beverages, pharmaceuticals, tobacco, confectionery, hotels, industrial cleaning, and security systems, provides one
such example. From its origins as a state-owned "holding" which
counted many large ailing companies in its portfolio, Procordia was
transformed during the 1980s into a robust, profitable growth company, with two core business areas—health care and consumer
products—and a loosely defined group of "service" businesses as a
third. Procordia's president at the time of this study, Sören Gyll,
had his own all-encompassing vision of Procordia as a "care" business. He frequently asked his top management collaborators if Pro-

cordia did not already have or could easily acquire the skills to become a "total health care provider" in addition to manufacturing pharmaceuticals. Procordia's strategic vision goes beyond just the makeup of the portfolio of corporate activity—it reaches out for a vision of the basic *mission* of the enterprise. Corporate strategic visions, if Procordia is anything to judge by, evolve over time, rather than being fixed targets—and as the company edges towards its vision step by step, new light is shed on the viability of the vision, the problems of its realization, and on other variations that might be considered.

At the level of an individual business, strategic vision is manifested primarily in terms of how the business might be defined in the future, what its focuses should be in product offerings and customers to target, standards to be achieved, and growth objectives to strive for. This was illustrated clearly by Heineken's general manager for Holland in the case of his vision for the Dutch subsidiary; by Caterpillar's manager of Power Systems in his vision for redefining that business, and by Schering's vision of a niche approach to very specific segments of the world pharmaceutical industry. Line of business strategic vision is not about "shape," but about the basis for customer satisfaction, the basis for sustainable advantage, and longer-term competitive positioning. We should also not forget that strategic vision at the line of business level is concerned with the "vertical" definition of the business. We have seen this earlier in the case of Benetton's vision of its position in the garment industry.

3. A Vision of Resources and Competences Needed

Strategic vision and a vision of needed resources and competences are, or at least should be, closely interrelated. It is indeed hard to say which of these two visions presupposes the other in an ideal sense. Articulating the two visions separately, as most companies seem to do, does at least assure that there is an implicit, if not explicit, check for internal consistency.

At the corporate level, competence *derives* from the scope of the corporate portfolio and synergies between the elements and at the same time plays an important role in *influencing* the shape of the portfolio. Acquisition and merger activity, as well as the building of strategic alliances, are a central part of vision because they affect the shape of the corporate portfolio—or the vertical definition of the business—at the same time that they add to core competences. Perhaps that is why this plays such an important role in most top managers' definitions of their tasks. Through acquisitions, mergers, and alliances, managers have a very direct way not only to realize their visions, but in fact to acquire the competences to realize them as they go along.

Some "core" competences are specifically denominated as being under headquarters purview, while others are envisioned as being under the jurisdiction of individual business units or functions within them. Core technologies with broad application, as well as certain areas of managerial know-how—particularly in the financial, control, information systems, and human resources areas—appear to be important objects of corporate vision when it comes to building for the future.

Although we have used the words "capabilities," "competences," and "resources" somewhat interchangeably, the distinction should be drawn between those preparatory activities that require specific financial outlays and those that do not. Building a new plant, investing in better warehousing, or improving product availability by field inventories are in the former category; so are "discretionary" investments in R&D, advertising, market development and process development. Upgrading managerial know-how and improving processes and procedures may be just as important but do not have such identifiable financial costs. Both must be considered in preparing for the future.

4. A Vision of the Future Organization

Organizational vision combines two separate dimensions—a vision of improved organizational *structures,* and a vision of improved organizational *functioning.* Firms appear to put different weight on these two components of organizational improvement, partly perhaps related to their own corporate culture and the styles and preferences of individual leaders; partly perhaps because of the perceived nature of the organization's present shortcomings. Nestlé was apparently therefore focusing on structural solutions; Caterpillar, while also changing organizational structure, was seeking new processes which would make centralized design and engineering departments more responsive to market forces felt at the individual dealer level.

Organizational *functioning* can encompass processes, systems, corporate culture, and leadership styles, among other things. Any or all of these may affect an organization's ability to be market-oriented, entrepreneurial, creative, and dynamic—terms in which visions for organizational improvement are often expressed.

5. A Vision of How to Proceed

How to get from point A (where we are now) to point B (where we want to go) is a critical aspect of vision. It is analogous to a driver finding his way from point A to point B in a complex maze of city streets. Some drivers conjure up a vision of the city street map as they drive and have a clear picture in their heads of the main turning points, obstacles, and shortcuts along the way. Others, even though they have an equally clear vision of the destination, proceed from street to street much more by trial and error. The former may be said to have a clear vision of the path of change; the latter, lacking such a clear vision of the path, depend much more on signals which are interpreted along the way. If their vision of the destination is also fuzzy, they may go completely off the track!

One important condition for tracing a path from A to B is to know where A as well as B lies! An important part of developing organizational consensus around a vision for the change process itself is therefore to establish consensus about the real nature of the point of departure. This means taking a hard, objective look not only at current performance, but also at everything that lies behind it—the current competitive position, presence or absence of real strategic advantages, and the real strengths and weaknesses underlying these, as described in Chapters 7 and 8.

While companies often appear to emphasize one or a few aspects of these five separate elements of vision, in reality they are all part of a larger whole. None should be singled out for special attention without considering the implications for the other four. Among the ten multinationals that were studied in depth, future visions were expressed quite forcibly and clearly on all of the first four elements—albeit with differing degrees of attention in different companies. Most top managements were also quite realistic in their appraisal of their current situation (point A) as well as the point B they were trying to reach in terms of organization, strategy, and competences. Strikingly, however, few of the top executives interviewed volunteered much in the way of a vision about how to get from A to B. Either they are like the city drivers who proceed from street to street by trial and error, or these are closely guarded corporate secrets. One might perhaps hope for the latter, but the former seems to be a more likely hypothesis!

One of the characteristics of some of the managers interviewed, which obviously helped them navigate their way even in the absence of an overall visual map, was a well-developed instinct for at least looking around the next bend. These managers were able to articulate and then do what was essential—they were ready for obstacles and opportunities that they instinctively knew would be on top of them in a period of a few weeks to a few months. Thus even without an overall map, they were seldom caught completely flatfooted by unexpected twists and turns in their path.

BEHIND VISIONS

In Chapter 11, four broad perspectives were seen to be behind specific choices of segments to pinpoint:

–what *could* be done

–what *can* be done

–what *should* be done

–what management *wants* to do

These same four underlying perspectives also determine future direction—but the constellation is fundamentally changed by the longer horizon involved. The "can do" now becomes a variable— and given time, imagination, and resources, new competences can be built to allow the realization of opportunities which in the short run cannot be contemplated.

The "could do's," that is, the opportunities that exist and might be exploited, are also no longer so fixed or defined. Opportunities can in fact be *created* by an imaginative definition of the business—as Benetton, IKEA, Canon, and others have done, and to at least some extent as Komatsu did in the earth-moving machinery business by taking the lead to open up the market for smaller, lighter, cheaper machines.

Entrepreneurship may be defined as the identification and creation of new opportunities on the one hand, combined with the assembly and management of resources required to do the job on the other. One characteristic of successful entrepreneurs is their ability to work with the resources of others in the accomplishment of their own particular visions. Entrepreneurial management in a corporate setting is no different—it is a matter of defining and creating new opportunities to connect with customers, and defining and building the resources to turn these visions into reality—resources from within but also resources beyond the immediate boundaries of the firm.

With much more flexible definitions in the longer term of what could be done and what can be done, the two other dimensions take a *heightened* importance. What management *wants* to do, and what management believes it *should* do to satisfy long-term, diverse stakeholder interests can become controlling factors in setting long-term directions. Passion and commitment take over from "fit" as the basis for laying the foundations for the future—a future that is less forecasted than "arranged" to suit management's ambitions and stakeholder's interests.

FROM VISIONS TO PLANS TO ACTIONS

No statement better describes the time-dependent nature of vision than that referred to earlier by J. A. Dörig, manager of Power Systems at Caterpillar. It is worth repeating here: "We have a clear vision for the near future; a half-clear vision for the medium term; and 'dreams to be clarified' for the long term."

While dreams may best describe one end of the scale, visions that are concrete enough to serve as the basis for specific plans and actions must describe the other. Visions that cannot be constituted as anything but dreams remain just that. For a vision to be transformed into a plan, three things are required:

–a clear, detailed specification of the starting point

–a clear, detailed specification of the destination

–a clearly formulated set of action steps for moving from the starting point to the destination.

Plans have to be formulated for each of the three main aspects of change, namely, organizational change, strategic change, and the development of new competences within the firm itself, or between the firm and its partners. Although it may sound trivial, a plan to build or acquire technological competences to fit a future strategic vision via outside alliances may itself be a very considerable undertaking. Plans have to be developed for each of the major functions of the business as well as each of the key resource areas—human resources being a critical one.

These plans for acquiring future competences and resources are quite different in character than the functional plans needed to define the role of a particular function in executing the *present* plan. Getting ready for the future implies putting in place the basis for future success; pinpointing today's opportunities is a matter of using as effectively as possible competences and resources already in hand.

Plans are blueprints for moving from A to B. For anything to actually happen, a set of action steps has to be laid out. Actions denote responsibilities and timetables—the *who* and the *when*. Until these are specified and broadly communicated, none of management's visions can actually be achieved.

ANTICIPATORY AND REACTIVE CHANGE; EVOLUTION AND REVOLUTION

As already described, a substantial proportion of the change that companies are engaged in appears to be reactive rather than anticipatory. It also appears to be "evolutionary" as opposed to "revolutionary." There are however exceptions. The following diagram illustrates all four possibilities, of which "normal" adjustment processes are only one:

	Anticipatory change	Reactive change
Revolutionary change	Redefinition of the business	Turnaround
Evolutionary change	Preparatory	Adjustment

Companies like Canon, Apple, and Benetton clearly anticipated the future and redefined the business they were in or entering in a revolutionary way. None of the ten multinationals that were studied could be said to be changing in such an anticipatory or revolutionary way—with the possible exception of Heineken which was clearly anticipating its future and contemplating far-reaching change.

Nor were any of the ten companies faced with what might be classed as a turnaround situation. "Turnaround" implies a relatively sharp and dramatic reversal in the trajectory of the firm—usually because it is in, or at least entering, a period of serious financial crisis. Caterpillar and Sulzer, if they had failed to act when they did, would probably have confronted turnaround conditions within a relatively short period.

By and large, the companies interviewed could all be said to be somewhere between "preparatory change" in anticipation of an emerging change in their environment, or "adjustment" to changes that had already taken place. If these large companies are in any way representative, we must assume that this is characteristic of the way the need for change is registered, how it is experienced, and how it is dealt with. Reactive, evolutionary processes outweigh both anticipation and revolution in getting ready for the future.

Given the fast-changing competitive world we are living in, it is safe to say that for most firms the successful management of reactive and evolutionary change is a minimum condition for success in the future. Failure to evolve continually will certainly confront the firm with a high likelihood of having to confront a more fundamental turnaround at some future date.

But is seems that the surest road to success is to go beyond just evolutionary change, at least in some areas of the corporation's overall activities. Revolutionary change, when well-managed, can redefine standards of customer satisfaction, redefine the basis of competition, redefine key success factors, and redefine the way the firm meets these new requirements. This can provide the competitive distance to secure the current earnings required to prepare for yet future challenges.

PART IV

NEW WAYS TO MANAGE

CHAPTER 14

TURNING THE ORGANIZATION INSIDE OUT AND UPSIDE DOWN

An organizational revolution is taking place. Perhaps we all tend to underestimate it because we are part of it. Living with it everyday, we often fail to register the extent of changes that are going on in organizational structures, processes, systems, and corporate cultures, and in the management of human talent, participation, delegation, and leadership. A revolution is indeed also *required* in many organizations if they are really to master the present while simultaneously transforming themselves for the future. The unfocused, slow-moving, nonadaptive organizations of yesteryear are not particularly effective at running or changing the business, let along doing both simultaneously.

Many attribute this revolution to computer systems, "information technology," and the like, but these are not the real causes; they are only among the means. Behind organizational changes are two fundamental driving forces: the new demands placed on organizations by the more competitive markets they already confront and are likely to confront in the future, and the steadily expanding responsibilities of people at progressively lower levels in the organizational hierarchy—with the result that the very word "hierarchy" no longer fits many organizations.

We shall examine these two driving forces separately at first, then bring them together to understand the nature of several common organizational improvement themes around which change is often sought. These usually require turning the organization not only inside out and upside down as the title of this chapter implies, but also heightening its capacity for "automatic focus" as it constantly has to zoom in and out on the present and future. Whatever the theme, the underlying intent is usually to improve the organization's overall capacity to perform well today and adapt for tomorrow. Finally, we shall look at some very specific organizational choices which enhance a dual approach, namely the assignment of specific roles and responsibilities for present and future.

MARKET INFLUENCES

The years following World War II saw many companies change from functional to divisional structures in response to growing product, market, and geographic diversity. Parenthetically, companies in East and Central Europe were embarking on the same road in the 1990s that their Western counterparts first embarked on nearly half a century earlier—in their bid to develop a much greater responsiveness to the needs of their markets.

Divisionalization proved for most Western companies, however, to be only a first step on the way to being market driven. Many companies found that divisions had been established on the basis of acquisitions or existing plant arrangements, or, as was often the case, because a business had reached a certain specified size limit, and had to be split. Thus these "divisions" did not always have a strategic logic, that is, they were not business units with a well-defined product market and a well-defined set of competitors. In consequence, many companies redivided the corporation into SBUs (strategic business units)—resulting sometimes in the aggregation of previously autonomous units, sometimes in the disaggregation of larger units, and sometimes in a total redefinition of the very basis for divisionalization, for example, from geographic to product-defined units, or from product-defined units to customer-defined units.

Further market-oriented restructuring has been taking place *within* divisions or business units as the struggle for competitive advantage in the marketplace has gathered in intensity. Hand-in-glove with this effort to improve competitive advantage has come increased market segmentation—with each competitor looking for his own particular niche in an ever more complex segmentation patchwork. And segmentation in the market has had its counterpart in segmentation of the organization, as each segment has not only to be separately planned for but also separately managed. So-called "matrix" organizational forms have resulted as functions, product lines, and geographic and customer-defined units increasingly share in the responsibility for overall business success.

Matrix Organizations

Matrix organizations are the inevitable consequence of splitting up the organization in more than one way. The simplest form of organizational matrix occurs when a company is organized simultaneously by functions and product lines—which is often the first step in the *subdivision* of a consumer goods business or division which comprises distinctly different product activities. Figure 14–1 shows the relationship in such a case between product/market strategy and organizational structure.

When a business is best segmented by end-user markets instead of by product, which is often the case in industrial product markets, the situation is exactly analogous—with market management re-

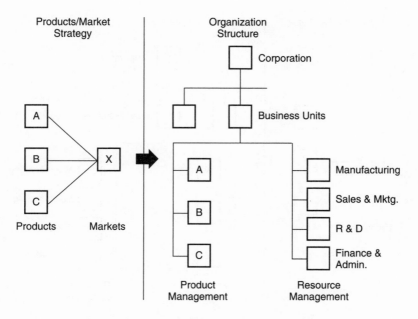

Figure 14–1. Product–Function Matrix Organization

placing product management as the appropriate organizational form. This is shown in Figure 14–2.

The situation becomes more complex when both product and market dimensions of segmentation are important. Such a circumstance occurs often when companies find they need to attend to the needs of a specific market segment while retaining product management. Computer manufacturers like IBM and DEC, recognizing that large computer systems need a different approach than small computer systems, and that banks, local government, educational institutions, and manufacturing industries also need differentiated approaches, are organized this way. The result, known as a bilateral matrix form, is shown in Figure 14–3.

When geography as well as end-user customer segmentation enters the picture, as it does in a multinational, then a trilateral matrix structure can result.

One may ask why functional activities are not subdivided also and simply "attached" to the various product market or geographic subunits within the overall business. This would seemingly preserve the conventional wisdom that accountability can only be re-

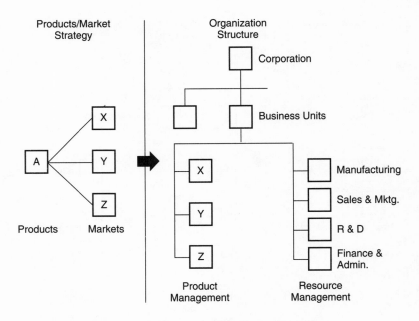

Figure 14–2. Market–Function Matrix Organization

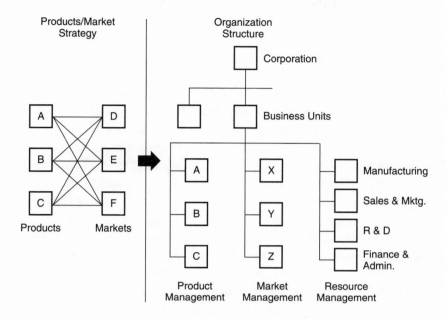

Figure 14–3. Product–Matrix–Function Matrix Organization

lated to responsibility—and would result in structures where each manager had one and only one clear boss, which is not the case in a matrix set-up. It would have the added advantage that presumably dedicated manufacturing facilities, separate sales forces, and in-house R&D would be more effective than shared facilities, "pooled" sales activities and centralized R&D. The dilemma is, however, that on one side this brings with it a great deal of duplication and added cost; on the other side functional resources often require a minimum scale to become efficient. While decentralization of functional activities might enhance focus and responsibilize lower levels of management, the possibilities for scale, technology, or experience gains create pressure for sharing or pooling critical resources.

Recognizing these counterpressures, many companies choose a middle ground. Companies like Dow Corning and Du Pont, for example, both of which face highly segmented markets, have tried to get the best of both worlds. Some functional resources are decentralized to individual businesses or subunits, while others are pooled. Today, in these and similarly segmented industries, many companies have centralized basic research (given its role in overall corporate success and the large sums involved) while decentralizing some business-specific development and marketing tasks. These semi-matrix organizations may be hard to manage, but may be the only workable organizational form in highly segmented markets.

Some managements are abandoning matrix structures for reasons both of cost and complexity. But the other side of the coin may be to lose focus on individual product or market segments. This leaves the door open for an aggressive, often smaller, focused competitor to challenge the more centralized giant, "cherry-picking" his most profitable pieces of business. Matrix organizations are certainly not ideal to manage but they may nevertheless represent the best structural possibility available for managing complex, segmented markets. Matrix organizations "mirror" market segmentation, and as such provide an organizational schema for implementing as well as drawing up plans by segment.

Matrix structures can best be understood by distinguishing "program" responsibilities from "resource" responsibilities. A "program" is the company's overall approach to a particular product or market segment. "Resources" are each of the functional activities— manufacturing, sales, R&D, service, and others—that contribute to the realization of a program in a particular segment. Using this terminology, we may call product managers or market managers "program managers." Manufacturing, sales, R&D, and service managers are "resource managers."

Program managers seldom have large numbers of people reporting directly to them, unless they manage dedicated resource departments such as sales or service staffs. But they do carry the final bottom line profit responsibility. To succeed they have to be skillful in bringing to bear resources which they may not have complete and direct control over. Theirs is a job that requires a special kind of leadership—based more on personal qualities than on hierarchical position. Negotiation and influence are therefore more important than command and obedience. Resource managers often have much larger numbers of people reporting to them directly, but theirs is the responsibility for the quality of the functional inputs and their cost—not profit itself. Resource managers are often called the "grizzly bears" of modern organizations, because their organizational weight derives from their organizational size and not from having the final word on activities associated with a particular program—a role reserved for program management.

The overall horizontal and vertical scope and definition of a business unit are, of course, determining factors in how it can be subdivided. Although we have used here, as an example, "product management" and "market management" forms of program management, it is quite possible also to imagine program management tasks corresponding to segments based on customer groups, customer functions, or technologies, that is, on one of the three underlying segmentation dimensions. Resource management responsibilities likewise do not have to be defined as falling strictly *within* the boundaries of the organization. They can extend to responsibility for horizontal or vertical partner organizations—and resources and competences within them which are brought to bear.

PEOPLE INFLUENCES

While organization *structures* relate closely to markets and market segmentation, other important elements of the organization—notably its informal structures, styles, processes, systems, culture, human resource practices, and patterns of leadership and followership—relate more closely to the people who make the organization work. Structure is the organization's skeleton; the human elements provide its systems, style, and soul. An organization can be well structured with respect to its markets but lack viability, creativity, and flexibility. In other words, structure is a necessary ingredient, but it is far from sufficient. We can only understand the *functioning* of an organization if we understand both its structural hardware and its human software. Both are important, as we shall see later, in an organization's ability to achieve excellence today while changing for tomorrow. Each of the elements of organizational software— namely, informal structure, styles, processes, systems, culture, and patterns of leadership and followership—is affected by the new roles that people are taking on at all levels as they are given more responsibility.

While program and resource units in the organization provide a useful typology for describing organizational structures, we are harder put to find ways to describe organizational functioning.

While catchall terms like "entrepreneurial," "market-driven," "lean," and "flexible" give us a mental image of an organization, they are not very exact. Even if it is agreed that these are positive organizational attributes, it is hard to tell, in the absence of an agreed-upon schema of measurement, how well an organization is endowed with these characteristics. This probably goes some way to explain the popularity of a number of recent management books that focus on organizational functioning.

No attempt will be made here to even summarize this excellent and burgeoning literature, but no one can doubt that many managements are searching for ways to improve the functioning of their organizations via people. For some, in fact, organizational functioning takes precedence over strategic direction as a key factor underlying corporate success.[1] While both are generally agreed to be crucial, it can be argued that a well-functioning organization takes precedence simply because it will "evolve" good strategies in response to the challenges before it; an organization that has formulated a clear strategic direction but has difficulty functioning is unlikely to accomplish its strategic ends.

The greater responsibilization of people, which is the decisive factor in all organizational improvement efforts, appears to have two origins. The first is a growing tendency for people to *seek* responsibility—which carries with it a certain degree of autonomy and control over one's own destiny. This has its roots in deep-rooted social and educational trends which appear to be taking place worldwide in the latter years of the twentieth century. The other strong force for responsibilizing lower levels of the organizational hierarchy is that it works! Senior management, faced with diversity and complexity, may sometimes see no alternative but to push responsibility further down the organization. Having done so, most agree that their organizations are much better for it. The reader will not have forgotten the admonition of R. F. Domeniconi, Nestlé's executive vice president for finance: "To get excellence, the greatest source of untapped resources is from middle management down. . . ."

Domeniconi's views of how to release this untapped source of organizational energy ranged from communications, to teamwork, to providing leeway for people to do things their own way, to changing boss-subordinate relationships, to breaking down "classical" organizational boundaries. In his mind, "If you can get an organization to do these things, it is like getting all the deposits out of your bloodstream."

ORGANIZATIONAL IMPROVEMENT THEMES

Having looked separately at the structural (hardware) and people (software) sides of organization, it is time now to put these back together. As we look at organizational form and functioning in those companies that are generally reckoned to be leaders in their fields, they are usually found to be working on one or more of six main organizational improvement tasks:

–to become more "market-driven"

–to become more "entrepreneurial"

–to become more participative

–to become "flatter and leaner"

–to become quicker

–to become more integrated internationally

Each of these, it should be remembered, can affect both the quest for excellence today, and the capacity for change for tomorrow.

Becoming More Market-Driven[2]

Failure to be market-driven can affect every aspect of a company's operations—from vague telephone responses, to poor customer service, to inappropriate manufacturing priorities, to misallocation of R&D efforts, to badly devised human resource management policies. The end result is usually red ink, but by the time it appears, the hour is often late for remedying the situation.

Examples abound of companies that suffer from failure to be market-driven. In the late 1970s and early 1980s, a large mechanical engineering company with seventy-five years of worldwide superiority in industrial product quality and underlying technology experienced a sliding market share, loss of its competitive product edge, and a widening gap between its prices and those of competition.

For nearly five years, the company anguished over slipping sales and market share while profits turned to losses.

Eventually management defined its problems as a basic failure of manufacturing, engineering, and product design to understand the new demands of the marketplace. In particular, none of the key "technical" functions had a clear view of the changed segmentation of the marketplace. New combinations of high value added products, technology, and service had emerged in some segments, while in more mature parts of the market, the key factors for success hinged on low cost and prompt delivery for products that had become largely standardized. In the late 1980s management reduced costs all around and improved manufacturing efficiency, but by the early 1990s they still felt that a long-term effort would be required to change the basic orientation of the company and make it more responsive to its market.

The failure of this company, and many others like it, can be attributed not only to the fact that the organization structure of the company failed to reflect the changed structure of the marketplace, but that the individual businesses had no "middlemen" between their particular market and all the internal functions of the firm—manufacturing, R&D, engineering, administration, finance, and even sales and marketing.

For companies in industries where marketing is a key function, the task of middleman can best be fulfilled by the marketing function. Marketing managers are usually better equipped than either R&D or manufacturing managers to take on the role of middleman. Marketing people understand the marketplace and its evolution, they are oriented towards competitive and environmental forces, and they have close contact with the customers themselves.

But even for companies in technology-intensive industries, technical managers may exercise marketing functions, whatever their titles. In such circumstances it is these managers who must play the middleman role.

For marketing management to play the middleman role and effectively orient the entire company towards the market, new organization structures and processes are often needed. Above all, the organization structure must mirror the segmentation of the market, and responsibilities must be well defined for each major target segment. These "segment managers" then become the middlemen between the market and the rest of the organization.

Unfortunately, many companies completely fail to recognize key shifts in market segmentation and to reflect these changes in their organizations. Many simply lag behind in changing their internal structures as the market evolves and segments are redefined.

By contrast, market-driven organizations stay abreast of, or even lead, changes in market segmentation. They create structures that lead the way to redefinition of the market. Only then can segment managers act effectively as middlemen between the marketplace and various functions of the firm which together provide the customers with products, services, or other benefits.

The talents of conventional marketing managers often fall far short of what is required if the middleman function is to be effectively performed. Limited or specialized experience, resulting in a narrow and often product-driven view, effectively prevents the achievement of a market-driven orientation. A broader outlook and broader knowledge of the business is required, including:

–a broad view of the whole business system and a strategic sense of the business as a whole

–comprehension of how all the functional activities of the business fit together and how each contributes to providing a competitive edge by meeting key factors for success better than any other supplier

–a practical and conceptual understanding of each of the various functions of the business at a level that assures easy working relationships with various functional heads within the firm; in addition, implementation skills are essential

–strong interpersonal and negotiating skills in order to manage the relationships between customer markets and functional managers inside the firm

–an instinct for management processes and organizational politics

–entrepreneurial skills in order to identify and exploit new opportunities

–leadership skills, since little will happen unless managers at
several levels and in diverse organizational functions can be
mobilized in an integrated way to address the marketplace

In sum, a broader managerial profile is needed than for a conventional marketing manager. Career evolution along specialized lines
often fails to produce the right kind of person. Frequently, careful
selection, a broader-than-normal pattern of managerial assign-
ments, and planned periods of management development are the
only ways to provide and hone the kinds of credentials required.

Becoming More "Entrepreneurial" (or "Intrapreneurial")

As noted earlier, the word "intrapreneurship" has been coined to
describe the concept of entrepreneurship as it is applied in the context of larger corporate enterprises.[3] I shall use the words entrepreneurship and intrapreneurship interchangeably here, since the underlying sense is identical, and only the setting is different.

Howard Stevenson, a professor at the Harvard Business School
and a luminary in the field of intrapreneurship, makes the following observations:

> The question is what entrepreneurship really means. It is not just
> small companies or start-ups, because the people who have grown
> some fairly good-sized businesses are still very entrepreneurial. It is
> certainly also not just the high-flying, fast-living, unscrupulous pro-
> moters. They will never create anything with sustaining value. It is
> an approach to management and it starts with opportunity.
>
> At Harvard, entrepreneurship is defined as the pursuit of oppor-
> tunity beyond the resources you currently control. Both parts of this
> definition are important. Opportunity depends on seeing and envi-
> sioning a future state. But as an entrepreneur, you know also that
> you have to use other people's resources, like finance, technology,
> and capital equipment, and that there are many different ways of
> getting resources. The key is to convince the possessors not only that
> it is an opportunity for you but also for them.[4]

Stevenson's words clearly describe what it is that most larger corporate organizations are now seeking as an alternative to the older,

bureaucratic, hierarchical management structures and processes. I held up some similar visions of more entrepreneurial organizations in Chapter 8, to which the reader may want to refer back. Most have discovered, however, that it is *people* as well as structures and processes that result in an organization become more entrepreneurial. When the right people are empowered by their superiors and given the room to make mistakes—and even sometimes to fail—an organization starts to behave like a tennis player with racket at the ready, rocking gently from foot to foot, every sense tuned to where the ball will land and how to turn it to advantage. Flatfooted, listless organizations, lacking entrepreneurial spirits are like flat-footed, listless tennis players—losers not winners.

Becoming More Participative

Participation is a further extension of decentralization. Whereas decentralization is usually understood as shifting decision making from the center, that is, from headquarters outward and downward to the *management of units,* participation implies the inclusion of employees other than managers in the decision-making apparatus. These may include "blue collar" as well as "white collar."

Participation may take two very different forms, however. The first is participation of lower-level employees in their role as important stakeholders. This has been widely practiced in some European communities—Scandinavia, Germany, and Holland being prime examples—where there is even a legal requirement to include "worker" representation on supervisory boards. This went furthest in Eastern Europe where in varying forms and degrees, "self-management" practices were widespread. In countries other than the former Yugoslavia, however, "self-management" was often a deception since the real decisions were made behind the scenes by local party bosses.

The second form of participative practice has nothing to do with stakeholder representation—it has to do with involving people in areas where they are often the ones best-placed and with most experience to make a contribution. Quality circles—pioneered by Japanese management and now widely imitated in the West—are one such example. Beyond any shadow of doubt, qualified plant operating personnel, when given the opportunity and training, are more productive and creative in terms of designing and suggesting improvements to practices they themselves are responsible for than management levels not directly involved in the daily work.

What quality circles have done on the shop floor is being replicated in virtually all aspects of the workplace—from R&D, to services, to distribution, to administration. Management itself has been able to streamline and improve managerial practices through similar approaches.

Central to the idea of "contributory participation," as opposed to "stakeholder participation," is teamwork. Creative solutions to workplace problems may be sparked by an individual, but their implementation usually requires wider commitment. Teams can also refine, redefine, and materialize ideas in ways which the individual originator seldom can.

The gains from contributory participation have proven to be very substantial. New ground is being broken now by organizations that are looking for benefits not only *within* functional departments or specialized resources areas but *across* and *between* functional areas. One example is the dramatic speeding up and improvement of new product development processes resulting from the formation of cross-functional teams who work in parallel rather than sequentially from the birth of an idea to its eventual commercialization. Joint participation of manufacturing, engineering, design, marketing, and sales personnel in the earliest stages of prototype R&D work sets the stage for eventual success in the marketplace.

Management's own role in companies that are committed to participative practices is changing dramatically. Instead of managing only the substance of whatever functional area they are responsible for, they find themselves managing participative *processes* designed to produce the desired result—a result that often greatly exceeds their own visions or expectations of what was possible. Management's role is also to focus the attention of participative practices on those areas that are "key success factors." New solutions reached via participative methods then have the highest leverage in the marketplace.

Communication, as I have stressed at several junctures in this book, is particularly important to the active participation of lower levels of management and staff. People further down the organization and particularly those "on the firing line" cannot be expected to guess how the company defines its business, how it wants to be positioned vis-à-vis competitors, and what particular features of customer satisfaction require emphasis for each targeted segment. Nor can they search for improvements if they are not provided with regular feedback and yardsticks of performance by which to control and measure progress. Designing and implementing appropriate communications up, down, and sideways in the organization are also therefore a key management responsibility.

Getting positive results from participative practices is not automatic. There are three basic preconditions. First, a management must be willing to "let go of the reins" enough to allow the process to even take place—and to be willing to support initiatives that may emerge without choking them off too early "because it won't work." Second, a well-educated workforce must have the experience and background to make real contributions. Third, continued investment in coaching and training is needed. In this latter case, much can be achieved by diffusing and spreading "best practice" from one well-functioning participative team to others. This internal "benchmarking" serves to upgrade practices company-wide.

Lastly, the effects of participation on motivation should never be underestimated. Even if *specific* new approaches are not forthcoming or not forthcoming with high frequency, the process itself may still be worthwhile. Participatively managed companies, like the entrepreneurially driven companies described above, appear to be standing on their toes rather than flatfootedly waiting for someone else's initiative. In fact, participation *is* a form of entrepreneurship, not from the top down but from the bottom up.

Becoming Flatter and Leaner

Faced with falling profitability caused by recession and even tougher international competition, many companies have started to take a long and hard look at their own internal managerial structures and personnel costs. Many don't much like what they see. Excess layers of management and staff have been surgically removed as a result. The declines have been dramatic. Philips, the Dutch electronics plant, counted only 45,500 employees in early 1992—down from more than 100,000 a decade earlier. Many others have made, or contemplate making, cuts of a similar magnitude—reducing workforces by 50 percent or more overall.

Some of these cuts represent contraction of business or abandonment of certain "noncore" activities. Other cuts go to the depth of the management hierarchy itself. Companies that may have operated previously with ten to twelve or even fifteen layers of seniority have reduced them to only four or five. The result is often not only lower costs, but faster, more responsive decision making. Communications up and down the organization are vastly improved in amount, timeliness, and accuracy. Like the old parlor game in which a message is repeated from one participant to the next out of earshot of the others, the relationship between what is heard and what was originally said is closely related to the number of intermediate participants!

The result of cutting out layers of management that do not create real value is not only to reduce the distance between top management and operating personnel but to "flatten out" the organization at the same time. Managers find themselves handling more reporting relationships, and consequently delegating more responsibility to each subordinate. Just like the participative processes described earlier, a precondition is the managerial capability and experience at lower levels to take on these enlarged tasks—and senior management's capability to "let go" without loosing complete control. Delegation does not mean *abrogation* of responsibility.

Some companies have, to their misfortune, "overshot" in terms of creating leaner, more horizontal structures. Either because lower levels were ill-prepared or because upper levels became overextended or both, important tasks may remain undone or start to fall between the cracks. Finding the right *sustainable* degree of organizational flatness and leanness is a critical judgment that management must continually be making as it goes along.

Becoming Quicker

Competition is not only fiercer but quicker. Doing the right thing used to go a long way to assuring success in the marketplace; doing things right as well as doing the right thing almost guaranteed it.

Today doing the right thing right must be accompanied by doing it *faster* than anyone else too. Neither of the other two prerequisites for winning have lost any of their original importance, so that speed cannot substitute for quality. But speed must be combined with quality to satisfy customers ahead of competitors and to stake out a durable market position.

Time is a factor that can be applied to each and every organizational process. It starts with something as mundane as the number of rings necessary to get a reply from the telephone receptionist, to the number of days, weeks, months, or even years to get an order processed, to the time it takes an organization to introduce a new generation of products from initial conceptualization to launch. It affects bill paying and bill collecting. It resides in attitudes as well as in procedures.

Time is a new competitive weapon of the 1990s, and many old lumbering corporate dinosaurs are not well prepared to meet the time challenges with which they are confronted.[5] Improvements in process time must be made first in those areas that provide the biggest marketplace leverage, namely, in those organizational areas and processes that represent "critical success factors" from a customer perspective. This may be the speed of getting a spare part to satisfy a service need; it may be on-time and prompt delivery schedules; it may be the speed with which a new product can be brought to the market ahead of competition—or it may literally depend on the speed with which an organization returns calls. As far as speed is concerned, all activities should probably be done quicker, but some—those critical to success—should be done quicker than others!

Becoming More Integrated Internationally

An important theme of organizational change running through nearly all the companies that were studied as background for this book was to find improved ways to manage increasingly region-wide or worldwide market participation.

Integration does not necessarily imply standardization.[6] Many companies are in fact finding that they need to develop more standardized approaches for some products worldwide, while at the same time differentiating their approaches even more sharply country-by-country for others.

Faced with such complexity, the relatively easy and simplistic formulas which put the final decision-making power and profit responsibility in some companies squarely in the geographic markets, and in others squarely in headquarters product divisions, are giving way to more delicately tuned organizational arrangements and balances. Companies like Nestlé are, as we have seen, fine-tuning the relationship between product line management and country management on a regional and product-by-product basis. And Heineken is centralizing some powers, while Caterpillar is decentralizing. None of these is contradictory. Each makes perfect sense given the particular setting involved, the strategic objectives of each company, and the historical point of departure that each has inherited. When growth has been largely organic from the center, a priority is usually to increase country-by-country differentiation. When growth has been via local acquisition, regional integration often appears as the main priority.

Whatever the direction of change, the issue of regional and global integration is a crucial one for most multinationals as they enter the last decade of the century—and will probably remain so well into the next millennium.

EXECUTIVE RESPONSIBILITIES
FOR TODAY AND TOMORROW

Becoming more market-driven, entrepreneurial, participative, leaner, flatter, timely, and integrated internationally all enhance an organization's capacity for duality. Organizations that can turn their inside outward to the marketplace certainly have a better chance of getting the right signals for the short term and long term than those that do not; and organizations that turn themselves upside down by empowering lower hierarchical levels have a much greater chance of interpreting the signals correctly and acting on them. But dealing simultaneously with today and tomorrow also usually requires an appropriate focus of executive attention—from top to bottom of the organization. For some managers this means a dual focus; for others it means a primary emphasis on either running the business or changing it.

Dual Responsibilities at the Top

Some organizations, recognizing the dual nature of the top management challenge, in fact split the job in two—one part being managed by the CEO (chief executive officer) and the other by the COO (chief operating officer). According to Warren Bennis, who observed a number of such arrangements in close up,

> On paper, the differences are very clear. The CEO is the leader; the COO the manager. The CEO is charged with doing the right thing; the COO with doing things right. The CEO takes the long view, the COO the short view. The CEO concentrates on the what and the why, while the COO focuses on how. The CEO has the vision, the COO hands-on control. The CEO thinks in terms of innovation, development, the future, while the COO is busy with administration, maintenance, the present. The CEO sets the tone and direction, both inside and outside the company, while the COO sets the pace. . . ."[7]

But Bennis remains skeptical of this solution to managing the dual tasks for a series of reasons, a central one being succession. As he says:

> While the CEO has to take tough positions on long-range issues, must plan ahead and articulate a vision, the COO has been working on short-run, ad hoc, and often simply expedient decision-making. The COO has been trained to act like a mechanic, a problem-solver, basically maintaining an efficient status quo. Is it any wonder then that boards discover, almost always too late, that the "natural" successor to the CEO is inadequately prepared for the top job?

Bennis's solution to the split leadership problem is to combine the responsibilities of CEO and COO in a "CEO-in-chief"—at the same time leader *and* manager of managers. This "CEO-in-chief" would "be responsible for seeing that the short view was compatible with the long view, that things done today would lead to tomorrow's goals."[8] He would define the "whats" and "whys" and assign the "hows" to associates; would have the vision and primary hands-on control, thus ensuring that the vision was always realistic; would think in terms of innovation, development, and the future while his associates took care of administration, maintenance, and the present, and would set "tone, direction, and pace for the company."

This is one solution, but certainly not the only one. Another is to look for the split in a single individual; yet another is to have a chief executive who himself coordinates *two* top managers—one responsible for planning and delivering excellence today; the other responsible for getting ready for tomorrow.

R. F. Domeniconi, Nestlé's executive vice president for finance, had this to say about the dual nature of the top management challenge: "People are overworked and do not think much about tomorrow; and many managers are not visionary by nature. But in a general management group of ten, maybe you only need one or two visionaries. You need at least four or five with hard noses!"

While these points of view from a leading academic and a leading practitioner respectively provide us with considerable insight, many questions remain. The challenge, while it is not new, is a growing one and company experiences are not yet well documented. Two conclusions do, however, seem to stand out.

First, the *chief* executive had better be ready to encompass *both* excellence today and change for tomorrow. This characteristic may in fact be one of the distinguishing criteria to be applied to candidates for the company's highest office.

Second, just below the top, there may be room for somewhat more specialization, with the *accent* being applied either to today's management or to preparations for tomorrow. Nevertheless, in the top management team, *all* managers have certainly got to be able to wear both hats on occasions.

But whatever the solutions at the very top, this is only a part of the whole story. What is needed is organizational duality further "down the line" also. Just how far down, and to what degree, we shall not consider.

Dual Responsibilities Below the Top

Further down the organization, *primary* concerns may become more divided. To take an everyday example, as I was walking recently past a construction site, it was obvious that one gang was already putting up shuttering and pouring concrete for the lower level main walls; a quite separate gang was erecting the giant crane that would serve as a key resource for later construction.

"Operating" personnel will certainly have their plates full meeting customers' needs today, but if they do not understand at the same time how the company is trying to change for tomorrow, they may not be capable of adjusting their operating procedures when the time comes. Internal communications about the company's strategies and goals with respect to the present and future are an essential part of accomplishing this "dual thinking."

The in-depth studies undertaken for this book indicate that change is often managed on a *project* basis. At Nestlé, the Nestlé 2000 project was one of the main preoccupations of corporate management in the early 1990s, alongside their normal "operating" responsibilities. But change projects were also underway at each individual country, at the regional level (the European region counted four or five such projects), within specific functional areas, and within product divisions. At Heineken, some twenty projects had been defined within the overall change process, to assure that the implications of centralizing more management responsibility for major international brands was reflected in every corner of the organization. Project teams at Heineken all comprised corporate staff as well as country management—assuring that all maintained a comprehensive involvement in changing the company as well as running it.

Project and "task force" forms of organization seem particularly appropriate to the management of change. By definition, change is time-delineated, and each change initiative should have a defined starting and ending point. Project teams or task forces can therefore be specially assembled for the task and then disbanded once the task is completed. A "temporary" organizational device of this nature also provides important opportunities to mix different functions, business perspectives, and levels in a single team, but also to "force" those who work normally on either present or future tasks to give due consideration to the other. For this reason, project team and task force organizational forms are likely to be used with increasing frequency—and will provide important organizational learning possibilities as well as serving their more specific task objectives.

Sometimes getting staff below the top to focus more on excellence *and* change simultaneously is best accomplished by a major team exercise. This may start with five to ten managers at the top but "cascade" further down the organization to involve hundreds

or even thousands eventually. Such an exercise can bring about a
new universally shared comprehension of both current market
plans on one hand, and the forces for change on the other. It can
become the basis for establishing clear current strategies and priorities, as well as working through the changes that will be necessary
for the future. Such a one-time company-wide group effort has
some risks but many rewards, as companies like SAS that have tried
it can testify.[9]

ORGANIZATIONAL CONTRASTS
IN MANAGING PRESENT AND FUTURE

I have hinted earlier that program and resource manager responsibilities may have to be differently balanced depending on the time
horizon of the task. This can now be placed in a large organizational
context. Bearing in mind that all functions and all levels of the organization have to have an eye to both present and future, there are
nonetheless some important shades of difference depending in the
task at hand.

For Excellence Today

A bottom-up approach appears to be more effective in both formulating and implementing strategies to achieve the highest standards
of customer satisfaction. This of course has to be blended with an
appropriate degree of "top-down" management—especially to ensure that cross-function, cross-business, and partner synergies are
most effectively utilized.

Program managers must lead in defining what has to be done
with excellence, and functional managers must follow. As uncom-
fortable as this is for many functional managers used to a certain
degree of independence, there must be a clear working understanding of who is calling the shots.

Finally, when it comes to the present, organizational structures
clearly follow strategy. Most important, as we have seen, is to put in
place structures that "mirror" market segmentation. But in addition, organizational systems, particularly compensation, motivation, and reward systems, must be carefully designed to encourage
strict implementation of chosen strategies.

Changing for Tomorrow

A substantially greater degree of top-down involvement in the strategic process is likely to be required in planning for the future. It results not only from the broader vision of the situation which is needed, but also from the fact that its fundamental purpose is to take a broader view of the company and its resources. A corporate-wide and even interorganizational perspective is needed.

In contrast to market planning for the present, functional managers are likely to be more important than program managers in planning for future change. Only they have the intimate knowledge of what is possible. While program managers provide important inputs in terms of what will be needed, what "can be done" takes on a larger importance than what "might be needed" as we look to the future. Market strategy becomes proactive rather than reactive. Opportunities have to be created as well as just fulfilled. Nowhere is this clearer than in the case of those companies quoted in Chapter 1 —companies like Apple, Benetton, Canon, IKEA, Sony, Club Med, and Polaroid—who at one time or another broke away from the conventional wisdom of their industry and redefined the way of doing business in it. General management provides the glue that is needed to join the creative visions of functional managers about the possibilities, to the market-oriented view of program managers about needs.

When it comes to organizing for the future, existing organizational structures are more likely to determine strategies than strategy determining structure. Whatever the existing segmentation, it becomes the organizational lens through which the future is viewed. This can be a limiting factor—particularly with respect to the ability of existing product managers or market managers to view the future in new ways. Major redefinitions of a business seldom originate within existing structures, and general management needs to be aware that structures that are well-designed to implement strategies for the present may at the same time hobble the organization's ability to think flexibly about its future.

CHAPTER 15

MOVING TO DUAL PLANNING

Part III of this book highlighted differences between management's short-term and long-term tasks, and made suggestions with respect to analytical approaches that can be employed to support decision making for each of the two time horizons. This chapter turns to the planning process itself, and particularly how it should be designed to ensure that the short term and the long term are given proper attention.

"Dual" planning systems provide the necessary planning framework for pinpointing today's opportunities while at the same time preparing for tomorrow. The two are tightly related because it is only with plans for change in mind that the plans for achieving excellence today can be projected forward. The opportunities that can be pinpointed *tomorrow* depend very substantially on resources and competences that have been built in anticipation of tomorrow.

Management is interested not only in the specifications of such a dual purpose planning system, but on how to put it in place. This depends very largely on how, in any particular organization, planning works currently. In this respect, there are wide variations from company to company—in the way they tackle planning for today as well as for tomorrow.

The first part of this chapter is devoted to a description of how planning has evolved over the last several decades. This provides a basis for readers to establish where their own firm currently stands. Only with such a determination in hand can a course be set to change to something better.

THE EVOLUTION OF PLANNING

Planning has evolved not only because managers and planners have developed new insights about what works and what does not work; it has evolved also to meet the needs of the day. When enterprises were small, relatively undiversified, domestic in orientation, and simple in structure, planning was also relatively simple and straightforward. As enterprises have increased in size, complexity, and geographic scope, planning tasks have also multiplied, and have become correspondingly more difficult. Planning systems have become more complex.

The smaller, single-product single-market domestic firms of yesteryear were in fact often led by owner-managers and characterized by entrepreneurial management styles. Many such firms still exist today, and indeed in sheer quantity vastly outnumber the multinational giants. Formal planning in such firms is often minimal; instead, they move forward through a process of trial and error, guided, in the best examples, by "visionary," "passionate" leadership from the top. Decision making tends to be quick, and intuition about strategy is developed by frequent face-to-face contact with customers, suppliers, and the trade. Management is by "walking around." Planning and implementation may, in fact, be difficult to distinguish from one another. Nonetheless, since much rests on the shoulders of one man—the entrepreneur and owner—a longer-term view is often a natural one. It is seldom incorporated, however, into formal plans.

One result of the steady trend towards increased size, product and market diversity, and technological complexity has been to push the job of general management further down the organization. Instead of a single boss at the top, diversified multiproduct, multi-market, multinational companies count scores of "bosses" at strategic vantage points throughout the organization. This started with the wave of reorganization that took companies from functional to divisional structures in the 1950s and 1960s, and continued with the further refinement of SBU (strategic business unit) structures and matrix substructures in the 1970s and 1980s.

This internal segmentation of the firm and the accompanying decentralization of managerial responsibility led inevitably to the need for planning *systems*—both to provide a decision-making "tie" between corporate and business unit management, and also to allow top management to manage the whole as more than the simple sum of each of the pieces. These systems may exhibit more or less sophistication and complexity depending on the firm's own particular environment, and on the stage of evolution of planning that has been reached.

In its most basic form, planning in these companies is no more than simple budgeting based on some rudimentary short-term forecasts of sales. Larger companies that do little more than this closely resemble their smaller entrepreneurially driven counterparts as far as their business planning practices are concerned.

Normally, however, the larger diversified enterprise is soon forced to plan more systematically and for a longer term. Three- to five-year plans replace one-year plans if for no other reason than to support physical capacity planning and capital investment decsions. And simple sales and financial forecasting is replaced initially by the development of marketing planning which recognizes that the firm is not just a victim of its destiny, but can indeed influence it. Nonetheless in many firms a strong emphasis remains on the financial dimensions of such "long-term" plans and praticularly the annual budget—which becomes the basis for financial control.

The 1970s witnessed the further development of planning systems in some large diversified firms in two distinct ways. First, market*ing* planning evolved into *market* planning, that is, into the development of a more complete *business* plan covering all aspects of the firm's approach to a particular market or market segment. Second, growing limitations on *external* cash resources prompted firms to fund growth businesses that needed capital investment from more mature and profitable businesses with cash throwoff.

As planning evolved into these more complex forms, at least in many large multinationals, the systems themselves often became so complicated and bureaucratized that general management threw up its hands in dismay, and left the planning detail to "staff" planners and financial controllers. Plans often lost their pragmatic, issue-oriented character and took on a life of their own. The output of the planning process was frequently a thick book, replete with the most detailed budgeting information, which once "approved," quickly found its way into the general manager's filing cabinet, to be consulted rarely or not at all during the course of the year. In fact, key decisions were often made *alongside* the plan through a parallel *managerial* process—a process which in the best cases involved regular cooperation and contact between corporate and divisional management, and in the worst cases not autonomy but something closer to anarchy. In the absence of either a relevant plan or proper communication, business units were managed highly independently of one another—and opportunites for overall corporate synergy ignored or overlooked.

This state of affairs produced a predictable backlash in planning practices in the second half of the 1980s. Finding that planning had become ineffective as well as expensive and overly time consuming, many leading companies fired the bulk of their planning staffs, and insisted that *general management* once again take over the planning responsibility—using planning staff help sparingly. Plans had to focus on the key issues confronting each business and the main strategic options before it. This has gone a long way to help—but it also may partly explain why few companies today, even those who are counted among the very best worldwide in their industry, have well-functioning dual purpose planning systems in place.

Instead, these firms often manage the dual tasks of trying to manage with excellence today and lay the foundations for tomorrow by using a number of *parallel* systems and approaches. It is not at all uncommon, for example, to find, under one roof, any combination of the following: a three- to five-year "long-term" planning process; a capital budgeting process; a series of project-based change activities; a "total quality management" project or projects; benchmarking; and, last but not least, an annual budgeting process. Since all of these activities should actually bear a close relationship to one another, it is no wonder that many firms do not yet fully have their planning act together—either for today or tomorrow.

SOME TYPICAL PLANNING SHORTCOMINGS

Although many companies have made large strides forward with their planning efforts over the last two or three decades, much remains to be done—particularly with respect to incorporating into planning the dual nature of management's tasks. On the positive

side, most multinationals now have in place organizational structures that allow balanced attention to product and market sides of
the matrix; most have made considerable progress in incorporating
industry analysis, competitive analysis, and business system analysis into their thinking and planning, and many are dealing increasingly with the "strategic" aspects of technology, human resources
planning and cost management.

But on the negative side, the problem of dealing simultaneously
with today and tomorrow as change becomes more and more ob-
trusive is manifested by many other kinds of complaint: planning
systems are too bureaucratic—and technocratic; there is too much
attention to strategy and too little on implementation; there is a lack
of entrepreneurship (or intrapreneurship as it is often called in the
corporate setting); and heard more and more frequently, "we don't
move fast enough."

Some of these complaints do indeed have their origins in the lack
of distinction between planning for today and preparing for tomorrow; others have their roots elsewhere. To set the stage for the next
section of this chapter which takes a more normative view of planning, it is worthwhile to go in detail through the list of potential
shortcomings and pitfalls with today's planning systems. I like to
divide these into three broad categories: analytical problems; planning process problems; and implementation problems. In each category we can make a distinction between the present and future horizons of planning.

Analytical Problems

In planning for the *present,* the most frequent and important shortcomings is a failure to segment the market creatively or effectively.
When this is not done well, the value of all subsequent aspects of
the plan is in serious doubt. Further, but not much further, down
the list in my experience, are failures to think broadly enough about
ways to improve customer satisfaction, an overestimation of internal capabilities for providing something truly distinctive, and an
underestimation of competitors—often because they are not inves-
tigated carefully enough. Other common problems are to consider
only one or only a very few options, and not to surface enough re-

ally *strategic* issues from the bottom up. It is simply too easy to hide these away from top management "under the rug" of the annual budget document.

In preparing for the *longer term*, many analytical problems arise from insufficient managerial experience in recognizing patterns of change. In fact, not all business situations are different, and in many cases history *does* repeat itself. Foreward planning is not so much the application of a process of analysis to a unique problem to get a unique answer as it is of *recognition* and *defintion* of problems based on generalized experience.

We do not need, for example, to engage in analysis of the movement of the planets to make plans to get up in the morning, go to bed in the evening, or fix dates for summer and winter vacation. We rely instead on our knowledge that the patterns of planetary movements are highly predictable. By contrast, in forecasting future stock price movements, it is necessary to do a thorough analysis of the economy, industry, and individual companies, as a basis for investment decisions.

Where does preparatory planning for the future fall on this spectrum? I would argue that, while the future includes both reasonably predictable as well as unpredicatable elements, many executives rely too heavily on analysis and too little on relevant experience— bounded in experience as they are in many cases by their own function, company, industry, and geographic setting. One of the great assets of good executive education programs is, in fact, to widen this experience, and by exposing participants to patterns of change with which they have had no direct exposure previously, get them to decipher patterns in their own industry.

Process Problems

With respect to planning for the *present*, three problems frequently appear: first, performance *objectives*, rather than performance *guidelines*, are handed down by corporate management without the benefit of a more realistic bottom-up view of the market situation. The result is often dysfunctional behavior with respect to the long term as business unit management complies in any way it can. A second process problem is separation of the annual budgeting process from the real strategic thinking process—with the result that budgeting leads planning rather than vice-versa. A third problem is focus on the planning *document* rather than on planning. Planning can then easily become a mindless ritual, with form filling by planning staffers and frustrated lower-level managers, rather than a strategic exercise by general management and top corporate management. Only those responsible for leading the organization can properly weigh the "can do" and "could do" with the "want to do" and "should do."

In preparing for the *longer term*, quite other problems show up in many planning processes. First, the distinction between short and long term may not be clearly made, nor are the true differences between the two properly highlighted. Many firms confuse the long-term *projection* of sales and costs with the quite different process of laying future foundations. Second, there is frequently a lack of discussion, and therefore lack of a broad consensus, on what kind of future the firm should be preparing for. This extends from lack of shared vision about the future situation the firm will find itself in, to lack of shared visions for organizational, strategic, and resource changes, to lack of shared vision about the path forward. Thirdly, the "softer" organizational aspects of the change process are often given too little attention relative to the "harder" strategic or operational aspects. Many firms today are recognizing that they suffer from bureaucracy, overstaffing, and lack of vitality, and that what worked well enough in the 1906s and 1970s cannot work in today's much more competitive global markets.

Implementation Problems

Implementation problems bedevil the realization of both short- and long-term plans: A common one is that internal, organizational structures do not adequately mirror the segmentation of the market—with the result that implementation responsibility is not clearly defined, even for extremely well laid plans. This subject was taken up in detail in Chapter 14.

A second problem is that the proper management systems and processes are not in place to support the implementation of plans—in the worst case even discouraging rather than encouraging effective implementation. Control and reward systems, and human resource management systems, are extremely important when it comes to effective implementation. This is taken up in Chapter 16.

Finally, many good plans fail at the implementation stage for lack of a well-thought-out communication program. Communication concerning what is required, why it is required, who is responsible for implementation, and when it has to be done is needed internally at all levels, and particularly by those on the "firing line"—namely, sales, service, and customer relations personnel. But communication is also an essential part of implementing strategies with and through alliance partners and other members of the vertical business systems with whom the firm cooperates.

Last but not least, communication is important to the market itself—to predispose customers to our plans for how they will be satisfied, and to stake out our particular claim on the market vis-à-vis competitors.

IMPROVING PLANNING

The foregoing problem areas provide some strong indications of general areas for planning improvement in virtually all organizations. We may summarize the main ones before turning to the specific question of how to integrate short- and long-term planning together. These are:

1. The planning process must have a human as well as technocratic face:

   –It must have an entrepreneurial, creative flavor.
   –It must be *led* by line management and *supported* by staff.
   –It requires a lot of "management by walking around." Line management, and particularly general management, are the eyes and ears of the firm.
   –Rigorous analysis has to be coupled with intuition and managerial experience.[1]

2. The planning process must gain commitment to action:

   –Planning and management should become integrated, not separate undertakings.

–The planning process itself should become a powerful agent for change.

–Implementation should be used as a way to refine strategy.

–Thinking about implementation has to start early on in the process.

–Communications must be used to get commitment and follow-through, especially in those parts of the organization (or "extended organization") furthest from headquarters.

3. Planning should be viewed as a continuous learning process:

–Plans should be updated regularly as new information becomes available (budgets may remain fixed, but plans cannot).

–Plans should be flexible enough to allow room for action; action in turn provides new insight into planning.

–Strategies should be "crafted" through experience rather than designed in their entirety on the drawing board.[1]

4. The planning process should become the backbone of all other management processes:

–Total quality management and benchmarking should be integrated into planning; not left as "free-standing" programs.

–Operational budgeting and capital budgeting should be tied in with short-term and long-term planning.

–"Project" activities should be related to the overall planning activity.

5. Last, planning should be kept simple!

With these general observations in hand, let us now turn to the specific problems that this book raises: how should companies plan to properly accommodate the needs for mastering today's markets, and laying the foundations for tomorrow? As we have seen in Chapters 11, 12, and 13, companies handle these two parallel tasks in a variety of ways. If we now put on a normative rather than purely descriptive hat, what should be recommended?

DUAL PLANNING

"Planning for today," in the sense of identifying current opportunities, cannot rest only in the present. Today is soon replaced by tomorrow, and the company must carefully pinpoint its target segments and decide how to serve them tomorrow too. The difference between tomorrow and today is that new opportunities will present themselves, or be generated, and new capabilities will have been built to exploit them.

The process described in Chapter 11 for planning for today's markets is therefore valid for tomorrow also. The only differences are that information will be less predictable, the way the market will evolve may still be a largely unknown quantity, and assumptions have to be made about our future capabilities and strategic intentions, as well as those of our competitors.

It is here that the two planning approaches described in Chapter 11 and 13 respectively have to be brought together. The future plan that spells out organizational change, strategic change, and competence building initiatives now becomes the *input* to the following period plan for pinpointing specific opportunities. These can take into account not only today's competences and resources, but also plans to expand and upgrade these. The two plans are therefore tightly interrelated—one dealing with the pinpointing of present *and* future opportunities; the other dealing with the changes necessary to make such pinpointing possible. Diagrammatically this is shown in Figure 15–1.

Not one but two plans are thus needed: one to deal with the pinpointing of opportunities, and the other to deal with change. The pinpointing of opportunities requires a vision of the present, and as we project it into the future, visions of what *will* be possible as the plans for change are actually realized. The "change" plan requires a vision of organizational, strategic, and resource futures. And it requires a clear strategic intent—as referenced and described already in Chapter 8.

In practice, the plan devoted to pinpointing current opportunities need not look ahead more than three years. To do so is to stretch

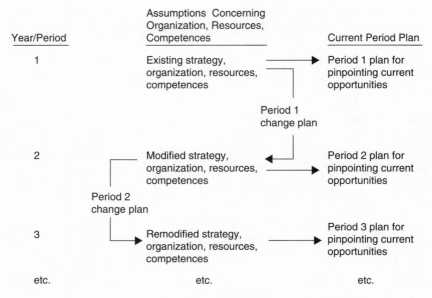

Figure 15–1. Dual Planning

the imagination about the precise shape of the future too far. Even if we assume that all *our* change plans will be realized as intended, external events may still overtake our own internal assessments.

The "change plans" should, however, have a considerably longer horizon. Five-to-ten-year timetables are not at all unreasonable when it comes to fundamental organizational change, strategic change, or resource reorientation. Of course, some defined change projects within these plans will have shorter duration, but the vision of the future should be long enough overall to allow fundamental change to be contemplated, and implemented. Note that the long planning horizon does *not* necessarily imply forecasting a very uncertain future; it does imply laying out a thorough long-term timetable for change—change which may well be prompted by events that have already occurred.

The various types of plan and their likely horizons may then be summarized as shown below: change plans have a medium- to long-term focus; plans that pinpoint specific opportunities typically have a short- to medium-term focus. The annual plan is dedicated to pinpointing today's opportunities but also contains any short-term plan to correct obvious weaknesses or reinforce strengths in the short term.

Planning Horizon

	Short-Term (annual)	Medium-Term (3 years)	Long-Term (5–10 years)
Plan Type Pinpointing Opportunities	Annual plan	Mid-term plan	–
Change	–	Mid-term plan	Long-term plan

One might well ask how this dual planning approach affects the botton-up, top-down processes that characterize most modern planning systems (see Figure 15–2).

The answer is that *both* the plans for pinpointing of current opportunities and the plans for change *relevant to a business unit* have got to travel this negotiated three-cycle path on the way to approval. Change plans that are directed at corporate-level change will normally be developed *within* corporate headquarters—but quite possibly with the inputs and counsel of senior line managers in the individual businesses or divisions. Here the main requirement is that once approved they are broadly communciated throughout the company, so that business-level plans can be developed, taking the corporate visions and plans into account.

From my own observations, few companies are explicitly practicing this kind of dual planning, although all those studied had apparently recognized the need and were edging towards their own unique solution. Heineken and Caterpillar, to name just two, were both well on the road to distinguishing, but also interrelating, short-term plans and long-term plans for change. If the pace of change accelerates, and the qualitative impact of change continues to rise, we can reasonably expect that the need for such solutions will become even more pressing. This brings us to the question that many practitioners must now be asking themselves. "Even if I see what has to be done, how do I get there?"

OVERHAULING THE CURRENT PLANNING APPROACH

I have deliberately used the word "overhauling" here since in nearly all cases, installing a dual planning approach should be com-

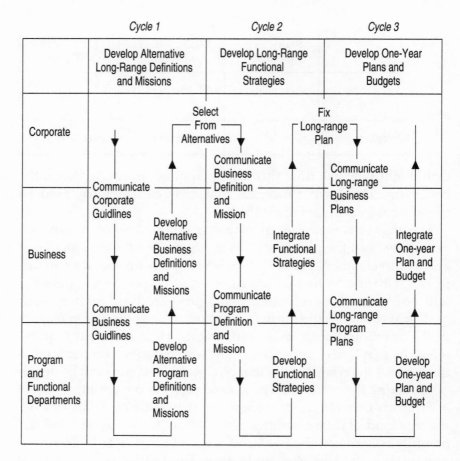

Figure 15–2. Top-down, Botton-up Planning
SOURCE: From Derek F. Abell and John S. Hammond, *Strategic Market Planning,* © 1979, p. 451. Prentice-Hall, Englewood Cliffs, New Jersey. This graphic presentation was based on a similar illustration presented originally by Peter Lorange and Richard F. Vancil in *Strategic Planning Systems* (Englewood Cliffs, N.J.: Prentice Hall, 1977), p. 26.

bined with other improvements. Few companies can claim to be immune from *all* the problems raised earlier in this chapter, or to have already incorporated into their own systems all of the suggested ways to raise planning effectiveness.

Like any other overhaul, it is important to start the process with an *audit* of the firm's current planning systems and approaches. This will enable the experienced manager or consultant to identify, as step one, where his own organization stands in terms of the various stages of evolution described earlier. Is planning still at a stage which characterized many leading companies in the 1960s and 1970s, or has it moved beyond this? If there has been a discrediting of planning, as has happened in many companies, has the "baby been thrown out with the bathwater" or do key elements remain in place? Is the process being driven by line management or by staff, and what is the relative importance of the "top-down" and "bottom-up" in the whole process? Finally, and most importantly, how are the two agendas and time horizons for mastering the present and preempting the future handled? These and many other questions which have been suggested in this chapter should allow an objective audit of where the company is currently situated.

With this background, alternative paths and timetables from the current position to a desired future position can be planned and evaluated. Changing the planning approach becomes a plan in and of itself—and its accomplishment will depend like all other plans on a clear definition of needed changes, actions, timetables, and responsibilities.

Rome was not built in a day—and neither are effective dual planning systems. But the pressures for dealing with change as well as achieving excellence today have never been greater. They do not favor an overly drawn out, step-by-step approach to installing more effective planning processes.

For most companies, the limiting factors will not be technical ones but the ability of the management team to comprehend what is needed and then make changes. Comprehension must start at the top, and the requirement for leadership to make such changes suggests that it should be a high priority on the agendas of every general manager from the president downward.

CHAPTER 16

CONTROLLING PERFORMANCE AND MONITORING CHANGE

This chapter provides a relatively cursory treatment of a complex subject. There are two explanations. The first is that both the theory and empirical research on the *nonfinancial* aspects of control are relatively sparse. Conclusions and implications from the foregoing chapters on this subject are therefore necessarily somewhat speculative.

The second explanation is that what needs to be said can be said briefly, as long as the assumption is made that *detailed* implications and procedures are excluded. This is the tack that I have taken here. Mindful of Voltaire's reputed comment to his correspondent: "I am sorry to be writing you this long letter . . . I did not have the time to write you a short one!", I have tried to avoid longwindedness—even in the somewhat speculative vein which characterizes this chapter.

FINANCIAL CONTROL AND "STRATEGIC" CONTROL

There is a literature—in fact quite an extensive one[1]—on why companies apparently concentrate their attention on short-term financial control at the expense of longer-term so-called "strategic" controls. Among the usual explanations are:

–difficulty in "measuring" strategic accomplishments

–concentration on short-term performance as opposed to long-term development

–the dysfunctionality that may occur from being too "rigid" about the future, with resulting loss of flexibility

–strategic management requires a "holistic" approach; concentration on a few selective measures of performance may "trivialize" management's response

While these reasons may each have some validity, another possibility may be that an appropriate conceptual framework to tackle questions of strategic control has been absent. By and large, the existing literature tends to gloss over some important distinctions: between, for example, *control of performance,* and *monitoring the progress of change;* and between the *operational* and *strategic* sides of *current* performance measurement. There are, in fact, four quite different types of control data—not just the two that are most usually quoted, namely, short-term budgetary ("operational") control on the one hand, and long-term "strategic control" on the other.

BROADENING THE CONCEPT
OF STRATEGIC CONTROL

As we have seen, vision and strategy are required both to perform with excellence today as well as to change in preparation for tomorrow. We have also seen that these two quite different concepts of strategy have to be "operationalized." The table below summarizes the resulting four broad areas for measuring performance and/or monitoring progress:

Control Measure

		Operational	Strategic
Time Horizon	Today	1 Budgetary control	2 "Strategic" control against key success factors (visible distinctions)
	Tomorrow	4 Detailed progress reports	3 "Strategic" control against milestones (hidden distinctions)

An effective overall control system comprises the tracking of important performance indicators, and their comparison with predeter-
mined yardsticks, in each of these four cells. They are all very different as we shall now see. In each case we shall ask: Who is it for?
What should they get? What should it be compared with? and How
often should it be done? I shall not, in this chapter, attempt to enter
the debate about motivation and reward aspects of control. I leave
that as part of the details to be filled in later and elsewhere.

1. BUDGETARY CONTROL

This is the most familiar to managers, yet many companies still fail
either to provide the right data, or to present data in the right format, to be really useful to management as a control device.

Who Is It For?

There are three different audiences for budgetary control data:

-program managers

-functional managers

-their bosses

What Is Needed?

In Chapter 7, I said that a more complete analysis of performance
requires not only an understanding of profit levels, but how profits
are used—which in turn requires an understanding of tradeoffs between cash flow and market performance as measured by market
share and growth. In other words, the measurement of current performance has both financial and market performance components,
and an experienced manager looks at the overall picture, not just at
one measure or another. Sad to say, this runs contrary to the practice in many companies where often only financial data is presented. When market data is also reported, it often originates not in
the controller's office but in marketing or sales so that the two reports are never looked at together. A complete view of current performance is therefore obscured.

As far as financial performance is concerned, it is important to recognize that *balance sheet* data is also important to current performance measurement. It provides the basis, when put together with the income statement item "cash from operations," for assessing cash sources and uses. It also provides the basis for measuring return on investment or return on assets.

And as emphasized in Chapter 9, income statements should be presented where possible with fixed and variable costs separated, allowing the measurement of contribution margins. The more "static" presentation of total "cost of goods sold" which lumps fixed and variable costs together—and allows only the measurement of gross margins—is usually much less useful to managers. It should be reserved primarily for reporting to the outside world.

Current performance measures are needed for each line of business, and within this for each segment of activity for which the company has a separate program. As pointed out in Chapter 9, this poses certain problems when segmentation schemes are very "fine," but either through sensible allocations or the use of contribution accounting these problems can be circumvented.

Performance data is most useful when it already provides explanations. Thus we prefer to break down the data into its underlying components wherever possible, as shown below.

Program managers, functional managers, and their bosses all need the same performance data—but their focus will be different. Functional managers will be more focused on costs; while program managers will be concerned with overall profit results, though of course interested in the cost components of these profit figures as well.

Basis of Comparison

Current performance must be compared with *something*. The main alternatives are:

–previous performance

–budgets

–competitors' performance (to the extent that it can be gathered)

–the performance of other lines of business, divisions, or country markets within our own corporation

–agreed-on targets, which may be more ambitious than budgeted performance

–"par" performance, i.e., what might normally be expected given the strategy followed and the characteristics of the particular market.[2]

All of these comparisons are useful but each serves a somewhat different purpose. Comparison with the past gives a sense of trajectory; comparison with the budget provides a perspective on how closely we are adhering to our plan; comparison with competitors gives us information on our relative standing (many companies look at their own performance complacently—forgetting that while it may be satisfactory by usual internal standards, it may fall short of what is possible in that particular marketplace); internal comparisons provide an element of internal rivalry which may motivate higher all-around performance (there is an obvious danger, however, of comparing "apples" and "oranges" when a company has two lines of business with very different characteristics); comparison against targets, as opposed to budgets, can provide a "stretching" dimension to the control process which negotiated budgets may not do; and finally comparisons with some "par" levels—just like a golf par—provide some more objective standards of what can be reasonably achieved.

Frequency

Comparisons should be made with whatever frequency is needed to control effectively the particular process being measured. "Control" is different than "reporting" in that it implies the possibility for management intervention if and when things go out of control. Control implies feedback in which management is actively involved. Reporting, on the contrary, is passive. For control to be effective, therefore, data must be timely and provided at intervals that allow effective intervention. This may be daily with respect to the cost of defective parts; it may only need to be weekly or monthly with respect to cash flow, and no more than quarterly with respect to overall profit reporting.

2. STRATEGIC CONTROL AGAINST KEY SUCCESS FACTORS
Who Is It For?

The same three audiences are concerned with the strategic control of current activities as with budgetary control—but the main users are likely to be functional managers, program managers, and their *immediate* bosses, in that order. Upper-level management will typically concentrate on results, unless there are very large variances that need strategic explanation.

What Is Needed?

The control of current performance is useful for identifying problems, but often by the time they show up on the income statement or balance sheet, the problems may be far advanced—sometimes to the point of being chronic. As a doctor needs a way to find a cancer that has eluded her superficial probe, companies need early warning "imaging diagnostic" systems that can look below the surface at the problem's origins.

The most important factors to control are "key success factors"—to establish whether those things that have to be done with excellence are indeed being done 100 prcent. These are *not* usually factors that are measurable in financial terms. If, for example, speed of service is a key success factor, the measurement should be in hours or days; if delivery punctuality is a key success factor, the "slippage" rates should be measured; and if retailer push is a key success factor, then indicators should be constructed to measure the marketing effort going on in the channels of distribution. Strategic control should also extend to the regular measurement of *customer satisfaction* on the various dimensions that our positioning in the market implies are important. This is not the same as our *internal* evaluation of how well we are doing on each key success factor. It asks the customer how well he or she thinks we are doing. It may combine several key success factors together into an overall evaluation, or it may make separate evaluations of each main aspect of customer satisfaction where we are looking for competitive distinction.

It is surprisingly rare to find such controls even in the best-managed companies, which may explain why there is often considerable slippage between what is actually done and what management implicitly knows needs to be done—segment-by-segment—to satisfy customers properly. Making key success factors explicit and measuring their achievement is considerably more important from a control point of view than measuring the final result in financial or market terms. The latter is equivalent to a doctor registering elevated temperature or blood pressure but not doing any deeper searching to understand their cause.

The explanations for companies' failure to control causes as well as results lie partly with controllers—who tend to overemphasize budgetary control and the financial side of budgetary control in particular—and partly with general management who fail to communicate clearly what the key success factors are segment-by-segment, and what level of performance on these key success factors is required.

Basis of Comparison

Strategic control of performance on key success factors should be two-pronged:

1. Comparison with *expectations* for each factor.

2. *Benchmarking* against others who are managing similar key success factors in other settings. This may mean benchmarking against other units within the same company, or benchmarking against other high performing companies. Benchmarking can not only become the basis for new standards, but can provide new ways to *define* standards. It can also provide insight on *how* standards of performance on critical success factors can be improved.

Frequency

Key success factor comparisons are likely to be needed at least as frequently as budgetary control comparisons of final performance, and in many cases more often. There are no fixed rules. Measurements have to be frequent enough to catch and correct deviations, yet not so frequent that management is drowned in reports. Frequent reporting on *critical* factors is more important than indiscriminate reporting—even if the frequency is lower.

3. STRATEGIC CONTROL OF THE CHANGE PROCESS

Who Is It For?

The change process, as we have seen, is primarily in the hands of general management and top management, although its success depends on broad involvement. The *primary* audience, as far as possible intervention is concerned, is therefore those levels of general management who are orchestrating the change process. All levels of management and employees all the way down to the operating level should, however, be the beneficiaries of regular communications about progress as key milestones are passed.

What Is Needed?

In Chapter 12, five different aspects of vision were discussed:

–a vision of the future *situation*

–a vision of the future *organization*

–a vision of the future *strategy*

–a vision of future *competences and resources* needed

–a vision of the *path* connecting the present and future of the firm

The last of these, the vision of the path connecting the present and future, has to be reduced to a set of concrete program and action steps for organizational change, strategic change, and changes in resources and competences, as described in Chapter 13. It is these steps which become the focus of strategic control.

In addition, it is wise periodically to recheck the assumptions underlying the change process. Is our vision of the future situation in which we are likely to find ourselves still valid? Is our vision of the future organization, future strategy, and future competences needed still valid, and is our designated path for getting to these destinations still the best one? Strategic control of the change process differs substantially from strategic control of current performance in this respect. With strategic control of key success factors, we have to assume that in the short term our assumptions are normally correct; with strategic control of change, assumptions should be regularly revisited and revised as we navigate the way forward with better and better information about the future as we approach it. Like marine navigation, distant land masses which are only blurs on the horizon fall into sharp relief as the ship approaches its landfall.

Being explicit about long-term "strategic intent" can be an important ingredient in the strategic control of change.[3] Strategic intent is not the same as vision. It is an expression of some high-level goals and objectives which the firm is trying to achieve in the mid- to long-term. These may be expressed in terms of goals for product superiority, market superiority, or broader societal objectives, for example. Progress towards these long-term intentions is usually marked by meeting separate "challenges" along the way; each challenge leading to the next. Such progress can usefully be reported and integrated into the strategic control process.

Basis of Comparison

There can only be one basis of comparison—our visions and assumptions, and our plan for achieving them. Making these *explicit* is essential for the strategic control of the change process.

Frequency

Milestones have to be matched with target dates for achievement. The frequency of control is therefore driven entirely by these timetables for completion or partial completion.

Construction managers are very familiar with the kind of control processes needed to assess progress, and other companies can learn a lot from their experience. The whole paraphernalia of Gant charts, critical path analyses, and project progress reviews can be borrowed extensively, and will not be repeated here.

4. OPERATIONAL CONTROL OF THE CHANGE PROCESS

"Operational" control of the change process may be a misnomer, since almost by definition change is a strategic process. By operating control, we mean, however, tracking the change process in sufficient detail to show up departures from the plan at the operating level. This means that major milestones have to be further subdivided into important marker points function-by-function and department-by-department.

Who Is It For?

The main users of operational control data related to the change process are middle and lower level management. In most cases, these are the individuals actually making the needed changes, rather than those who are orchestrating change.

What Is Needed?

Detailed data on how the change process is actually progressing is required for each function and department. This may involve data on organizational variables, resources, and competences. With respect to such technical functions as R&D or engineering, for example, it may involve detailed assessments of technological competence; with respect to marketing, sales, and distribution it may involve assessments of market position, customer franchise, and relationships with channel members; and with respect to human resources it may involve detailed assessments of capabilities.

Basis of Comparison

Assessments of actual progress with respect to planned changes can only be made if detailed marker points have been laid out in advance. While top management may have set specific milestones with respect to major strategic objectives to be reached, too often these are not reduced to more operational measures relevant to lower level management. As noted earlier, there is much to be learned from project management practices in the construction and engineering industries, where progress is monitored in fine detail as the project advances.

Frequency

Quarterly, monthly, and even weekly progress reports can be of great help to management in flagging when change is falling behind schedule, or when important elements of the overall change process are not getting adequate attention. Operational control of the change process should usually be on a month-by-month basis at the very minimum.

SOME TENTATIVE CONCLUSIONS

Control of performance and the monitoring of change processes are totally different in character. Both are needed. The operational and strategic aspects of controlling current performance are also totally different in character: The former focuses primarily on results, the latter on what lies behind the results. Both are also needed. Financial control is therefore only a part of the control processes that companies need if they are to deliver excellence today and, in parallel, change for tomorrow.

The research that was conducted for this book provided ample evidence of the dual nature of modern managements' task—to look after excellence today and to change for tomorrow. It also provided ample evidence of changes going on in organization and planning to accommodate this duality. In the area of control, there appears, however, to be a need to go further in recognizing the dual task that management confronts. I hope these few suggestions will provide at least some pointers for what seems to be needed.

NOTES

Preface

1. Derek F. Abell, and John S. Hammond, *Strategic Market Planning* (Englewood Cliffs, N.J.: Prentice Hall, 1979).
2. Derek F. Abell, *Defining the Business: The Starting Point of Strategic Planning* (Englewood Cliffs, N.J.: Prentice Hall, 1980).

Chapter 1. The Dual Nature of Management

1. Charles O. Rossotti, *Two Concepts of Long-Range Planning: A Special Commentary* (Boston: Boston Consulting Group, 1968).
2. This point was raised initially by Rossotti in *Two Concepts of Long-Range Planning*. It was made again by Henry Mintzberg in "The Design School: Reconsidering the Basic Premise of Strategic Management," *Strategic Management Journal*, March–April 1990.
3. Original source unknown. I am indebted to J. B. H. M. Beks, formerly corporate director of finance, Heineken, who brought this quotation to my attention.
4. R. W. Wuttke, finance director, Caterpillar Overseas S.A. (COSA).
5. Theodore Levitt, "Marketing Myopia," *Harvard Business Review*, July–August 1960.

Chapter 3. There's More to Customer Satisfaction Than Meets the Eye

1. See the video by Thomas J. Peters, *A Passion for Customers*, Video Publishing House, Inc., Schaumburg, Illinois.

Chapter 4. Market Segmentation

1. See Daniel Yankelovitch, "New Criteria for Market Segmentation," *Harvard Business Review* (March/April), 1964.
2. See Abell, *Defining the Business*, p. 15.
3. See Abell, *Defining the Business*, for a more complete coverage of the ideas contained in the next three sections of this chapter.
4. See Abell and Hammond, *Strategic Market Planning*, pp. 49–50.

Chapter 5. Markets in Motion

1. "Swatchmobile" is a planned entry into the automobile market by a joint venture between SMH (the Swatch parent company) and Volkswagen.
2. See Derek F. Abell, *Competitive Market Strategies: Some Generalizations and Hypotheses*, Report No. 75–107, Marketing Science Institute, Cambridge 1975.

Chapter 6. Defining an Industry

1. Wendell R. Smith, "Product Differentiation and Market Segmentation as Alternative Marketing Strategies," *Journal of Marketing*, July 1966.
2. Philip Kotler, *Marketing Management: Analysis, Planning and Control* (Englewood Cliffs, N.J.: Prentice Hall, 1975), 3rd Edition, pp. 151–154.
3. Michael E. Porter, *Competitive Strategy* (New York: Free Press, 1980).
4. Abell, *Defining the Business.*
5. Abell, *Defining the Business.*
6. Martha E. Mangelsdorf, "Broken Promises," *Inc.*, July 1991, p. 25.
7. "EC's Car Components Supply Base Lagging Behind Japan," *Financial Times*, March 25, 1991, p. 6.
8. Porter, *Competitive Strategy*, p. 4.

Chapter 7. The Company and Its Competitors: Visible Differences

1. See previous chapter and Abell, *Defining the Business.*
2. "La Vache Qui Rit" (The Cow that Laughs) is the brand of a well-known cheese.
3. Thomas J. Peters, Panel Discussion, Strategic Management Society Annual Conference, Toronto, 1991.
4. Gary Hamel and C. K. Pralahad, "Strategic Intent," *Harvard Business Review* (May/June 1989).
5. Attributed to Robert Frish, Vice-Chairman, Bank of America, 1980.
6. Parts of this text originally appeared in Abell, *Defining the Business,* which should be consulted for more complete coverage of this subject.

Chapter 8. The Company and Its Competitors: Hidden Differences

1. Gary Hamel and C. K. Pralahad, "The Core Competence of the Corporation," *Harvard Business Review*, May–June 1990.
2. "Grand Ambitions," *Time Magazine*, July 15, 1991, p. 32.

3. Ibid.
4. Michael E. Porter, *The Competitive Advantage of Nations* (London: The Macmillan Press, 1990).
5. See Derek F. Abell, "Leadership in the Organization of the Future," *IMD Perspectives for Managers* No. 1, 1990.
6. Thomas J. Peters and Robert H. Waterman, Jr., *In Search of Excellence* (New York: Harper & Row, 1982).
7. See Abell and Hammond, *Strategic Market Planning*, pp. 6–7.
8. Gary Hamel and C. K. Pralahad, "Strategic Intent," *Harvard Business Review*, May–June 1989.

Chapter 9. The Dynamics of Costs

1. "Dumping" is a term used to describe the systematic selling of products (usually in foreign markets) at prices below costs.
2. See Abell and Hammond, *Strategic Market Planning*, pp. 106–133 for a more complete coverage of this topic.
3. Jerome Chauncy, *History of the American Clock Business for the Past Sixty Years: Life of Chauncy Jerome Written by Himself*, (New Haven: F. D. Dayton, Jr., 1860).
4. Staff of the Boston Consulting Group, *Perspectives on Experience* (Boston: Boston Consulting Group, Inc., 1972).
5. Winfred B. Hirschmann, "Profit from the Learning Curve," *Harvard Business Review*, January–February 1964, p. 125.
6. William J. Abernathy and Kenneth Wayne, "Limits of the Learning Curve," *Harvard Business Review*, September–October 1974, pp. 109–119.
7. The experience effect can be thought of as making an equivalent product for less cost, a product of greater value for the same cost, or a combination of the two.
8. N. Baloff, "Start-Up Management," *IEEE Transactions in Engineering Management*, EM7, No. 4, November 1970.
9. And there are those who would include experience as a part of scale effect. For instance, Pessemier refers to what we have called scale effect as static scale effect (since it is achieved at isolated points in time) experience is a dynamic scale effect (since it is achieved over time). See Edgar A. Pessemier, *Product Management: Strategy and Organization* (New York: John Wiley & Sons, 1977), pp. 51–99.

Chapter 10. Managing Costs for Competitive Advantage

1. Abell and Hammond, *Strategic Market Planning*, pp. 129–130.
2. William E. Fruham, "Pyrrhic Victories in Fights for Market Share," *Harvard Business Review* September–October 1972, pp. 100–107.

3. "Hewlett-Packard: Where Slower Growth is Smarter Management," *Business Week,* June 9, 1975, pp. 50–58.

4. One can also argue that HP is in a different market segment (high quality and performance) than TI and DEC and thus is not a direct competitor of either. Further, HP's experience in its segment is far greater than its competition's; it dominates its segment and thus has the greatest profitability as the experience curve model suggests.

5. William J. Abernathy and Kenneth Wayne, "Limits of the Learning Curve," *Harvard Business Review* September–October 1974, p. 109.

Chapter 11. Mastering the Present

1. I first heard this expression from one of its most ardent exponents, Danica Purg, Founder and Director of the International Executive Development Centre, Brdo pri Kranj, Slovenia. More than anyone I know, she epitomizes the never-ending quest for excellence.

2. From Derek F. Abell and John S. Hammond, *Strategic Market Planning* (Englewood Cliffs: Prentice Hall, 1979), p. 214.

3. See Abell and Hammond, Chapter 6.

4. Michael E. Porter, *Competitive Strategy* (New York: Free Press, 1980), p. 4.

5. Henry Mintzberg, "The Design School: Reconsidering the Basic Premises of Strategic Management," *Strategic Management Journal,* March/April 1990.

6. Gary Hamel and C. K. Pralahad, "Strategic Intent," *Harvard Business Review,* May–June 1989.

7. "Nothing important can be accomplished in the world without passion." (G. W. F. Hegel, *Vorlesungen über die Philosophie der Weltgeschichte,* first part: *Die Vernunft in der Geschichte.)*

8. "Time Warner Takes Heat Over Rappers 'Cop-Killer Song,'" *International Herald Tribune,* July 18–19, 1992, p. 1. The Cop-Killer song was viewed by some as inciting the murder of police officers.

9. For a complete description of how to use portfolio analysis methods, see Abell and Hammond, pp. 182–184.

10. Abell and Hammond, p. 180.

11. See for example Abell and Hammond, *Strategic Market Planning,* particularly pp. 223–226.

12. See Derek F. Abell, "Strategic Windows," *Journal of Marketing,* July 1978.

13. See Scott-Air Corporation Case Study, Darden School, University of Virginia, Ralph Biggadike and Derek A. Newton, 1974. UVAM 132R.

14. See Tex-Fiber Industries Petroloid Products Division (A) and (B), Harvard Business School Case, Derek F. Abell, 1979. 9.576 188/189.
15. Gould Inc. Graphics Division, Harvard Business School Case, Ulrich Wiechmann and Ralph Sorenson, 1971. 9.571.071.

Chapter 12. Agendas for Change

1. H. G. Wells, *An Outline of History* (London: Georges Newnes Ltd), Vol. II, p. 664.
2. I am indebted to John S. Hammond for this and the following two examples.
3. Thomas J. Peters, *Thriving on Chaos: Handbook for a Management Revolution* (New York: Harper & Row, 1988).

Chapter 14. Turning the Organization Inside Out and Upside Down

1. See Thomas J. Peters and Michael E. Porter, *Proceedings on the Strategic Management Conference,* Toronto, 1991, Opening Plenary Session.
2. This section draws heavily on "'The Middleman': An Imperative for Market-Driven Organizations," *IMEDE Perspectives for Managers,* Derek F. Abell, Number 2, 1988; Lausanne, Switzerland.
3. See Clifford Pinchot III, *Intrapreneuring: Why You Don't Have to Leave the Corporation to Become an Entrepreneur* (New York: Harper & Row, 1986).
4. See Howard Stevenson, "The Nature of Entrepreneurship," pp. 3–4, in Derek F. Abell and Thomas Köllermeier, Eds., *Dynamic Entrepreneurship in Central and Eastern Europe* (Amsterdam: Delsey, 1993).
5. See Joseph A. Blackburn, *Time-Based Competition. The Next Battleground for American Manufacturing* (Homewood, Ill.: Dow Jones Irwin, 1990).
6. See Kamran Kashani, *Managing Global Marketing* (Boston: PWS-Kent Publishing Company, 1992).
7. See Warren Bennis, "The Split Brain at the Top," *Across the Board.* Conference Board Commentary September 1984—excerpted from the book *Why Leaders Can't Lead: The Unconscious Conspiracy Continues* (San Francisco: Jossey-Bass, 1989).
8. Bennis, Ibid.
9. Jan Carlsson, *Moments of Truth* (New York: Harper Business, 1987).

Chapter 15. Moving to Dual Planning

1. Henry Mintzberg, *Mintzberg on Management* (New York: Free Press, 1989), "Crafting Strategy," chapter 2.

Chapter 16. Controlling Performance and Monitoring Change

1. See for example, M. Gould and J. J. Quinn, "The Paradox of Strategic Controls," *Strategic Management Journal*, Volume II, No. 1, January 1990, as well as the bibliography to this article.
2. Par financial performance is analogous to par performance in golf. It was first proposed in the "PIMS" project. See Abell and Hammond, chapter 6.
3. See Chapter 8, and Gary Hamel and C. K. Pralahad, "Strategic Intent," *Harvard Business Review*, May–June 1989.

INDEX